DATE			

BAKER & TAYLOR

American Foreign Policy

Carter to Clinton

American Foreign Policy
Carter to Clinton

John Dumbrell

Senior Lecturer in American Studies
Keele University

St. Martin's Press
New York

AMERICAN FOREIGN POLICY: FROM CARTER TO CLINTON
Copyright © 1997 by John Dumbrell
For information, address:

St. Martin's Press, Scholarly and Reference Division,
175 Fifth Avenue, New York, N.Y. 10010

First published in the United States of America in 1997

This book is printed on paper suitable for recycling and made from fully managed and sustained forest sources.

Printed in Hong Kong

ISBN 0–312–16395–9

Library of Congress Cataloging-in-Publication Data
Dumbrell, John, 1950–
American foreign policy : Carter to Clinton / John Dumbrell.
p.   cm.
Includes bibliographical references and index.
ISBN 0–312–16395–9
1. United States—Foreign relations—1977–1981.   2. United States–
–Foreign relations—1981–1989.   3. United States—Foreign
relations.   4. Cold War.   I. Title.
E872.D859   1996
327.73'009'045—dc20   96–9310
                                                          CIP

Contents

v

055015

Acknowledgements

I wish to acknowledge valuable help from the following: Tony Badger, series editor; colleagues in the Department of American Studies at Keele University, especially Chris Bailey; John Thompson of Cambridge University; Simon Winder, editor at Macmillan; and Jenny Williams, who word processed the manuscript.

JOHN DUMBRELL

1 Introduction

In February 1987, Secretary of State George Shultz told an audience in Denver, Colorado, that 'the great ideological struggle that has marked this century ever since the Bolshevik revolution of 1917 has essentially been decided'.[1] Two years prior to the Eastern European revolutions of 1989, America's foreign policy leadership was already proclaiming victory in the 'great contest' of the twentieth century: the struggle between liberal, democratic capitalism and Soviet state socialism. The denouement of the Cold War inevitably constitutes one of this book's most prominent themes. Later chapters will examine various attempts to redefine the national purpose in the wake of the apparent victory described by Shultz.

Besides the ending of the Cold War, this book incorporates three other major themes: the legacy of the Vietnam War, American decline and the possibilities of democratic foreign policy. Throughout its long history, the Cold War was sustained by American democratic optimism: the belief that the democratic history of the US provides a model for the world. No-one expressed this view better than Presidential Cold Warrior, Ronald Reagan. In his memoir, *An American Life*, Reagan recorded his fantasy that he and Soviet Leader Mikhail Gorbachev would take a helicopter flight over an American working class neighbourhood. They would descend among the 'lawns and backyards ... not the concrete rabbit warrens I'd seen in Moscow', and American workers would tell Gorbachev of their attachment to the ideals of freedom, democracy and free enterprise. Reagan would proclaim: 'They not only live there, they *own* that property'.[2]

Ronald Reagan's fantasy belongs to a long tradition of American democratic optimism. Yet, by the 1980s – and despite America's apparent victory in 'the great ideological struggle' – this tradition had come under intense pressure. The most immediate challenge to consensual American democratic optimism derived from the defeat in Vietnam. It was the post-Vietnam President, Jimmy Carter who, in 1978, asserted: 'The hardest thing for the American people to understand is that we are not better than other people'.[3] Throughout this book, we will see memo-

1

ries of Vietnam shaping decisions and attitudes, both at symbolic and substantive levels. Even more profoundly, however, American democratic optimism was challenged in our period by the perception of relative American international decline, even weakness – a perception that continued into (perhaps even dominated) the post-Cold War period. Our final theme – the possibility of a democratic foreign policy – also relates to the fortunes of American democratic optimism. During the Cold War, the US evolved patterns of foreign policy-making far removed from anything that could conceivably be called 'democratic'. The years between 1977 and 1994 – between Carter and Clinton – called forth a questioning of this legacy, and elicited various attempts to restore American foreign policy's democratic deficit.

THE COLD WAR

Writing in the journal *Foreign Affairs* under a pseudonym, George F. Kennan, head of the State Department Policy Planning staff, wrote in 1947 that the US should take as the centrepiece of its foreign policy 'a long-term, patient but firm and vigilant containment of Russian expansive tendencies'. The US should apply 'counter-force at a series of constantly shifting geographical and political points'. In words that were to be frequently quoted some forty years later, Kennan held that such a policy would 'promote Soviet tendencies which must eventually find their outlet in either the break-up or the gradual mellowing of Soviet power'.[4]

Containment of Soviet power remained at the heart of US foreign policy until the late 1980s. Indeed, finding a doctrine with which to replace anti-communist containment as the driving force of American internationalism was to become a central concern for Presidents Bush and Clinton into the 1990s. In emphasising the centrality of containment to US Cold War policies, it is important to stress also that containment was never an entirely stable doctrine. At various times, it came under attack from right and from left. The globalised version of containment which emerged under President Harry Truman (especially after the onset of the Korean war in 1950) was a step well beyond the modulated, Eurocentric doctrine advocated by Kennan. During the early 1950s, Republican advocates of 'liberation' and 'rollback' assaulted containment from the right. Globalised containment policies eventually delivered the US into the Vietnam War. Anti-war critics in turn interpreted containment either in terms of American imperialism, or as an expression of the 'equivalence' in arms and outlook between Washington and Moscow. From the competitive coexistence between the superpowers which followed the 1962 Cuban missile crisis, President Nixon (1969–74) developed the most drastic operational revision of containment: 'detente'.

As conceived by Nixon and his National Security Adviser, Henry Kissinger, detente rested on the perception that the US was finding it increasingly difficult to sustain the demands made by militarised, globalised containment. The Nixon–Kissinger approach sought to release containment from its moralistic underpinnings and to inaugurate a power-oriented *Realpolitik*. The USSR would be given incentives, largely economic, to moderate its expansionism. It would thus practice a kind of 'self-containment'.[5] Relaxing international tensions would enable the US to extricate itself from Vietnam. Detente would also, in Kissinger's formulation, allow a new international balance of power (primarily involving the USSR, Western Europe, China, Japan and the US) to be achieved. (In his later years as director of US foreign policy under President Gerald Ford (1974–7), Kissinger developed a somewhat more complex 'world order' approach.)

By the time Carter came to the White House in 1977, American leaders were deeply concerned at the degree to which containment in its various forms had resulted in an imbalance between resources and commitments. The US had become a 'national security state' with a highly militarised economic base. In 1968, annual US defence spending had attained a high of 188.7 billion dollars. Following withdrawal from Vietnam, the figure fell back to 119.9 billion by the time of Carter's election in 1976.[6] Moreover, by the later stages of the Vietnam War, it was no longer apparent that the US had a strategic advantage over the Soviets. It also became clear in the 1980s that the Soviet economy had deeply rooted structural weaknesses. In the early 1970s, however, US leaders were content to accept, indeed to institutionalise, strategic parity with the Soviet Union.

American leaders from Truman to Reagan, with varying degrees of qualification and emphasis, accepted a 'Soviet threat' interpretation of the Cold War. They all saw American militarism, at least at one level, as a necessary response to a threatening and potentially expansive Soviet Union. At times, however, Presidents (such as Eisenhower in his 1961 Farewell Address on the 'military industrial complex') showed themselves aware of other forces. Detailed theoretical discussion of these forces is beyond the scope of this book. However, in putting the Cold War into context, and in attempting to explain its end, it is important to be aware of the rich theoretical literature on the origins and dynamics of modern superpower confrontation. Clearly, the Cold War had both ideological and geopolitical dimensions. The debate on its origins constitutes one of the fine set-pieces of modern historiography. In various formulations, 'orthodox' views (emphasising Soviet expansionism and the 'inviting in' of the US into post-1945 Europe) still vie with 'revisionist' perspectives (emphasising Soviet defensiveness, American imperialism and the US search for markets). On the dynamics of the Cold War, interpretations range through 'internalist' explanations, notably relating to shifting elite configurations in the US; through the putatively dynamic (though destructive) militarisation of the superpower economies; through notions of a symbiotic ('vodka/cola') Cold War system, serving elite interests in both powers; to various inter-systemic theories of superpower rivalry; and to various theories of mutual misperception, as Moscow and Washington viewed each other through a distorting mirror.[7]

THE LEGACY OF VIETNAM

Our period begins and ends with resonantly symbolic Presidential acts: Jimmy Carter's 1977 amnesty for draft evaders, and President Clinton's 1994 lifting of the trade embargo with Vietnam and 1995 normalisation of US–Vietnamese relations. President Nixon had been preoccupied with disengaging from Indochina, and with attempting to portray the 1973 peace (and US withdrawal) as a victory. Filling out Nixon's term, President Ford presided over the endgame in Indochina. Congress and the American people were in no mood to redeem promises made by Nixon and Ford to South Vietnam when Saigon was threatened, and eventually fell, in 1975. Jimmy Carter thus became the first President squarely to face the legacy of the war, rather than the war itself.

One of the war's legacies was a disaffected and uncertain American public. One disaffected young member of the 'Vietnam generation' was eventually to enter the White House, as President in 1993. Disaffection was not confined to American youth. Opinion polls, taken in the wake of the defeat in Vietnam and of Watergate, indicated an accelerating pattern of declining public trust in US governmental institutions. The war appeared to incline the American public away from global concerns. From about 1975, polls clearly identified domestic economic issues as the public's most salient concerns. (Earlier polling had tended to place containment of communism as either the foremost or equally strong concern.)[8] Equally troubling for post-1975 American leaders was the problem of re-building elite consensus. During the war, elite dissidence had affected virtually every facet of American culture and organisation: the creative arts, academe, Congress, the federal bureaucracy, organised labour, business – even the military itself. Some elite disaffections (like that of Senate Foreign Relations Committee Chairman J. William Fulbright) were spectacular; others (like that of President Johnson's Defence Secretary, Robert McNamara) more organic. By the early 1970s, all elite dissidents were questioning the 'Soviet threat' theory of Cold War. All were sceptical about the 'domino theory' (the version of globalised containment which insisted that communism must not be allowed to advance, even in countries remote from immediate American interests). Some saw Vietnam as primarily a mistake; others saw it as a crime. All agreed that never again should force be used so cavalierly and unreflectingly.[9]

Post-Vietnam leaders were cautious about the use of force. Reagan saw it as part of his mission to exorcise the 'Vietnam syndrome', which he defined as a national sense of uncertainty, involving extreme reluctance to revert to military force.[10] Yet Reagan himself was extremely circumspect about committing US troops to any conflict – as in Central America – which could conceivably be seen as 'another Vietnam'. As we shall see in Chapter 8, President Bush's handling of America's major post-Vietnam conflict – the 1991 Gulf War – involved a constant and elaborate determination to avoid parallels with Vietnam.

The war in Indochina not only shook American faith in the universal applicability of liberal democratic capitalist values and institutions – too often this faith looked too much like imperialism; it also earned the US a legacy of mistrust in the developing world. By the early 1970s, the 'can do' nation-building optimism of the Presidency of John Kennedy appeared facile. Too many Third World dictators had been supported in the name of a 'freedom', which subsisted merely as anti-communism. Vietnam-era US policy-makers had shown themselves quite unable to unscramble the interconnections between nationalism and communism in the developing world. Far from being identified with progress, anti-colonialism and democratic change, the US was perceived as the sponsor of corrupt elites and the instigator of covert warfare. 'Dependency' economists in Latin America and elsewhere traced the mechanisms by which liberal patterns of international trade – ultimately guaranteed by the US – kept the emerging world in a state of chronic, dependent underdevelopment.[11]

Suspicion of American motives and practices extended also to allies of the US in the industrialised world. In the US, this scepticism was directed primarily at the institution of the US Presidency. The Vietnam years saw new demands for democratic accountability, leading most famously to passage of the War Powers Resolution and Act (1973/4). (The Act put restrictions on the President's ability to deploy military forces abroad without Congressional consent.) These years also saw a new public and elite preoccupation with American weakness, internal dissension and decline.

AMERICA IN DECLINE?

In March 1971, a bomb exploded on Capitol Hill. An anonymous caller linked the bombing to the contemporaneous South Vietnamese invasion of Laos. Senator George McGovern, strong proponent of controls on the President's war powers and Democratic candidate for the White House the following year, proclaimed:

It is not possible to teach an entire generation to bomb and destroy others in an undeclared, unjustified, unending war abroad and not pay a terrible price in the derangement of our own society.[12]

The Vietnam era saw many such invocations of domestic 'derangement', embracing variously rising violence, youth disaffection, extreme racial tension and social dislocation. With the ending of the war, this widespread awareness of crisis tended to give way to a perception of secular international American decline. During our period, 1977–94, this perception became enshrined at various levels in American culture. As the US became a net debtor nation in the mid-1980s, Gore Vidal penned an address, 'The Day the American Empire Ran Out of Gas'.[13] That perceptions of decline influenced the outlook and behaviour of US leaders in our period is not in doubt. To most, the need was to appreciate and accommodate limits to American power. To Reagan, at least at the level of rhetoric, perception of decline – rather than decline itself – was the problem. While appreciating that 'perception' and 'reality' are interpenetrating concepts, it is now the intention briefly to review the debate about the 'reality' of American decline.

Theorists of American decline point to the Vietnam War as marking the beginning of the end of the (short) 'long cycle' of US international dominance following World War II. The war was not only a humiliating defeat for the United States and a severe test of its traditions of democratic optimism. It coincided with the achievement by the USSR of strategic nuclear parity. It was also the occasion of an inflationary and excess outpouring of dollars into the world economy. America's role, under the post-1945 Bretton Woods system, came under pressure and President Nixon was forced in 1971 to destroy the system by breaking the fixed link between the dollar and gold. Relative American competitiveness failed to keep pace with new challenges from Europe, Japan and newly industrialising Pacific nations. The 1973 oil crisis clearly demonstrated America's weakness. Still a vast over-consumer of the world's energy, the US showed little willingness or ability to adjust to new circumstances. The United States was no longer able to act as a stabilising hegemon for the global economic system. The world's economy was now manifestly characterised by interdependence, rather than by American dominance. In fact, it showed every sign of collapsing not into a stable interdependence regime, but into protectionism and fragmentation. During the 1980s, according to the declinist thesis, America's plight was camouflaged by the far more spectacular implosions taking place in Eastern Europe and the Soviet Union. Yet the US situation also worsened, through improvident military expenditure, chronic over-extension and failure to adjust psychologically to changed circumstances. A 'crippled giant', the US was prey to a series of humiliations at the hands of unpredictable forces in the developing world, especially in the Middle East. By the later 1980s, the US had become the world's largest debtor nation. The US political process did not adapt well to international financial deregulation and economic interdependence. All these various ills were compounded by a reluctance to invest in America's infrastructure, including education.[14]

Though baldly presented and an amalgam of different viewpoints, the foregoing narrative of decline is essentially persuasive. However, important qualifications do have to be made to this declinist analysis. Firstly, by the late 1980s, the US had, at least for the time being, as George Shultz told his Denver audience in 1987, won the Cold War battle of ideology. Liberal capitalist values were in the ascendant and

Soviet-style communism in apparently terminal decline. Moreover, as the USSR imploded, the US arguably became as dominant a military superpower as at any time in the post-1945 period. Secondly, it may be that the whole concept of national 'decline' in an era of global interdependence is misleading. The 'United States' needs to be defined, not in narrow territorial terms, but as a 'soft shell' state.[15] Hegemony in an interdependent world has cultural, as well as economic and security, dimensions. Analogies with British experience earlier in the century are not entirely appropriate. As Stephen Gill writes:

> ... the sheer size and weight of the US within the international system substantially affects the psychological, cultural, economic and political conditions under which others must operate, not just their policy responses.[16]

'Power' in an interdependent world is 'soft' (involving the ability to co-opt rather than to coerce, to set the assumptional and organisational framework for international activity) as well as 'hard'. Lastly, even in relative economic terms, some writers challenge the thesis of long-term decline. Susan Strange, for example, has pointed to the huge share of global output 'under the direction of U.S. companies'. US companies producing outside the territorial United States constitute a new, 'nonterritorial empire'.[17] According to Joseph Nye, writing in 1990:

> America is rich but acts poor. In real terms, GNP is more than twice what it was in 1960, but Americans today spend much less of their GNP on international leadership. The prevailing view is 'we can't afford it' despite the fact that US taxes are a smaller per cent of GNP than in other OECD nations. This suggests a problem of domestic political leadership in power conversion rather than long-term economic decline.[18]

Anti-declinist writers are correct to point out the rather puzzling way in which perceptions of decline were exaggerated precisely at the time of America's Cold War triumph. The Spenglerian overtones of the debate instigated by Paul Kennedy's *The Rise and Fall of the Great Powers* (1987) were a little overblown. Decline has not been absolute, and to a large degree it has been a function of qualitative change in the international environment. Above and beyond this, however, it is important to bear in mind that, during the 1977–94 period, the US stood in a very different relationship to the rest of the world in comparison with the period before the Vietnam War. The major problem for foreign policy-makers in our period was that of managing the transition from pre-Vietnam hegemony to the achievement of a leading role for the US in an altered, interdependent global environment.

DEMOCRATIC FOREIGN POLICY

At the Republic's birth, the Framers deliberately drafted a Constitution of shared powers and balanced institutional participa-tion, fully aware of the risks that arrangement posed to the nation's international well-being. By mandating that separated institutions share powers in foreign as well as in domestic affairs, the Framers determined that we must sacrifice some short-term gains from speed, secrecy and efficiency in favour of the longer-term consensus that derives from reasoned interbranch consultation and participatory decision making.[19]

The constitutional tradition here described by Harold Hongju Koh has not fared well alongside the growth in American internationalism, espe-cially in its Cold War phase. Building on the vision of Presidential foreign policy dominance enshrined in the Supreme Court's 1936 *Curtiss–Wright* decision,[20] post-1945 Presidents successfully moved to extend executive discretion. The exigencies of crisis decision-making in the age of nuclear power were held to militate against meaningful Congressional, much less public, intrusions into the process. The Cold War could not, many argued, be waged through open diplomacy and constant democratic accountability. During the Cold War, according to Dean Rusk (Secretary of State, 1961–9), the US – especially its Central Intelligence Agency – had to vie with the Soviets 'in the back alleys of the world'.[21]

Presidential domination of Cold War foreign policy was especially acute in the area of crisis management. As the National Security Council (NSC) system evolved after its inception in 1947, not only Congress but also the State Department became excluded from a crisis-driven process dominated by the President and his NSC staff (espe-cially the National Security Adviser). Individual Secretaries of State,

like Rusk, could still be powerful, and Congress continued to be important in incremental administration of long-term commitments (notably
the annual defence budget). Congress also showed more resilience in
the case of foreign economic issues, including the increasingly central
'intermestic' agenda, embracing energy and environmental, as well as
trade, issues. Yet, at least until Vietnam, Presidential influence over
strategic security issues remained strong.

As we have seen, the Indochina war did lead to a profound questioning of Presidential discretion. It stimulated efforts to open up and to
subject the CIA to democratic control. Nevertheless, the war's later
stages coincided with what was in some respects the zenith of the NSC
system: Henry Kissinger's tenure as National Security Adviser
(1969–76) and Secretary of State (1973–7). As Nixon's National
Security Adviser, Kissinger effectively shut the State Department and
Congress out of key decisions (such as the military incursions into
Cambodia). His move to the State Department was largely cosmetic,
and, even under President Ford (1974–7), Kissinger was allowed to
continue his 'Lone Ranger' style. Nixon and Kissinger had more or less
open contempt for what they saw as antiquated constitutional checks,
and inappropriate majoritarian democratic influences, on elite foreign
policy calculations. Regular bureaucrats and Members of Congress
were seen as similarly unable to rise above parochial concerns and
narrow, 'turf' wars. As Kissinger wrote as an academic at Harvard, the
statesman in foreign policy was bound to conflict with 'those whose
primary concern is with safety and minimum risk'.[22] Ford's 1976 decision to remove Kissinger from his White House post was a response to
criticisms of the secretive, authoritarian and self-dramatising diplomatic style. For George Ball, sometime foreign policy adviser to
Presidents Kennedy and Johnson, Henry Kissinger was 'the Master
Player' on the global chessboard:

> The Master Player must not only keep foreign nations in the dark,
> awaiting surprising moves, but he must also conceal his tactics from
> the State Department bureaucracy, the American Congress, and, of
> course, the American people. A democratic system will tolerate such
> practices for only a limited period of time.[23]

2 Jimmy Carter and 'Global Community'

On his first full day in office, 21 January 1977, Jimmy Carter issued an amnesty for Vietnam War draft resisters. Despite the efforts of peace activists at the 1976 Democratic convention, the amnesty did not amount to an absolute pardon. It did not, for example, apply to deserters.[1] Nevertheless, Carter's signal was clear. Here was the President as national healer: a 'born again' President inaugurating a 'born again' Presidency. Carter's critique of the Vietnam War was couched not in terms of a glorious crusade gone awry, but attacked the underlying assumptions of preceding Democratic and Republican Presidents. In May, 1977, the new President delivered a speech at Notre Dame University, Indiana, in which he declared that his foreign policy would be 'free of that inordinate fear of communism' which had for so long underpinned US support for dictators in Southeast Asia and elsewhere:

> For too many years we have been willing to adopt the flawed and erroneous principles of our adversaries, sometimes abandoning our values for theirs. We have fought fire with fire, never thinking that force is better quenched with water. This approach failed, with Vietnam the best example of its intellectual and moral poverty.[2]

Globalised containment and the 'domino theory' had left America exposed, over-extended, defending questionable moral positions abroad and demoralised at home. Two years after the Notre Dame speech, Carter sought to rekindle the 1976–7 'post-Vietnam' mood and sense of purpose. The 'crisis-of-confidence' address (15 July 1979) contained a litany of recent shocks to the confidence of the American people:

> We were taught that our armies were strong and invincible and our cause always just, only to suffer the agony of Vietnam.[3]

11

At one level, Carter argued in 1977, the recent war represented a hideous miscalculation of America's security interests. The war had involved the expenditure of blood and treasure 'in a distant place on Earth where our security is not even threatened'.[4] The *Realpolitik* of Nixon and Kissinger was no answer, however. Jimmy Carter had declared on the campaign trail that US foreign policy 'requires a balancing of tough realism on the one hand, and idealism on the other'. The 1976 'wheeler-healer' promised to restore 'those moral values that have always distinguished the United States of America from other countries'.[5]

Memories of Vietnam inevitably intruded on the confirmation process for Carter's foreign policy appointees. Cyrus Vance, the new Secretary of State, declared that 'it was a mistake to intervene in Vietnam', and that the US had illegitimately attempted to 'prop up a series of regimes that lacked popular support' and to impose its values on Southeast Asia. Pressed on his own role in the Johnson Administration, however, Vance fell back on the view that the war was a mistake, not a crime:

> The motivation and initial involvement were not based on evil motives, but were based on mistakes and misjudgments as we went along.[6]

Defence Secretary Harold Brown interpreted the lessons of Vietnam as including the need for caution 'in expanding our foreign policy commitments beyond our vital security interest'; the need to approach 'very cautiously' the use of military force; and the need to recognise that unpopular regimes abroad could not be made viable simply by extending American military backing to them.[7]

In developing its post-Vietnam foreign policy, the Carter Administration sought to adopt both the procedural and the substantive critiques of the Vietnam war: to produce a foreign policy based on democratic processes, 'global community', interdependence and human rights.

A DEMOCRATIC FOREIGN POLICY FOR GLOBAL INTERDEPENDENCE?

As a product of the Vietnam-era Democratic party reforms, the Carter Presidency was more concerned with evolving a 'democratic' rather than a 'Democratic' foreign policy. Carter occasionally portrayed himself – as he did when he dedicated the Kennedy Library in Boston in 1979 – as standing in the great Democratic tradition of New Deal, New Frontier and Great Society. But Vietnam stood as a fire-break between Carter and his Democratic predecessors. (Even in the 1979 Boston speech, the President described the new Democratic era as requiring 'a keener appreciation of limits'.)[8]

The new era could, declared Carter and Secretary of State Cyrus Vance, produce a new 'democratic' foreign policy. In 1982, Carter recalled:

> ... the reason why I was elected was because I was the epitome of an adverse reaction to secrecy and misleading statements and some-times betrayal by the president of the public, since Watergate and Vietnam and the CIA and so forth.[9]

Carter promised a new 'openness of government, a closeness between the President and the people themselves'.[10] The dismissal of George Bush as head of the Central Intelligence Agency indicated the determination to break with the old order. Jimmy Carter was the first incoming President to fire an incumbent Director of Central Intelligence. The Administration decked itself out in populist symbolism. Cabinet members were to drive their own cars. Carter began dropping in on 'ordinary' American families: for example, staying with an Irish-American family in Massachusetts prior to issuing his 1977 statement on Northern Ireland. Energised public discussion of international issues – so damagingly absent in the early Vietnam years – became the Administration's stated goal.

The commitment to an open and democratic process involved an undertaking to respect, and share power with, Congress. Cyrus Vance assured the Senate Foreign Relations Committee that he would always 'come completely clean' with them.[11] The early 1970s had seen a new mood of assertiveness on Capitol Hill, combined with internal reforms which increased Congressional fragmentation and made the national legislature an extraordinarily difficult institution with which to do business.[12] House Speaker 'Tip' O'Neill warned Carter, his fellow Democrat, in January 1977:

> With the War Powers Act and the new budget process, Congress is proving that it is capable of operating on an equal footing with the executive ...[13]

The 'post-imperial' Congress – albeit with Democratic majorities in both houses – would have presented problems for any Democratic President assuming office in 1977. Carter found himself pinioned between left-wing, 'post-Vietnam' Democrats on one side, and 'neo-conservatives' led by Senator Henry Jackson of Washington on the other. The former group, best represented by Congressmen like Tom Harkin of Iowa but also including Senators such as Edward Kennedy, sought defence cuts and the application of human rights tests to US dealings with its traditional allies. To 'neo-conservative' Democrats, 'post-Vietnam' attitudes, especially when applied to the Soviet Union, looked alarmingly like appeasement. The Carter Administration frequently contended that the categories 'liberal' and 'conservative' were outdated. The new era of scarce resources and awareness of limits to American power had made old labels redundant. Nevertheless, it was to the right that the Administration initially looked as a focus for opposition. Hamilton Jordan, architect of the 1976 campaign and close aide to the President, advised Carter in 1977: *'Conservatives are much better organized than liberals and will generally oppose our foreign policy initiatives.'* [14] Senator Henry Jackson led the Senate fight against the confirmation of Paul Warnke as Carter's chief arms control negotiator. Hamilton Jordan described the confirmation and 'deep *mistrust between liberals and conservatives*' in Congress as '*potentially explosive*'. [15] Warnke, a well known opponent of unrestricted arms accumulation by the superpowers – he referred to the US and USSR in a 1975 article as 'apes on a treadmill' [16] – was confirmed by the Senate, 58–40. The vote thus ominously fell short of the two-thirds majority required for approval of any major arms treaty.

If any President would have had problems with Congress in the late 1970s, Carter and his White House staff undoubtedly brought along their own particular difficulties. Carter's gubernatorial experience in handling the legislature in Georgia was inappropriate. The President and his staff (including legislative liaison head Frank Moore) also lacked much sympathy with the folkways and culture of Capitol Hill. [17] The Administration's initial instincts, however, suggested that frankness was the key to good relations. The 'deep cuts' arms proposals which Vance took to Moscow in May, 1977, were disclosed in advance to the relevant Congressional committees. Efforts were made to include Members of Congress in subsequent delegations negotiating a second Strategic Arms Limitation Treaty (SALT) – (no doubt as much to co-opt potential opposition as to consult and inform). Hamilton Jordan outlined to Carter in early 1977 a detailed plan for consulting Congress on SALT, the Middle East and the Panama Canal.[18] However, it will become apparent in the next chapter that the promise of always 'coming clean' to Congress, along with other aspects of the democratic foreign policy, did not survive intact the international shocks of 1978–9.

Vance soon emerged as a strong defender of the democratic foreign policy. He later criticised Carter on the grounds that the President 'should have involved himself much more with the Congress than he did'.[19] The commitment to break with the ways of Henry Kissinger was far less clear, however, in the case of Zbigniew Brzezinski, the new National Security Adviser. Both appointments – Vance and Brzezinski – indicated the limits of discontinuity with the past. The 1976 'peanut brigaders' were disappointed by the appointment of 'establishment' figures in the foreign policy hierarchy. (Hamilton Jordan famously promised in 1976 to resign if a Carter Administration included Vance and Brzezinski.)[20] Where Vance, former servant to the Kennedy and Johnson Administrations, self-consciously proclaimed his 'post-Vietnam' credentials, Brzezinski – Polish-born academic – cultivated the image of the Cold War defence intellectual. He did little to disguise his misgivings about what he saw as the post-Vietnam paralysis which had gripped traditional elite figures like Vance. (Shortly after the 1980 Presidential election, Brzezinski denounced those Democrats who had become 'traumatized by the experience of Vietnam'.)[21] Despite his criticisms of his predecessor's 'Lone Ranger' diplomatic style, Brzezinski stood in the Kissinger tradition. In remarks broadcast in 1990, Zbig averred: '... operationally, I have no objections to Kissinger's role'. From Brzezinski's perspective, the State Department was slow and incapable of transcending its narrow, bureaucratic interests; '... large bureaucracies', Zbig declared in 1990, 'do not produce strategies – they produce shopping lists'.[22] As for Congress, the 'new oversight' – for example, of the CIA – looked very much like irresponsible interference: '... like the liberum veto in the Polish Parliament'.[23]

The more advanced supporters of democratic foreign policy within the Carter Administration saw it as the necessary counterpart to changes in the international environment. A disaggregated foreign policy process matched a disaggregated, 'post-realist' world policy arena. Here, in a commitment to ideas of global interdependence, Brzezinski seemed initially to be a firm supporter of the new approach. The new National Security Adviser presented Carter in 1977 with a list of ten objectives for his first term: enhanced economic cooperation with Western Europe and

Japan; development of bilateral US ties with 'regionally influential' states across the globe; a new prioritisation of North–South dialogues, with a restoration in 'America's political appeal to the Third World'; strategic arms limitation; 'normalization' of relations with mainland China; a Middle Eastern settlement; the promotion of multi-racial democracy in Southern Africa; restrictions on international arms transfers; promotion of human rights; and the development of a defence posture which would both deter Soviet aggression and reflect 'broad changes in the world'. These changes amounted, in a key phrase of the period, to an emergent 'complex interdependence'. Brzezinski's agenda was predicated on 'an unstable world' still organised on the basis of national sovereignty 'yet increasingly interdependent socially and economically'.[24]

The growth of new technologies, America's loss of oil self-sufficiency, economic internationalization, the rise of non-governmental organisations (from multinational corporations to international crime cartels), the rise of the 'intermestic' agenda (notably energy and environmental issues): all these combined with the 'lessons of Vietnam' to produce a foreign policy based on 'leadership without hegemony' and the 'management of complex interdependence'. America could no longer dominate the world, but still had an interest in and ability to promote stability. Here, the notion of 'regional influentials', especially oil producers like Saudi Arabia, Nigeria, Venezuela and Iran, was crucial. There were pre-echoes of this in the later Kissinger years, as noted in the previous chapter. Yet the Carter approach was far more concerned with economic interdependence, with North–South dialogues, with human rights issues and with moral values generally. The new agenda stood in the tradition of Woodrow Wilson and moralistic, 'world order' liberalism. It offered a revised union between interests and ideals.

The agenda reflected the 1970s academic focus on interdependence, a focus to which Brzezinski himself had been an important contributor.[25] It also embraced the 'post-Vietnam' reorientation of American business interests. Carter and all of his major foreign policy advisers were members of the Trilateral Commission, a Rockefeller-backed offshoot of the Council on Foreign Relations. An elite study group, the Commission promoted cooperation between the US, Western Europe and Japan, along with a transnational programme of environmental, trade and energy issues. From the viewpoint of the Trilateralists, Henry Kissinger had failed to appreciate the possibilities of a revivified economic alliance between the main capitalist powers. The major danger facing the US was a collapse into myopic protectionism and isolationism.[26]

The Trilateralist, interdependency and 'global community' agendas drew the Administration into a confusing amalgam of economic, nuclear proliferation and non-security issues (such as the long, frustrating search to revise international agreements regarding the world's oceans). As Madeleine Albright of the National Security Council (NSC) staff later testified,[27] however, Carter's premier initial commitment was to values rather than to theories of world order. What gave the new foreign policy its credibility and sense of purpose, and distinguished it from the Nixon-Kissinger-Ford policy, was its attachment to human rights.

HUMAN RIGHTS

In the Inaugural Address, Carter proclaimed an 'absolute'[28] commitment to human rights as the centre of his foreign policy. The commitment had its roots in the President's religious beliefs, in various 'post-Vietnam' Congressional initiatives (notably the 1973–4 hearings held by Representative Donald Fraser's subcommittee of the House International Relations Committee, and the 1975 Harkin foreign assistance amendment), and in the complex Washington DC human rights lobbying networks of the mid-1970s. It also served immediate, practical purposes. First and foremost, as NSC staffer William Odom later recalled, it 'offered some basis of a new domestic US foreign policy consensus'.[29]

The great triumph of the human rights policy was in holding together a consensus which survived until the shocks of 1979. For liberals, the policy promised a crusade against right-wing dictators (especially the military governments of Latin America), and embodied an atonement for Vietnam. For conservatives, the policy offered a lever against communism and its abuses – also a way, in Odom's words, 'to really beat up morally on the Soviets'.[30] At the 1976 Democratic convention, the Carter team found that human rights was the only basis for party unity at the platform drafting meetings. Senator Daniel Patrick Moynihan, from the Henry Jackson wing of the party, entered a dialogue with the party's left: 'We'll be against the dictators you don't like the most ... if you'll be against the dictators we don't like the most.'[31] In December 1977, Hamilton Jordan advised Carter of the policy's consensual strengths:

I agree with Zbig that we need to be more visible and active on the human rights issues. Of our numerous foreign policy initiatives, it is the only one that has a broad base of support among the American people and is not considered 'liberal'. With Panama and SALT II ahead of us, we need the broad-based, non-ideological support for our foreign policy that human rights provides.[32]

Beyond the achievement of consensus, the human rights policy was seen as a way to improve America's image in the developing world, as focus and guarantee of the new internationalism, and as a means of enhancing US leverage in a range of regional contexts. If the policy presented opportunities, it raised a host of concomitant difficulties. Three problem clusters stand out: problems of definition, problems of consistency and problems of reconciling ideals and interests.

The Carter Administration never achieved a satisfactory operational definition of human rights. Did human rights include the right to eat? To live in peace? Or were human rights essentially negative – freedom *from* torture, arbitrary arrest and political censorship? Was America simply seeking to impose culturally relative values on other countries? Members of the Administration continually quarrelled over these questions. Cyrus Vance offered a three-part definition in 1977: 'integrity of the person's rights (notably in relation to torture, and arbitrary arrest); the 'right to fulfilment of such vital needs as food, shelter, health care and education'; and 'civil and political liberties' (especially regarding voting, travel and freedom of speech).[33] In operational terms, the Administration tended to accept the injunction of the 1974 Foreign Assistance Act that the US should not extend aid to countries with 'consistent pattern(s) of gross violations' of 'internationally recognised human rights'. (The Administration sought refuge from the charge of cultural imperialism by appealing to international legal codes.) Recognised infringements included 'torture or cruel, inhuman, or degrading treatment or punishment', including 'prolonged detention without charges'. White House aide Lynn Daft commented:

> The trick, of course, is in defining a ... 'consistent pattern of gross violations of human rights' and, once defined and the countries identified, figuring out a way to deal with the 'hit list' diplomatically and constructively.[34]

The policy achieved the unlikely distinction of being both even-handed and inconsistent. It was even-handed in the sense that a country's ability to 'escape' the policy did not depend upon the ideological complexion of that country's government. It depended on other factors. These included the unpredictable outcomes of unceasing bureaucratic warfare within the Administration. (The State Department's Human Rights Bureau, under Patricia Derian, found itself opposed by more traditionalist elements both within and beyond the State Department.) Also of importance was the degree of leverage available to the United States. After all, countries not in receipt of foreign assistance could hardly have aid withdrawn! The degree, and highness of profile, of domestic lobbying on behalf of various regimes was also relevant. Regarding countries who were in receipt of aid, the Administration also had to consider whether withdrawal of assistance might simply harm needy populations, rather than governmental abusers of human rights. Policy outcomes depended also upon wrangles within the international development banks and lending institutions. In some cases, there was a simple problem of American ignorance, or of awareness of abuses not making its way up the bureaucratic ladder. Mostly, however, 'escaping' the policy depended upon the invocation of some overarching US 'national interest'. The roster of 'escapees' is long and various. It includes: Romania (seen as a plucky country standing up to the Soviet bear); 'regional influentials' like Indonesia, Pakistan (especially after 1979) and oil-rich Iran; mainland China (where 'normalization' proceeded with little concern for Beijing's human rights record); and the Philippines (whose President Marcos used the US naval base at Subic Bay to extract concessions). To a large degree, the human rights policy became a policy for South Africa, the Soviet Union and, especially, for Latin America, where the US enjoyed particular leverage. Argentina, Bolivia, El Salvador, Guatemala, Haiti, Nicaragua, Paraguay and Uruguay all had security assistance cut off at some stage during the Carter Presidency due to human rights violations.[35]

Carter's rhetorically 'absolute' commitment to human rights was misleading and disingenuous. An inter-agency bureaucratic forum, chaired by Deputy Secretary of State Warren Christopher, existed precisely for the purpose of adjusting ideals to interest on a case-by-case basis. Human rights legislation explicitly provided for exceptions to be made on the basis of 'security' considerations. Even Patricia Derian, the supposed human rights firebrand, testified:

> ... human rights objectives do not determine each and every foreign policy decision. They are ... considered along with other vital U.S. interests such as the promotion of national security, trade and arms control.[36]

Yet it was not simply an issue of *force majeure* compelling policy retreats. Cynicism was not entirely absent within the bureaucracy. It also rapidly became apparent that the human rights/'global community' agenda was not the first concern of the National Security Adviser and his close associates.

For Jessica Tuchman Matthews, human rights officer on Brzezinski's staff between 1977 and 1979, the 'bottom line' of the human rights policy was its 'seriousness vis-a-vis the Soviet Union'.[37] The conservative wing of the human rights consensus was anxious that the Carter Administration should condemn Soviet human rights abuses and build on the 1975 Helsinki agreements on human rights (the so-called 'basket three' provisions). Before the 1976 election, Carter had already reversed his earlier opposition to the Jackson-Vanik amendment, which tied trading favours to the USSR to the loosening of restrictions on Jewish emigration. High profile human rights activism was resented by the Soviet leadership as an improper interference in the internal affairs of the USSR, and threatened to endanger detente and arms control. Carter, although he had criticised President Ford for giving away too much in the name of detente, wished detente to continue and to underpin a new arms control treaty. The Administration's answer to this conundrum lay in a separating out of human rights (support for Helsinki monitoring groups and for prominent Soviet dissidents like Andrei Sakharov and Anatoly Shcharansky) and arms control. Rejecting linkage, the Administration would pursue both goals. One problem with this was the extent to which leading American actors embraced different positions. For Vance and his close adviser Marshall Shulman, the prime goal was always arms control. For Brzezinski, traditional, hard-nosed containment doctrines became increasingly attractive. For Malcolm Toon, retained as Ambassador in Moscow from the Ford era, human rights activism from Washington had only the potential to destroy detente, without which the Soviets would be 'even less concerned about world public opinion'.[38] The parallel pursuit of human rights and arms control also exposed Carter to accusations of cynicism. (A 1977 memo to Carter from Jody Powell, press secretary and close Presidential confidant, illustrated the thin dividing line between cynicism and mature, realistic policy:

It seems to me that the Soviets should understand your feeling that it is necessary to build domestic political support for initiatives in arms

control and for detente in general ... . Surely the Soviets are sophisticated enough to understand ... the domestic flexibility we need to
make progress ... .)[39]

Yet it is going too far to suggest that Carter's support for Soviet dissidents was not conducted in good faith. The dissidents themselves welcomed the support, rejecting the view that it merely encouraged the
Soviet authorities to repress with more energy. Despite overtones of
cynicism, public backing for Soviet dissidence also demonstrated
Administration convictions that the new foreign policy should be cen-
trally concerned with values.

THE DEVELOPING WORLD

(a) Regionalism

The post-hegemonic policy for the developing world contained contradictions. Robert Pastor (Latin American specialist on the NSC), for
example, asserted in 1979 that Latin America should no longer be
regarded as the US 'region of influence', or indeed as an homogenous
region at all.[40] Yet the reason why the human rights policy became so
much a policy for Latin America was precisely because this was the
region, above all, where the US had the power to influence the behaviour of governments.

To critics on the left, the policy amounted simply to imperialism in
new clothes. As a good Trilateralist, Carter saw American business
investment in the Third World as a progressive force. There was no
'incompatibility between a belief in the free enterprise system' and a
'belief in enhancing human rights'.[41] Administration spokesmen denied
that the structural power of US-based capital precluded autonomous
decision-making in developing countries. According to Vance: 'Each
nation must decide for itself the role that private investment should play
in development'.[42] Unregulated lending to developing countries in
these years, it is now clear, was to accelerate the Third World debt
crisis of the 1980s.

The 'global community' approach to foreign policy, ascendant in the
early Carter years, embodied a 'regionalist' explanation of conflict in
the Third World. Disputes should not be seen through a Cold War lens:

that had been the problem in Vietnam. Legitimate nationalist aspiration was not to be equated with communism, even if nationalist or separatist movements had Soviet backing. Carter held that, since Vietnam, 'we've learned that this world ... is too large and too varied to come under the sway of either one of two superpowers'.[43] As a responsible superpower, the US had an interest in and a duty to seek resolution of regional conflict. However, in a complex world of limits, the US must seek the assistance of allies and 'regional influentials' – 'leadership is increasingly in need of being shared'.[44] Above all, America must back progressive, democratic change, and avoid becoming identified – as so often in the past – with tyranny and reaction. Identification with a democratic future in the developing world would serve American interests as well as American ideals.[45] The new approach required sensitivity, a reluctance to use either military power or covert CIA action; a commitment to preventive – rather than 'reactive'[46] – diplomacy; and a willingness to promote development through directed aid. Vance told the Paris Conference on International Economic Cooperation in May 1977 that Carter would 'seek from the Congress a substantial increase in the volume of new bilateral and multilateral aid programs over the coming five years'.[47] In fact, foreign economic aid increased from about four to about seven billion dollars annually between 1976 and 1980. In its first year, the Administration also moved to accommodate Third World positions on commodity prices and trade preferences. The Carter Administration certainly did not support any major redistribution in resources from rich North to poor South. Apart from anything else, worries about recession at home would have turned Carter against any such policy. Nevertheless, by the end of 1977 a combination of 'global community' and 'regionalist' statements appeared to presage a new era of what Pastor called 'cooperative multilateralism'[48] in US–Third World relations.

(b) The Panama Canal Treaties

Aware of the legacy of suspicion about US interests in the developing world, the Administration sought to prove its good faith: to demonstrate that it was serious about its post-hegemonic attitudes, even if policies were not yet fully developed nor free of contradiction. The key, and profoundly symbolic issue here involved Carter's determination to break the impasse surrounding US relinquishment of sovereignty over the Panama Canal. According to Robert Pastor, Carter spent more time on this than on any other issue during his first two years in office. Panamanian nationalism was to be recognised as a legitimate force. 'Imagine,' asked Vance, 'that a foreign country controlled and administered a ten-mile-wide strip of the Mississippi River. How long do you think the people of this country would willingly accept such a situation?'[49]

As well as sending signals to the developing world, Carter sought to defuse anti-American sentiments within Central America. Such sentiments threatened to deliver the Canal and Canal Zone to less predictable hands than those of the Panamanian leader, Omar Torrijos. Settlement of the Canal issue thus became a test of preventive diplomacy. Torrijos warned that if no treaty were signed, the Canal Zone might soon be without 'water, light or gringos'.[50]

In September 1977, treaties were drawn up to establish a US–Panamanian partnership in controlling the Canal until the year 2000. Subsequently, Panama would operate the Canal, but the US would have a right to 'defend' its neutrality. The treaties faced a tough path to acceptance in Panama, as well as in the US Senate. Carter's battle against the perception of many Senators that all this was a humiliating American give-away, was prolonged and bitter. The issue witnessed complicated interest group mobilisation, characteristic of the politics of interdependence. Carter's victory involved frenzied bargaining (notably in relation to the crippling 'reservation' offered by freshman Senator Dennis DeConcini). The victory was, as Brzezinski noted, 'politically costly'.[51] Yet it revealed Carter as – in David Skidmore's phrase – 'a skilful and flexible political improviser'.[52] The President was criticised for not pulling back from this difficult issue (as Gerald Ford had done); possibly he could have postponed it until a second term. Yet the treaties were accepted by the Senate (both by a 68–32 margin, in Spring 1978), Canal security was apparently guaranteed, and a signpost for the new foreign policy erected.

(c) Africa

'Regionalist' approaches to African policy were promoted by Secretary Vance and by Andrew Young, US Ambassador to the United Nations. Vance told the National Association for the Advancement of Colored People that a policy 'that seeks only to oppose Soviet or Cuban involvement in Africa would be both dangerous and futile'.[53] The Secretary of State was also particularly anxious that superpower confrontations in Africa were potentially destructive of arms control agreement. Andrew Young, civil rights veteran and the leading African–American in Carter's entourage, saw himself representing – as he put it in his 1979 resignation speech – those who suffered 'some kind of oppression in the world'.[54] Young saw US interests as dependent upon a strong commitment to change. US corporations could lead this change by investing in black Africa and promoting fair employment (the Sullivan Code) in South Africa. 'I see Africa,' Young told a House subcommittee in 1979, 'as a potential market ... that is asking for involvement with the United States.'[55] US accommodation with white conservative regimes in Rhodesia or South Africa would only push black Africa towards the Soviets.

Policy in Africa was the product of the encounter between this Vance-Young regionalism and the Cold War concerns increasingly being prioritised by Brzezinski. Even in 1977, Zbig saw his role as 'making certain that we did not ignore the Soviet-Cuban military presence', which had to be interpreted in the global Cold War context. American appeasement would, in any case, simply make 'the conservative whites in South Africa' even more 'fearful of accepting any compromise solution'.[56] The Vance-Young approach bore fruit in the Rhodesia/Zimbabwe settlement. (The agreement, which built on Henry Kissinger's 1975–6 policy, was finalised in 1980, after Young's departure from the Administration.) It was evident also in early efforts to persuade South Africa to quit, or at least hold free elections in, Namibia; in a muted American reaction to the April 1977 invasion of Zaire by secessionist forces from Angola ('Shaba I'); and in an extension of South African trade restrictions, notably to commodities destined for police use. Cold War considerations prevailed in continued non-recognition of the MPLA regime in Angola; in a much tougher reaction to the 'Shaba II' invasion of Zaire in 1978; and in a softening of America's stance towards South Africa and its occupation of Namibia in 1978–80. The extension of aid to mineral-rich Zaire also seemed to contravene the human rights policy. Above all, conflict in the Horn of Africa brought the antagonism between the Vance and Brzezinski approaches into the open. Brzezinski's anti-Sovietism had clearly triumphed by 1979, with the US opposing the Soviet-backed regime in Ethiopia and supporting Somalia. A military assistance pact was agreed with Somalia in 1980, again with little apparent concern for that country's human rights record. The tensions in policy towards Africa caused no little embarrassment to the Administration's defenders. David Newsom of the State Department argued in 1979 that Cold

War policies in Africa were an extension, rather than an abandonment, of human rights policies. It was Soviet underwriting of 'insecure and repressive regimes', like that in Equatorial Guinea, which had led to 'ghastly crimes against human dignity'.[57] In 1980, Richard Moose, the State's chief Africanist, tried to defend apparent easing of pressure on South Africa (seen, for example, in abandonment of any effort to make the Sullivan Code mandatory). Rather uncomfortably, Moose tried to adapt 'post-Vietnam' arguments about the limits on American power. Americans must realise that 'our ability to influence events is limited' and that 'dependencies between Western economies and South Africa's are mutual'.[58] Such arguments could not conceal profound policy inconsistencies.

WESTERN EUROPE AND JAPAN

Part of Carter's critique of the Ford-Kissinger regime centred on the supposed exclusion of Western Europe from the processes of detente. The Trilateral agenda promised close transatlantic collaboration, especially on economic issues. Early on in 1977, Carter sounded out West German Chancellor Helmut Schmidt on the prospects for cooperative economic management.[59] By 1980, some progress had been made – at least from Washington's viewpoint – on allied defence cooperation. Yet deep rifts had also opened between Bonn and Washington, and the Trilateral agenda of economic coordination had achieved little.

Among the major Western European allies, Anglo-American relations alone remained relatively free from strain and personal rancour. British Labour Foreign Secretary David Owen felt Carter to be 'the first US President to understand that in future America would lead more through persuasion than domination'.[60] Strains did appear when Carter responded to domestic pressure and to his own human rights announcements by announcing, for the first time, a legitimate US interest in Northern Ireland. His 1977 statement on the province offered US investment as a reward for a Catholic/Protestant power-sharing 'solution' there. In 1979 the State Department announced a ban on arms sales to the Royal Ulster Constabulary. Yet shifting American attitudes towards Soviet power intermeshed with political changes in London. The post-1979 Conservative government, despite some reservations, were far more supportive of the growing anti-Soviet toughness in Washington than were Carter's other European allies.[61]

The Carter years saw a coalescence of interests between Paris and Bonn. One expression of this was the progress made on plans for a single European currency: a move generally distrusted in Washington. Both Helmut Schmidt and Giscard d'Estaing (French President, 1974–81) saw Carter as an amateurish interloper, unmindful of European interests – for example, in the Middle East – and a potential destroyer of detente. Giscard's semi-clandestine meeting with Soviet leader Brezhnev in May 1980 elicited extremes of anger from Secretary of State Muskie. As for Schmidt, his intense antipathy to Carter dated from early American opposition to West German–Brazilian nuclear technology transfers. At the London economic summit of 1977, Schmidt was, according to David Owen, 'bruised by Jimmy Carter's insensitivity in implying that Germany could not be trusted over nuclear matters'.[62] By the year's end, Schmidt was canvassing support for a Euro-strategic balance concept (instead of the traditional global strategic balance favoured by Washington). Schmidt's implication was that the US commitment to Western Europe could not be relied upon. Carter's 1978 cancellation of the battlefield neutron ('Enhanced Radiation Weapon') bomb, for which Schmidt had lobbied against hostile domestic constituencies, incited a virtual breakdown in relations between Bonn and Washington.

Yet Carter's handling of the difficult West German relationship was not entirely lacking in either guile or achievement. In 1978, the allies acceded to the President's request for defence spending increases. Even more crucially, the putative West German 'shift to the centre' – Schmidt's apparent desire to act as a kind of disengaged intermediary between the superpowers – was resisted. The main issue here concerned the deployment of new, accurate intermediate missiles in Europe, to balance the Soviet SS-20s. Schmidt preferred sea-launched cruise missiles. Responding to Schmidt's fears about destroying detente, Carter reminded the German leader that he, Schmidt, 'had initiated the entire discussion of a European missile imbalance'.[63] In December 1979, Schmidt acquiesced in NATO's decision to begin deployment of S72 Pershing II and cruise missiles on European soil – many in West Germany, designed to deter and/or respond quickly to a Soviet first strike. (The 1979 agreement provided also for cancellation of deployment before 1983, should any arms control agreement lead to substantial SS-20 reductions.)

The Trilateral economic management agenda involved attempts by the US to persuade West Germany and Japan to reflate their economies,

especially with regard to imports. Carter achieved promising statements
on the need for economic coordination, notably at the 1979 Tokyo and
1980 Venice summits. The Carter Administration was acutely aware
both of the problem of US energy over-consumption and of the increasing importance of international trade. In December 1977, a State
Department economist reminded a Los Angeles business audience that
the US, with 6 per cent of the world's population, consumed one-third
of global energy production 'at a rate of the equivalent of a barrel of oil
per week per person'.[64] Carter repeatedly made this point in his television addresses. A Congressional trade subcommittee was informed in
1980 that exports, as a percentage of Gross National Product, had
doubled over the preceding 15 years.[65] (The implication here was that
the US was not overly concerned with falls in the value of the dollar.)
Economic allies were not convinced of American good intentions. The
energy bills which passed Congress in 1979 and 1980 did nothing to
lighten German scepticism about Carter's commitment to cutting consumption. US market interventions to halt the dollar's slide in value similarly failed to impress. At Tokyo in 1979, the US was urged to halve its
oil imports and to strengthen its commitment to a strong dollar.

By 1978–9, the US was running an annual trade deficit worth approximately 40 billion dollars. Of this, 12 billion derived from the Japanese
trade surplus. By 1981, Japan had gained control of 23 per cent of the
American car market. Carter's attempt to extract trade concessions, channelled through special envoy Robert Strauss, were energetic but un-
productive. Interlinked with these economic concerns was another
Trilateralist priority: to move Japan away from constitutional inhibitions
on rearming and towards assumption of the role of guarantor of regional
security. Increasing Japanese defence spending would not only aid the
cause of burden-sharing in Asia, but would – in Richard Thornton's words
– 'curb Japan's economic resurgence … by channeling Japan's enormous
and growing financial reserves into … consumption and away from
capital construction'.[66] Enhancement of the Japanese security role was an
important American goal and the key features of Carter's Asian policies –
the undertaking (subsequently abandoned) to withdraw from South Korea,
rapprochement with China, encouragement of the Association of South
East Asian Nations – can only be understood in terms of their intended
impact on Tokyo. Japan welcomed closer ties between Washington and
communist China, along with greater apparent US interest in the Pacific
region generally. The 1980 Report on Comprehensive National Security,
coordinated by Japanese Prime Minister Ohira Masayoshi, addressed

sensitive security issues after prodding from Washington. It pointedly noted the 'termination of the clear American supremacy in both military and economic spheres'.[67] Yet the Carter years ended with no firm Japanese undertakings to expand commitments.

SEARCHING FOR A MIDDLE EASTERN SETTLEMENT

In its earliest weeks, the Carter Administration characteristically committed itself to the search for a comprehensive settlement in the Middle East. Such an approach had the virtue of signalling a public break with Kissinger's discrete, 'step by step' strategy. Anwar Sadat, President of Egypt, himself apparently a beacon of moderation in the Arab world, indicated to the United States that Arab leaders were ready for a settlement. Similarly, the Israeli Labour Administration, under Prime Minister Yitzhak Rabin, seemed amenable to negotiation. (Washington presumed that Labour would be returned at the May 1977 elections.) The leading actors in Washington were also especially disposed to comprehensive solutions. Carter himself had a particular commitment to the region, deriving from his religious beliefs. He also saw the future of the Palestinians as an important human rights issue. Brzezinski and NSC staffer William Quandt had authored a 1975 study which envisaged Israel returning to pre-1967 borders, a demilitarised zone to protect Israeli security, and the establishment of a Palestinian state.[68] On addressing the Middle Eastern issue immediately after assuming office, Vance rejected the 'damage-limiting' approach (one of the options drawn up for him by regional specialists at the State Department). All, according to Quandt, were also acutely mindful of the Middle Eastern crisis of October, 1973:

> ... memories of the near-confrontation between the United States and the Soviet Union, the nuclear alert, and the oil crisis were still very much in mind. Rarely mentioned but also present was the recognition that full-scale war in the Middle East could some day involve the use of nuclear weapons.[69]

The Administration's commitment to comprehensive settlement was made in a spirit of pragmatic optimism. Carter and Vance were aware that tensions with Israel, and hence with Jewish lobbyists and voters at home, were 'unavoidable'. Opting for comprehensive solutions also did not rule out 'falling back to ... partial agreements if that was all that appeared possible'.[70] Nevertheless, miscalculations were made regarding both the evolving political configurations within Israel, and about Sadat's ability to lead and shape Arab opinion.

Washington's initial focus was on a re-convening of the 1973 Geneva conference, with invitations being extended to the Palestine Liberation Organisation (PLO). (Sadat favoured a kind of plenary Geneva process, assembling in East Jerusalem, and involving all interested parties including all permanent members of the United Nations Security Council.) Israeli opposition to any implied recognition of the PLO, and certainly to the establishment of a Palestinian state, effectively destroyed American and Egyptian plans to revive the Geneva conference. Further problems arose from the Israeli parliamentary elections of May 1977. The Likud bloc defeated Labour, and in June Menachem Begin was unexpectedly installed as Prime Minister. Begin was to remain implacably opposed to a Palestinian state; to Israeli withdrawal from the West Bank – an area he referred to as Judea and Samaria; – and to the ending of Jewish settling in the occupied territories (especially the West Bank). The Carter Administration was hopeful that American Jewish opinion would divide over the issue of the West Bank. None the less, by October 1977, the 'political reality' was, in Quandt's words, that 'Carter was under great pressure from the friends of Israel, and the Israelis played on his discomfort with extraordinary skill'.[71]

Against this background, Sadat made his historic decision to travel to Israel and to address the Israeli parliament. The Egyptian leader's initiative effectively foreclosed the Geneva conference option, ending controversial US efforts to recruit Geneva co-chairman, the USSR, into the process. The Knesset address (of November 1977) produced little else of substance. Begin began, rather unconvincingly, to speak of a form of 'autonomy' for Gaza and the West Bank. Yet the Sadat–Begin meeting at Ismailia (December 1977) made no progress. Carter effectively charged Begin with intransigence when the two leaders met in Washington in March 1978. Continued settling of occupied territories and a major Israeli incursion into the Lebanon deepened the pessimism. Faced by complex Egyptian and State Department manoeuvring, and also aware of the imminence of Congressional elections at home, Carter acted. In almost as bold a move as Sadat's Knesset address, Carter invited the Israeli and Egyptian leaders to high-profile, 'do or die' talks at Camp David in September 1978.

In an August news conference, Carter acknowledged that Camp David was 'a very high risk thing for me politically …'.[72] Though Begin's position was dangerously strong, the American President felt that Sadat would have to be seen to emerge from the talks with some kind of agreement. The 1978 accords were, as R.C. Thornton has argued, 'a temporary compromise'.[73] Yet they were also, in terms of what was feasible and as the various memoirists of the event make clear,[74] an extraordinary achievement for Carter's personal diplomacy. Shaped by Carter's personally drafted 'frameworks', the accords provided for and defined Israeli–Egyptian peace; set a timetable for Israeli withdrawal from Sinai; and promised vague transitional arrangements for the government of Gaza and the West Bank.

Between September 1978 and March 1979, the US tried to convert the accords into a treaty. The crisis in Iran, accelerated Israeli intransigence over West Bank settlements and evidence of Sadat's isolation in the Arab world all impacted dangerously on the prospects of resolution. Brzezinski informed Carter in January 1979:

… for the good of the Democratic Party we must avoid a situation where we continue agitating the most neuralgic problem with the American Jewish community (the West Bank, the Palestinians, the PLO) without a breakthrough to a solution.[75]

The final treaty, signed in March 1979, was again the product of personal intervention by Carter. Both Egypt and Israel were promised new military assistance. Israel was assured that oil supplies would be guaranteed by the US. As Carter admitted in 1985, Begin was determined to 'finesse' transitional arrangements for the West Bank and Gaza.[76] As White House adviser Hedley Donovan noted in January 1980, there was little prospect of keeping even 'moderate Middle East regimes' behind the treaty:

If we are unwilling or unable to budge Israel … it calls into question (with many Americans, as well as the Saudis) our capacity to conduct an independent foreign policy based on national interest.[77]

In the end, the Carter Administration was forced to accept a peace treaty rather than a comprehensive settlement. As Quandt noted,[78]

Carter had difficulty even in understanding, much less turning to America's advantage, the views of Menachem Begin. For Begin, territorial and settlement issues were not simply reducible to security concerns. Certainly, Sadat was very successful in promoting Egypt's claim to the US aid budget. He was nevertheless, in Carter's view, a man of political vision. Yet the Egyptian leader could not deliver even moderate Arab opinion, often for reasons deeply rooted in the history of the region. (King Hussein of Jordan, for example, feared the consequences for his own Hashemite regime of any real 'autonomy' on the West Bank.) Even more profoundly, policy-makers in Washington and Cairo had taken insufficient account of those forces which were to erupt in Iran in 1978–9: the forces of fundamentalist Islam. (Sadat himself was to be assassinated by fundamentalist soldiers in October, 1981.) Second only to the Soviet relationship, Islamic militancy was to preoccupy American diplomacy in future years.

3 Carter in Crisis

In 1982, Madeleine Albright of the National Security Council staff recalled that Carter was always 'totally committed to human rights'. Carter's personal commitment did not diminish. He saw the policy shifts of 1979–80 as involving, at worst, a postponement rather than a negation of the early 'global community'/human rights agenda. By 1979, however, there was a pervasive awareness of crisis within the Administration. Albright recollected Carter's reaction:

> As the real world began to fall in on him, we all, other than Zbig did, didn't know how he would come down [*sic*].[1]

By the latter part of 1979, the Administration had essentially reverted to containment as its guiding principle. The triumph of containment was never total; individuals in the Administration like Patricia Derian (and, up to his 1980 resignation, Cyrus Vance) continued to fight the 'global community' corner. Nor was containment rediscovered overnight. Shortly after assuming office in 1977, Jimmy Carter was presented with worrying evidence about the vulnerability of the US Minuteman force to Soviet guided missiles.[2] Later in the year, Carter signed Presidential Directive 18, a measure designed to establish special forces for flexible, low-intensity conflict in the Third World. In January 1978, Carter urged NATO countries to accept 3 per cent defence spending increases. In March, the USSR was warned not to intervene in 'local conflicts'.[3] Above all, US reaction to the 1978 African conflicts (especially in the Horn) exposed the degree to which the Brzezinski wing of the Administration retained the assumptions of containment theory.

Prominent among the 'shocks' of 1979 – the 'real world' which Albright saw as crashing in on Carter – were two revolutions. The first, in Iran, resulted in the coming to power of a fundamentalist, fanatically anti-American, but also anti-communist regime. The second revolution, in Nicaragua, was mounted by a broad-based, nationalist coalition.

Revolutionaries in both countries saw themselves as opposing the agents of American imperialism. Reverberations from the Iranian revolution were virtually to paralyse the Carter Administration in its later stages. Repercussions from both revolutions seemed, some years later, set to destroy the Presidency of Ronald Reagan.

REVOLUTION IN IRAN AND NICARAGUA

(a) Iran

More so even than the Soviet invasion of Afghanistan (December 1979), events in Iran caused the Carter Administration to re-examine its thinking and its priorities. Stansfield Turner, Director of the CIA in these years, subsequently described everything being 'totally consumed by Iran'.[4] The revolution and fall of the Shah (January 1979) disrupted US oil supplies and heightened the sense of crisis – so acutely and damagingly expressed in Carter's 'crisis-of-confidence' address of July 1979 – within the Administration. The taking, by militant Islamicists, of 65 American hostages in November, 1979, precipitated a yet more intense sense of urgency, even panic. Agriculture Secretary Robert Bergland remembered the hostage crisis bringing 'everything to a screeching halt'.[5] The Administration's agonies were compounded by a tripling in world oil prices between 1979 and 1981, and by the failed hostage rescue mission of April 1980. Vance opposed the mission when he was belatedly informed of plans for it. The Secretary of State resigned after the mission was aborted by Carter, following the deaths of eight US servicemen. The timing of the eventual release of the hostages – almost immediately after President Reagan's inauguration in January 1981 – seemed somehow appropriate. Robert Strauss, chairman of Carter's re-election campaign, commented thus on his boss's fortunes: 'Poor bastard – he used up all his luck getting here ...'.[6]

Reviewing events in Iran, it is not easy to identify exactly how Carter's policy could have been altered so as to produce different outcomes. Few Western observers were prepared for the intensity of the militant Islamic upsurge. Nevertheless, some key questions about US policy demand attention. In relation to the period before the Shah's fall, these include: Should the human rights policy have been applied more conscientiously to Iran? Alternatively, did the Carter Administration send the wrong signals and neglect its valuable ally? Why was it not possible to make a more coherent response to the deteriorating situation? What was the effect of the Vance–Brzezinski rivalry? Could the fundamentalists have been conciliated?

The Shah was a long-established American ally. He owed his position to a CIA-backed coup, which had restored him to power in 1953. Under his rule, Iran emerged not only as a source of oil but as (by the mid-1970s) the consumer of over half of all American arms sales. During 1977 and 1978, Carter effectively consolidated this relationship, choosing to ignore the record of human rights abuses associated with the Iran secret police (SAVAK). Cyrus Vance personally guaranteed arms contracts and negotiated the sale of new, high technology military equipment. The Administration's view appeared to be that the Shah's human rights record was far from perfect, but that it was improving. Peter Tarnoff gave the State Department view in September 1977. The Shah now had 'a more open approach to the entire subject of human rights'.[7] Gary Sick, Iranian specialist on Brzezinski's staff, noted that, with Iran, the 'security relationship was paramount'.[8]

Despite all this, and even despite Carter's famous Tehran toast (in January 1978) to the Shah's leadership 'and to the respect and the admiration and love which your people give you ...',[9] the closing of the Kissinger era did send encouraging signals to Persian oppositionists. Liberals were encouraged. The exiled Ayatollah Khomeini was advised by his (naturalised American) associate Ibrahim Yazdi that the 'Shah's friends are out' and that it was 'time to act'.[10] Throughout 1978, the Shah's position deteriorated. Washington's reaction was confused, and bore the imprint of the Vance–Brzezinski division. The State Department tended to see the crisis as capable of resolution if the Shah were prevailed upon to press ahead with reform. Meanwhile – although this policy was strongly opposed, at least until November 1978, by America's Ambassador in Tehran – overtures could be made to the fundamentalists. Brzezinski's preferred solution was repression. As he testified in 1982: 'I favoured a military coup before things fell apart'.[11] The Washington response to the gathering crisis was, by turns, dilatory, contradictory, and manic. Reluctance to abandon the Shah competed with the perceived need to build bridges to the opposition. Arguing the latter course, George Ball (the Democratic foreign policy veteran who Carter called upon to report on the crisis in December 1978) again invoked memories of Vietnam. America should not, argued Ball, 'as we did with President Thieu' (of South Vietnam) 'become the prisoner of a weakened leader out of touch with his own people'.[12]

With the fall of the Shah, the State Department attempted to encourage 'moderate' factions in Tehran. Whatever the virtues of this policy, Washington clearly still did not fully comprehend the strength of the Islamic fundamentalist opposition. Any hopes for a 'moderate' succession were destroyed by the taking of the American hostages. Carter's allowing of the Shah to receive cancer treatment was the immediate trigger to the hostage taking. However, this was essentially the product of the complex inter-factional politics in Tehran, and could well have taken place whatever Carter's attitude to the former Persian ruler. The President's own opinion was that the Shah was 'as well off playing tennis in Acapulco as ... in California'.[13] Yet arguments (urged on Carter by, among others, Henry Kissinger) about the need to be seen to stand by former allies were heeded. There was certainly no question of Carter acceding to demands that the Shah be shipped back to face trial (and execution) in Tehran.

Carter's reaction to the hostage crisis was undoubtedly embedded in the President's personal commitment to do what was 'right'. Yet, the suspicion of politics-as-normal, and the promise not to campaign until the hostages were released, were also acts designed to demonstrate the Administration's moral seriousness. Yet panic rather than high moral seriousness characterised Washington's conduct in the election year of 1980. The rescue mission was bungled and riven with over-hasty planning, inter-service rivalry and top-level disagreements. Brzezinski actually favoured bombing 'the hell out of Tehran', even if this meant having the hostages killed.[14] Vance's preferred option – of opening contacts with Tehran (including via the PLO) – eventually did lead to the release of the hostages.

Many important facets of the Iranian crisis, especially in its latter phase, still require clarification. The Administration was constantly frustrated by the complex situation in Iran. Warren Christopher (who served as deputy to Vance and to Ed Muskie, Vance's successor at State) later wrote: 'the aspirations of the Iranians changed according to who among them was doing the aspiring'.[15] Frustration certainly led to something in the manner of a 'deal' being offered to Tehran. It has also been alleged, though hotly denied by Brzezinski, that Iraq was encouraged by the Carter Administration to invade Iran in September 1980. Gary Sick has also famously charged that Ronald Reagan's campaign/transition team connived with Tehran to postpone the hostages' release.[16]

What is clear is that the entire conduct of policy in Iran was adversely affected, as Vance has acknowledged, by 'internal policy divisions'[17] –

especially between the Secretary of State and the National Security Adviser. It is possible to conceive how the crisis could have been more poorly handled. The hostages *were* eventually released. A major goal of policy in 1980 – the shutting out from Iran of Soviet influence – was achieved. (The period after the Soviet invasion of Afghanistan was marked by a distinct softening of Washington's attitude towards the anti-communist fundamentalists in Tehran.) Yet Washington's errors far out-weighed any achievements. The extreme prioritisation of the hostage issue increased the Iranian's bargaining power. During the earlier period, the combination of human rights rhetoric with continuing backing for the Shah amounted to exceedingly short-sighted policy. To some extent, the damage had already been done during the Nixon and Ford years. Then, the Shah's modernisation drive had been unhesitatingly countenanced in Washington, with no complementary concern for developing democratic institutions. Yet the Carter Administration also neglected unequivocally to identify itself with the cause of reform. As Vance admitted:

> We dissipated our potential influence by trying to breathe life into the imperial constitution rather than seeking to mediate an under-standing among the army, the political establishment, and the Khomeini-controlled opposition.[18]

Washington may not have been willing in 1977–8 to do what its Iranian Ambassador (William Sullivan) urged in November, 1978: to 'think the unthinkable' and envisage an Iran with no Shah. Never-theless, clear US identification with the cause of human and democra-tic rights would have signalled that the 'new' foreign policy was not merely gestural; and would have encouraged democratic opposition-ists, without necessarily disappointing them. Whether any such identification would have been sufficient to conciliate the Khomeini supporters is very doubtful. Perhaps the 'moderate' centre in Iran was never powerful enough to hold. Certainly the Administration did underestimate the force of Islamic militancy. Yet the 1978 uprisings were not entirely of a fundamentalist orientation. In George Ball's phrase, they amounted to 'a revolution of a thousand discontents'.[19] As it was, disinclination to 'think the unthinkable' led steadily to polarisa-tion in Iran, to anti-American extremism, and to the collapse of the very security structure which US support for the Shah had been designed to guarantee.

(b) Nicaragua

Events in Iran demonstrated the difficulty faced by Washington in escaping past commitments. It also illustrated how problematic was the search for a post-revolutionary 'moderate' centre. Both themes were replicated in Nicaragua, where the dictatorial Somoza regime owed its position almost entirely to Washington's patronage. The original dictator, Anastasio Somoza, had emerged from the US-trained National Guard to seize power in 1934 and to murder Augusto Sandino, the Nicaraguan nationalist leader. Presenting themselves as guarantors of US economic and anti-communist interest, the Somozas remained in power until the fall of the younger Anastasio in July 1979.

As noted above, the human rights policy had more impact in Latin America than in other parts of the developing world. Lacking the obvious strategic and economic prioritisation of an Iran, Nicaragua did feel the effect of the human rights initiatives. During much of 1977, security assistance was terminated to Nicaragua; the US also opposed loans to the Somoza regime within the multilateral lending agencies. The struggle over policy was played out between pro- and anti-Somoza forces on Capitol Hill and within the executive bureaucracy. In mid-1977, the Administration made it clear that any security assistance agreement would have to await major human rights improvements before it received the Presidential signature. To some extent this policy was vitiated by skilful and cynical second-guessing in Managua. Adept at adjusting to changes in direction from Washington, the Somoza regime was prepared to make cosmetic changes in order to extract aid. In September 1977, for example, Somoza lifted his internal 'state of siege'. Such gestures put the Administration in a near impossible situation. Few people believed that Somoza would ever respect human rights. Yet the human rights policy was based on the assumption that all regimes were capable of reform, and that changes in behaviour should be rewarded. The unhappy consequences of all this were demonstrated by Carter's ill-judged letter of June 1978. President Carter urged human rights improvement upon Somoza, but congratulated the dictator for an apparent change of heart about allowing exiled democratic oppositionists to return to Nicaragua. Regional leaders in Panama, Costa Rica and Venezuela interpreted the letter as a guarantee of US support to Somoza, whatever the consequences for human rights. Somoza's apparent ability to orchestrate Washington's policy convinced some – notably Terence Todman, who resigned as Assistant Secretary for Inter-American Affairs in February 1978 – of the unviability of the entire human rights policy. To Todman's successor, Viron Vaky, it demonstrated that any pretence of 'neutralist' or 'post-hegemonic' relations between the US and Nicaragua should be abandoned. Somoza should be eased out of power, and a constitutionalist opposition eased in.[20]

The murder of constitutionalist leader Pedro Joaquim Chamorro in January 1978 led to a temporary cessation of American aid the following month. The Administration was by now deeply divided about how to handle the situation. At one level, the Vaky position clashed with the view held by Pastor and by Anthony Lake (State Department Director of Policy Planning) that – in Pastor's words – 'the United States should not pursue a policy of overthrowing governments'.[21] At another, human rights representatives like Patricia Derian and Mark Schneider vied with those who were now preoccupied with the 'security threat' raised by the radical Nicaraguan opposition: the Sandinistas or FSLN. In August 1978, the Sandinistas actually seized the Presidential palace in Managua. Douglas Bennet of the State Department informed Congressman Lee Hamilton in October that policies were needed to 'help steer developments towards a moderate, independent course which will avoid Marxist or revolutionary excess'.[22]

Washington's major initiative involved a rather muddled attempt to mediate between the various Nicaraguan factions through the main regional organisation, the Organisation of American States. The more independent-minded OAS leaders (notably Costa Rican President Rodrigo Carazo and Venezuelan leader Carlos Andres Perez) distrusted US aims in Nicaragua, and were engaged in shipping arms to the Sandinistas. The preferred US policy appeared to be '*Somocismo* without Somoza': a transfer of power from the dictator to the National Guard. Like US clients in Vietnam, Somoza was not prepared to bend to instructions from Washington. Mediation failed. As events unfolded, Washington's response degenerated into a confused panic reminiscent of policy in Iran only a few months previously. Brzezinski promoted unilateral American intervention. 'Moderate' centrists were courted. Anthony Lake was to recall 'desperate efforts to find a way to influence a flood of events that surged far ahead of Washington's real power or even understanding'.[23] Somoza resigned on 17 July 1979, to be succeeded by a Sandinista-appointed government, drawn from all sectors of oppositional opinion.

William Bowdler, who had attempted to lead the OAS mediation for the Carter Administration, later argued:

The sensible reaction to the Nicaraguan revolution would have been to avoid open hostility to it. Then the Sandinistas could not use the United States as an excuse for their own mistakes.[24]

In fact, the Administration was uncertain whether to co-opt, conciliate, support or oppose the new regime. Pastor's early reports emphasised that the Sandinistas were prepared to tolerate opposition; that the new government included Catholic priests; and that the new Nicaraguan ambassador 'pointedly indicated' that US aid 'would be channelled through the private sector'.[25] Many voices within the Administration argued that the best way of avoiding another Cuba was to integrate the new regime into international aid and lending networks. The US backed and encouraged multilateral loans in the latter part of 1979, and in June 1980 a major US aid package eventually passed Congress. US Ambassador Lawrence Pezzullo argued that, although not exclusively democratic, the Sandinista regime was 'home-grown'. As he told Congress in 1979, 'Sandino predates Castro'.[26] Above all, the US should not abandon its leverage by attempting to ostracise the new government.

Pezzullo was to resign his post in August 1981 in protest at the Reagan Administration's abandonment of leverage and increasing demonisation of revolutionary Nicaragua. Yet, here as elsewhere, the transition from Carter to Reagan was surprisingly smooth. Even as he reported to Brzezinski that the Sandinistas were committed to pluralist media, Pastor described a country 'largely directed by pro-Cuban, anti-American Marxists'.[27] In its very last days, the Carter Administration accused the Sandinistas of fomenting revolution throughout the region, diverted covert monies to destabilise the Nicaraguan regime internally, and restored 'non-lethal' aid to the rightist government of El Salvador. To some extent, increasingly hostile attitudes towards Managua were the product of events in Nicaragua itself: for example, the postponement of free elections and the opening of trade links to the Soviet Union. Primarily, however, hostility reflected the Administration's post-1979 reversion to containment thinking and attitudes. Of course, policy had earlier reflected muted anxieties about Soviet influence in Central America. Martha Cottam has analysed policy in terms of a three-way tussle between human rights promoters (notably in Derian's bureau), 'modified cold warriors' (like Vance and Vaky) and 'traditional cold warriors' (like Frank Devine, Carter's first Ambassador to El Salvador).[28] Derian's faction was able to influence policy early on, but essentially only due to the patronage of Vance and other leading State Department figures like Warren Christopher. As the Nicaraguan crisis developed it moved, in Vaky's phrase, 'a little closer to the front burner'.[29] The crisis-riven atmosphere of 1979 and 1980 ensured that it never, in fact, became entirely a 'front burner' issue; (Nicaragua is, for example, largely absent from the major Administration memoirs). Its translation from a 'human rights' to a 'security' issue was not straightforward, yet it mirrored the evolution of Administration thinking. By the end of 1979, the most important 'modified cold warrior' of all – President Carter himself – had changed his views about the nature of Soviet power.

FROM SALT TO THE CARTER DOCTRINE: ARMS CONTROL, THE USSR AND CHINA

(a) Arms Control

For the early Carter Administration, 'global community' ideas did not involve conciliatory attitudes towards the Soviet Union. Carter actually assumed office proclaiming a new toughness, rooted in claims of a new understanding of Soviet power. One dimension of the new toughness related to human rights concerns, considered in the previous chapter. Another involved the condemnation of the Ford-Kissinger version of detente. Brzezinski considered this too timid, 'essentially static, even conservative'.[30] In the second televised debate with President Ford, candidate Carter declared that, in the diplomacy of detente, 'we've been out-traded in every area'.[31] Rather paradoxically, the new toughness emanated from the view of the Soviet Union propounded by political and academic figures associated with the Trilateral Commission: the designation of the USSR as a 'status quo' power. According to this view, the Soviet Union was no longer a Leninist power bent on world domination. It was a mature, conservative actor in the international arena, beset by economic weaknesses and progressively enmeshed in global interdependence networks. A major Trilateralist goal was precisely to entice the Soviets further into such trading, cultural and technology-transfer webs.[32] The 'status quo' thesis also involved the assumption that the Soviets had deep anxieties about nuclear war, and were unlikely to risk all in a bid for world domination. Awareness of all this might release the US from past timidity and permit a new, tough directness in US–Soviet relations. Speaking for the 'hard' wing of Trilateralism, Brzezinski criticised the Kissinger approach in the following terms:

If you predicate your entire foreign policy on the assumption that any predetermined move you make in American–Soviet relations is fraught with the dangers of nuclear war, you are, in fact, declaring yourself unequal to the game Moscow is playing.[33]

In fact, Brzezinski, unlike Vance and other leading figures in the Administration, never fully accepted the 'status quo' thesis. Zbig's deputy on the NSC staff, William Odom, later testified to an early split within Carter's team, 'over whether or not the Soviet Union was a status quo power'. Odom and Brzezinski 'thought it was not'. Vance and Leslie Gelb (political-military officer in the State Department) saw the USSR – in Odom's rather tendentious phrase – as 'becoming benign ... and accepting the international order'.[34] For Brzezinski, the USSR was a malign force, but opportunistic and actually incapable of global domination. A major NSC staff study,[35] completed in Carter's first year, concluded that the Soviet Union was economically vulnerable. Zbig argued that the US should avoid 'excessive preoccupation with Soviet relations'. He felt that the 'Soviet threat toward global preeminence was less likely to lead to a Pax Sovietica than to international chaos.'[36] The USSR leadership was both malevolent and mature.

Henry Kissinger's policies, of course, had also been based on a recognition of the maturity of the Soviet system. His central doctrine, 'linkage', had come under severe pressure in the Ford period, and Carter's team tried to distance themselves from it. Defined as the delicate orchestration of trade, arms control and regional policy to influence Soviet behaviour, 'linkage' conflicted with the Carter-Vance determination to seek arms control for its own sake, and to pursue regional solutions to regional problems. Again, Brzezinski's stance was somewhat different. Always anxious – in fact, actually more so than Vance[37] – to distance himself from Kissinger, Brzezinski also condemned 'linkage'. Yet Zbig's programme for 'a carefully calibrated policy of simultaneous competition and cooperation'[38] was difficult to distinguish from his predecessor's. Where Vance, Brzezinski and Carter came together, however, was in the assertion that Kissingerian 'linkage' and detente had worked to the Soviet advantage. Under detente, Soviet leaders had sought 'to deter the United States from responding effectively to the changing political balance'.[39] Nowhere was this clearer than in the area of arms control.

The Carter Administration was soon to come under intense attack from conservative opponents of its own arms control policy. The President's cancellation of the B-1 bomber – seen, with some justification, by Carter as wasteful Pentagon excess – was an early occasion for such criticism. Yet the Administration was itself deeply concerned about the extent of Soviet defence spending during the era of detente. Defence Secretary Harold Brown advised Brzezinski in March 1978:

> ... the Soviets have been building up their forces steadily for fifteen to twenty years, while our real defence spending except for the period of the Vietnam War, has steadily dropped and is lower than at any time since 1950.[40]

Richard Thornton's thesis, that virtually every action taken by the Carter Administration was deeply affected by February 1977 intelligence reports about the vulnerability of its Minuteman force, strains credibility.[41] However, the alacrity with which the USSR fitted its long-range missiles with multiple, independently targeted warheads (MIRVs) did alarm Washington. The deployment of SS-20 missiles in 1977 also raised the possibility of disabling strikes against NATO targets in Europe.

Against this background, Carter decided to disown the 1974 framework agreement made at Vladivostok by Kissinger and Soviet leader Brezhnev. (The framework was designed to lay the foundations for a strategic arms limitation – SALT II – treaty.) The Carter Administration wanted something, in Brzezinski's words, 'more *comprehensive* and more *reciprocal*'.[42] Vance's 'deep cuts' proposal, which he and Paul Warnke presented to Brezhnev in March 1977, were designed both to restore concessions made at Vladivostok, and to redeem Carter's promise (made in his Inaugural Address) to lead the world to a non-nuclear future. Vance's proposals would have severely restricted Soviet land-based missile capability. In return, the US delegation offered to drop future MX (missile experimental) construction. Moscow's almost inevitable rejection was followed by some limited agreements and commencement of a complex negotiating process.

The 'deep cuts' proposal was a fiasco. According to Strobe Talbott, it:

> ... led the Soviet leadership to conclude that the new administration did not really know what it was doing – and to the extent that it did know, it was up to no good.[43]

'Deep cuts' had been enthusiastically advanced, for various reasons, by Carter, Harold Brown and Vice-President Walter Mondale. Vance and Warnke, in fact, had misgivings about abandoning the Vladivostok framework, but suppressed them in their zeal for cuts in nuclear arsenals.[44] For the next two years the superpowers struggled to produce an agreement which, when it came, was not all that different from the 1974 agreement. The SALT II treaty was signed by Carter and Brezhnev at Vienna in June 1979. By this time, Republican and conservative Democrat suspicion of Soviet intentions had overtaken those harboured by the Administration. Senator Henry Jackson condemned the Vienna agreement as 'appeasement in its purest form', comparing it to Neville Chamberlain's 1938 Munich agreement with Adolf Hitler. When Carter returned from Vienna, he stood in the pouring rain, declaring: 'I'd rather drown than carry an umbrella.'[45]

The tortuous SALT negotiations did involve some Congressional input, but were far more redolent of Kissinger-style 'back-channel' diplomacy than the open processes promised by the Administration in 1977. Inevitably, verification issues were especially troublesome. The final agreement had something for both sides. Strategic limits were fixed for both parties at 2400 maximum, with reductions in the early 1980s. Sub-ceilings were attached to MIRVed long-range missiles. However, the Soviets would not budge in the face of efforts to have them dismantle their 308 heavy missiles. Here, Moscow probably did achieve leverage from their perception that American negotiators were very unwilling to leave Geneva without an agreement. Facing the US Senate, Cyrus Vance was pressed to explain why the agreement included MIRV sub-ceilings, rather than a limit on Soviet heavy missiles. According to Strobe Talbott, the Secretary of State glossed over the reason for this:

... namely, that the Soviets had repeatedly refused to negotiate a limit on heavies, and the U.S. had finally decided that there was no point in continuing to butt its head into that particular stone wall.[46]

The treaty did not specifically mention the American intermediate Pershing II missile, although a protocol prohibited deployment of the intermediate cruise missile until 1982. Brezhnev made informal undertakings to restrict production of the Backfire bomber. Treaty provisions on heavy bombers tended to favour the American side. More important in terms of selling the treaty to the US Senate, however, was the scope which the treaty allowed for the US to develop the MX. Carter found decisions on destructive weaponry 'nauseating'.[47] In April 1978, he had announced that his Administration did not wish to proceed with the neutron (battlefield 'enhanced radiation') bomb. As the Vienna summit approached, however, he was convinced by Brzezinski of the political and strategic benefits of the MX. In effect, the MX represented America's response to the problem of Minuteman vulnerability: a possible first strike against Soviet long-range missiles.

The Administration nevertheless faced a bitter ratification battle in the Senate. The battle became, as Vance put it, 'the catalyst of a broadening conservative challenge to detente'.[48] These conservative forces grouped around Henry Jackson in the Senate and around the Committee on the Present Danger, an elite, bipartisan group (including Paul Nitze and Eugene Rostow) re-formed in 1976. Central to their concerns was America's 'window of vulnerability': the possibility of a concerted Soviet attack destroying America's land-based missiles. The 'window of vulnerability' thesis effectively ignored the extent to which US weapons systems had continued to develop in the 1970s, and discounted the retaliatory strike capacity of submarine-launched, manned bomber and European-based missiles. Critics of SALT argued also for the revival of 'linkage'. As Dan Caldwell has argued, Brzezinski himself explicitly linked SALT success to Soviet behaviour in Africa, and thus to some extent himself slowed down the prospects for ratification. For Brzezinski, arms control was always 'at best a secondary objective'.[49] But even Carter himself could not deny that Soviet behaviour across the globe was bound to influence the Senate vote. The case against 'linkage' was put to the Senate Foreign Relations Committee in September 1979 by Stanley Hoffmann, a leading academic initiator of the Administration's 'global community' agenda:

> Rather than as a deliberate, planned and masterly march toward world domination, Soviet policy is much easier to interpret as first a relentless attempt at achieving equality with the United States by breaking the American monopoly of control of the high seas, or of means to intervene all over the world, and imposing Soviet participation in the settlement of all major disputes, and second, as the skilful

exploitation of opportunities ... . To be sure, recent Soviet successes are profoundly irritating to Americans, but the idea of linking explicitly arms control agreements to Soviet good behaviour does not deserve being revived. It suggests that such agreements must somehow be in the Soviets' interests more than in ours, which is false.[50]

On 24 December 1979, Soviet troops invaded Afghanistan. The Administration abandoned SALT – although the Reagan Administration observed its limits until 1986 – and the treaty never came to a vote. As well as the treaty, the Administration also abandoned Hoffman's ideas about the nature of Soviet power.

(b) The China Card

Much of the difficulty in concluding a SALT agreement with the Soviet leadership, especially in the Winter of 1978–9, was traceable to the developing closeness between Washington and Beijing. Chinese communist leader Deng Xiaoping made no secret of his hostility to SALT, and did his best to undermine it. Brezhnev saw President Carter as taking up Nixon's policy of using China as a lever against Moscow. In mid-1978, the Soviet leader condemned America's playing of the 'China card' and developed his theme in his statement at the 1979 Vienna summit. In December 1978, a joint US-Chinese communique joined the two nations in opposition to 'efforts by any country or group of countries to establish hegemony or domination over others'.[51] In January 1979, full diplomatic relations were established and Leonard Woodcock (after Senate acceptance) became the first ever US Ambassador to the People's Republic of China.

Normalisation of Chinese relations had been part of the early 'global community' agenda. Brzezinski saw it as part of 'a new post-Eurocentric' policy.[52] Increasingly, however, the National Security Adviser promoted the policy, not in 'global community' terms, but as a way of establishing a Eurasian balance of power through the development of an anti-Soviet alliance. Here, Brzezinski moved to what he himself described as a 'head-on confrontation'[53] with Vance, who objected both to Zbig's arrogant assumption of policy leadership and to the policy itself. For a time, as Alexander Moens describes it, the two 'literally tore the process in two directions'.[54] Carter's adjudication was characteristically modulated, but essentially and increasingly the President favoured Brzezinski.

At issue was not only the Soviet reaction but also the question of American loyalty to the old Chinese nationalist ally in Taiwan. Rightist critics raised the loyalty issue, issued the cry of 'another Panama', and pursued the constitutional issue (of US termination of the Taiwan treaty) to the Supreme Court.[55] Yet Brzezinski's formula for dealing with the Taiwan issue won the day. Cleverly adapting Chinese tactics towards their treaty with the USSR (which China now wished to abrogate), Brzezinski's plan involved giving notice of termination of the US–Taiwan defence agreement. To some degree, the US–Chinese agreement on Taiwan was highly limited. The US right to supply 'defensive' arms to Taiwan continued to be contested by Beijing into the Reagan Administration. The Chinese undertaking to renounce the use of force against Taiwan was also rather ambiguous, and reflected complex intra-Politburo rivalries.[56] Nevertheless, Brzezinski's formula worked in the context of US domestic politics, with the new Taiwan Relations Act passing easily through Congress in March 1979.

Deng visited Washington in January 1979 and informed Carter of the Chinese intention to undertake a punitive invasion of Vietnam. Carter's protests were not heeded. China's action followed the Vietnamese invasion of China's anti-Soviet ally, Cambodia. As Gaddis Smith has written: 'If standards of human rights alone had prevailed, the United States should have supported Vietnam'.[57] America's old enemy had invaded its neighbour as much to save that country from the murderous onslaught of its own ruler, Pol Pot, as to fulfil the role of a Soviet proxy. To Brzezinski, the Vietnam–Cambodian war was the 'first case of a proxy war between China and the Soviet Union'.[58] Vance managed to ensure that no major arms sales were made by the US. Yet there was a clear American tilt towards China and Cambodia, in line with the accelerating commitment to anti-Soviet containment and with policies favoured by the leading 'regional influential' (the emergent industrial states represented in ASEAN, the Association of South East Asian Nations). Carter's early hopes of offering reconciliatory overtures to the recent foe in Hanoi were abandoned. (Mid-1979 also saw a retreat from the 1977 US commitment to withdraw ground troops from South Korea.) By the end of 1980, with containment in the ascendant in Washington, new US–Chinese trading arrangements were in place. These provided for the transfer of technology with possible military uses.

(c) Afghanistan and the Carter Doctrine

The relentless move towards the resumption of containment doctrines was bound up with Administration reactions to anti-SALT elite mobilisation and to perceived changes in public opinion. As Raymond Garthoff puts it: 'Rather than serving as a rallying point for the administration, SALT II became a lightning rod that attracted attacks on the administration, on detente, and on SALT.'[59] The SALT debate put the Administration on the defensive, as 'neo-conservative' Democrats and Republicans railed against the putative ascendancy of 'post-Vietnam' disaffected intellectuals, who offered 'defeatism masquerading as optimism'.[60] Public opinion had questioned the competence of the Carter Administration, but had appeared to support most of its foreign policy initiatives. In 1978, Carter was able effectively to use public opinion as a lever against conservative opponents of his policy towards Taiwan. Polls taken after the Iranian hostage seizure were generally supportive of Carter and the early 1980 Presidential primaries showed a clear 'rally-round-the-flag' effect. By late 1979, however, there were clear signs that the spillover from SALT was running against the Administration. Daniel Yankelovich and Larry Kaagan, in an article published in 1981, linked SALT to the oil crisis, to the 1980 Mariel boatlift (where Cuban leader Fidel Castro succeeded in having over 40 000 Cuban 'refugees' admitted to the US), to Iran, and to America's trade performance: the US public felt 'bullied by OPEC, humiliated by the Ayatollah Khomeini, tricked by Castro, out-traded by Japan and out-gunned by the Russians'.[61]

Throughout its final eighteen months in office, the Administration both provoked and reacted to this newly apparent public assertiveness. Public worries were exacerbated by the September 1979 'discovery' of a Soviet 'combat brigade' in Cuba. The affair was farcical: a combination of bureaucratic gaffe, panicky over-reaction and spin-offs from the Vance–Brzezinski rivalry.[62] The incident did nothing to reverse growing public perception of the Administration's incompetence.

Against this backcloth – the SALT debate, the playing of the 'China card', increasing worry in Washington about Soviet intentions, signs of a new US public unease, the crisis in Iran, bureaucratic victories for Brzezinski – the Soviets invaded Afghanistan. The Soviet leadership undoubtedly took into account the formation of what it saw as a hostile Sino-American alliance. It probably also made calculations about the likely fate of SALT. (The Soviets may have seen SALT as a lost cause, but the timing of the invasion scarcely bears out conservative views that the 1979 Vienna summit was a triumph for Moscow.) Undoubtedly the Soviets sought to strengthen their position in the destabilised Persian Gulf region. It was tempting to interpret the invasion as a return either to Leninist expansionism, or to the search for traditional Russian geopolitical goals (such as the acquisition of warm water ports). Conservatives argued that the perception of American weakness encouraged the invasion. However, far more immediate motives were apparent. The Soviets wished to restrain Islamic fundamentalism on their borders, and indeed within the territorial USSR. They may even have anticipated some sympathy in Washington in this respect. George Kennan, architect of containment in the 1940s, warned the Carter Administration against overreaction. A pro-Soviet regime *already* held sway in Kabul, and open Soviet incursions took place only when that regime was threatened. Kennan saw the Soviets as being 'sucked in' by the instability in the region.[63] They were concerned about the nature of the rural opposition to the Hafizullah Amin regime. Amin was murdered and replaced by Babrak Kamal, with the apparent intention of shoring up the country against Pakistan and China, as well as against the militant Islamic threat.

The American Administration's reaction was intense and extreme. This was the 'most serious threat to peace since World War II';[64] the first 'use of military power by the USSR in a nonaligned country' since 1945;[65] more serious than the 1968 Czech invasion, since Afghanistan was 'an independent country'; a threat to Pakistan and to '90 per cent of exportable oil supplies in the world';[66] 'a deliberate effort of a powerful atheist government to subjugate an independent Islamic people'.[67] In his January 1980 State of the Union Address, the President promulgated the Carter Doctrine:

Let our position be absolutely clear; an attempt by any outside force to gain control of the Persian Gulf region will be regarded as an assault on the vital interests of the United States of America, and such an assault will be repelled by any means necessary, including military force.[68]

A barrage of anti-Soviet measures was announced. Risking electoral retribution in the farm states, Carter proclaimed a suspension of grain sales to the USSR. Invoking memories of the 1936 Berlin Olympics, the President declared that the US would not take part in the forth-coming Moscow Games, and urged allies to follow suit. SALT II was to be withdrawn from the Senate. Defence spending was to be significantly increased. A Rapid Deployment Force was to be established, primarily to enforce the Carter Doctrine. Draft registration was to be re-introduced.

The resumption of containment as the cornerstone of Washington's policy was sudden and intense. Yet it admitted to renewed prominence a doctrine which, in reality, had never been abandoned, but merely sidetracked by the Administration in its 'post-Vietnam, global community' phase. Washington's arming of North Yemen in early 1979, for example, had essentially been predicated on the assumptions of containment doctrines, and provided almost a dry run for the 1980 policies. These policies were also, at one level, associated with personnel changes: not only Vance's partial eclipse, but also the firing of Andrew Young (in July 1979, following an unauthorised meeting with PLO representatives). Carter's own understanding of the nature of Soviet power had also changed dramatically. Ever since the Soviet dissident 'trials' of July 1978, the President had been increasingly inclined to picture Moscow as cynical – even, perhaps, as evil. Yet shortly before the announcement of the Carter Doctrine, the President declared that his 'opinion of the Russians' had 'changed more dramatically in the last week than even the previous two and a half years ...'.[69] Already sensitised to the importance of safeguarding oil flows, the Administration now displayed a new sensitivity to geopolitics. As David Newsom, Undersecretary of State for Political Affairs, put it in April 1980:

> No one outside the Politburo really knows why the Soviet Union made the decision to invade Afghanistan. The real reason is, perhaps, not as important as the fact that they are there.[70]

The new attitudes accelerated the adoption of a new nuclear doctrine, promulgated in Presidential Directive 59 (July 1980). Recognising the emergence of newly accurate nuclear targeting, PD-59 essentially broke with traditional strategic deterrence theory and embraced 'limited' nuclear war options.

Not everyone within the Administration agreed that the invasion was the greatest threat to world peace of recent times. White House adviser Hedley Donovan, for example, warned Carter against overreaction.

Donovan's Soviet sources told him that the invasion was essentially defensive in motivation. As for Afghanistan, the US could not 'do much of anything' there in any case.[71] In public, Administration spokesmen tended to link the new tough policies to Moscow's apparent post-invasion restraint. In April 1980, however, Undersecretary Warren Christopher admitted that the USSR had 'their hands full in Afghanistan' – a conflict which Christopher likened to Vietnam – and were now unlikely to push forward to the Gulf.[72] (Severe warnings were issued by Carter, however, when, in his Presidency's final days, it seemed as if the Soviets were preparing to invade Poland.)

Outside his Administration, Carter was faced by a familiarly double-pronged attack. Republicans contended that this 'post-Vietnam' Administration had stripped American arsenals bare, and that its eleventh hour conversion to containment was too little, too late. The new policies were welcomed in Congress and appeared to rest on public approval. Carter's victorious opponent in the 1980 Presidential elections supported the Carter Doctrine; yet Reagan was also able to exploit perceptions of Administration unpreparedness. On the left, Senator Edward Kennedy, challenging Carter for the 1980 Democratic nomination, questioned:

> ... is this really the gravest threat to peace since World War II? Is it a graver threat than the Berlin blockade, the Korean War, the Soviet march into Hungary and Czechoslovakia, the Berlin Wall, the Cuban Missile Crisis, or Vietnam?[73]

EVALUATING CARTER'S FOREIGN POLICY

Evaluation of Presidential direction of foreign policy is inherently difficult. It brings to the surface the evaluator's assumptions and values. Appropriate criteria for such evaluation cannot be hard and fast. However, in line with the focus of this book, the following criteria may be suggested: firstly, a President's managerial effectiveness and success in achieving stated goals; secondly, accordance with the principle of democratic accountability and adherence to constitutional procedures; and finally, and most problematically, the wisdom and morality of the policies pursued. Hovering over these criteria is our theme of putative American decline. To what extent have the post-Vietnam Presidents understood, reversed, overcome, managed, resisted or accelerated this decline?

The conduct of Carter's foreign policy was occasionally chaotic, and its coherence was badly damaged by the Vance–Brzezinski rift. Carter undoubtedly felt that a successful post-Vietnam foreign policy would have to embrace the positions advocated both by Cyrus Vance and by Zbig. Carter's approach to relations with the USSR, for example, emphasised both cooperation *and* competition. Operationally, however, the rift was debilitating. Neither Vance nor Brzezinski showed any inclination to observe the division of labour intended (according to Hamilton Jordan) by the President: 'Zbig would be the thinker, Cy would be the doer, and Jimmy Carter would be the decider'.[74] The relationship between Secretary and National Security Adviser was also marked by a personal bitterness which transcended any 'natural', bureaucratic tendency for these two senior foreign policy officers to clash. Vance actually accused Zbig of deliberately falsifying NSC committee summaries which Brzezinski produced for the President. Although Brzezinski never attained the status of a Kissinger, events tended to play into the National Security Adviser's hands. Prior to 1980, however, the top-level rivalry required firmer and more directed Presidential adjudication.

The 'global community'/human rights phase of Carter's Presidency represented – despite the contradictions discussed in Chapter 2 – an imaginative and intelligent attempt to restore consensus and purpose after Vietnam. Carter's new foreign policy was a sensitive and politically sophisticated attempt to respond to the erosion of American hegemony and to the rise of interdependence. In its 'global community' phase, the Administration was to some extent led astray – in the case of SALT and, arguably, also in the Middle East – by its desire for comprehensive solutions. Yet a new working consensus, rooted in the wide appeal of the human rights doctrines, was achieved. Moreover, the commitment to democratic foreign policy was not merely gestural. Carter's appointment of Stansfield Turner to head the CIA signalled a new determination to promote Agency accountability, and to accommodate Congressional demands for greater oversight.[75] All this failed to survive the shocks of 1979. During the Iranian hostage crisis, the Administration undertook, according to Harold Hongju Koh, 'one of the most dramatic exercises of presidential powers in foreign affairs in peacetime United States history' (for example, in unilaterally freezing Iranian assets in the US).[76] By 1980, containment had effectively replaced 'global community'. The CIA was engaged in covert operations in Iran, Central America, Afghanistan and Africa. The 'Second Cold War' had begun.

The policy turnaround of 1979–80 was not as sudden as it appeared to many contemporary observers. Carter's Annapolis speech of June 1978 foreshadowed the later, tougher line toward Soviet power. The President himself regarded 1980 as embodying a postponement, rather than an abandonment, of 'global community'. (Carter's 1981 Farewell Address significantly re-prioritised human rights concerns.) Post-Cold War writers have shown new sympathy for Carter's foreign policy.[77] Many of Carter's concerns – above all, the search for a consensual belief to replace anti-communism – were also to preoccupy American foreign policy-makers in the 1990s. It must also be remembered, however, that it was the Carter Administration which reversed the post-Vietnam decline in US defence spending. The total annual military expenditure in 1980 rose to 127.3 billion dollars.[78] (Reaganite charges that Carter left America defenceless were absurd.) By 1980, detente was extinct and nuclear war more of an immediate possibility than at any time since the 1962 Cuban missile crisis.

4 Renewing America: Reagan and the Cold War, 1981–5

Ronald Reagan was content to allow the 1980 Presidential election to take its course as a referendum on Jimmy Carter's performance in office. The hostage crisis, the second oil shock (resulting after the Iranian revolution in four hour gasoline lines in the US), domestic inflation, unemployment, appearances of disarray in the White House, the 'window of vulnerability': Reagan scarcely lacked opportunities to assault Carter's record. Reagan entered the immediate pre-election period with a clear lead on domestic issues. Yet on foreign policy issues, the signs were that the American public, though more assertive than previously, were alarmed by Reagan's bellicosity. Gallup polls taken in September 1980 suggested that Carter was ahead on foreign issues, and far more trusted to keep the peace than Reagan. (A year later, nearly two-thirds of Gallup respondents actually thought a nuclear war 'likely'.)[1]

Reagan's reputation as a warmonger had been made in his days as a roving lecturer to the Republican right, and as Governor of California. In October 1965, he attacked President Lyndon Johnson's (indeed disastrous) 'limited war' strategy in Vietnam:

We should declare war on Vietnam. We could pave the whole country and put parking stripes on it and still be home by Christmas.[2]

In his 1970 California campaign, Reagan addressed the apparent loss of national purpose. It was 'time we ended our obsession with what is wrong and realize how much is right ...'.[3] Aware of the dangers of reopening wounds, the Reagan team showed caution in its treatment of the Vietnam legacy ten years later. The word, 'Vietnam', took its place alongside 'Watergate' as an evocation of unnecessary and paralysing self-doubt. Yet when candidate Reagan spoke of 'no more Vietnams' it was in the context ('our front yard') that the US would stand by its friends.[4] In August, 1980, Reagan's emotional attachment to the old cause surfaced in a speech to the American Legion. Discussing the late war, Reagan declared it was 'time to recognize that ours was in truth a noble cause'; never again must young Americans be asked to 'die in a war our government is afraid to win'.[5] The Inaugural Address in January 1981 saw Reagan invoking 'a hundred rice paddies and jungles of a place called Vietnam', along with Belleau Wood and Omaha Beach, as the scene of heroic American deaths.[6] The contrast with Carter's immediate post-inaugural amnesty was palpable.

THE REAGAN APPROACH

(a) **Myth and Substance**

Received views of the Reagan Administration's foreign policy tend to focus on 'the Reagan paradox': the gap between words and deeds; between declaratory and operational signals; between New Right attitudes and pragmatic handling of concrete issues; between rhetorical warmongering and practical peace-making; between Reagan as the exemplification of rightist Republican provincialism (with overtones of nativism and isolationism) and Reagan the internationalist instigator of a new, post-Cold War order.[7] Such interpretations do tell an important part of the story. Reagan's words and deeds frequently did not connect. There was a manifest alteration in emphasis between the first and second Reagan Administrations. Analyses of the Administrations do have to disentangle symbol from substance. Yet some qualifications still need to be made to interpretations which stress the gap between Reagan's words and mythic language (especially in the early 1980s), and Reagan's deeds. Firstly, as will be seen below and in the following chapter, Reaganite warmongering was not entirely confined to windy speechifying. Secondly, 'symbols' clearly do impinge on the 'real' world and on 'real' behaviour. Soviet and European behaviour in the early 1980s was as much a reaction to Reaganite symbolism as to Reaganite 'substance'. Thirdly, 'symbol' and 'substance' are not – as postmodern cultural theory reminds us – entirely discrete categories: especially not in the context of contemporary American culture,[8] and certainly not in the mind of Ronald Reagan.

All American Presidencies aspire to symbolic leadership and to a declaratory reinvention of national purpose. Political culture in the United States is saturated with the urge of self-conscious re-creation: to proclaim New Deals, New Frontiers or (in the less well-remembered example of Jimmy Carter in 1979) New Foundations. Even more than other Presidents, however, Reagan manifestly regarded symbols neither as optional extras, nor as dangerous hostages to fortune. As Michael Schaller writes, he 'lived in a world of myths and symbols, rather than facts and programs'.[9] The liver of an archetypal 'American life', Reagan exemplified at least one version – in truth many versions – of the American dream. To quote Garry Wills:

> He is an icon ... He is a durable daylight 'bundle of meanings', as Roland Barthes called myth. Reagan does not argue for American values; he embodies them.[10]

Holding, embodying, reinventing American values, Reagan was, as William Schneider wrote in 1986, able to 'have his cake and eat it too'.[11] Living by potent myths, Reagan was able (at least until the Iran-*contra* story broke in 1986) to combine pragmatic crisis-avoidance with his role as orator of American values. 'America is Back!': the slogan of 1980 well expresses the heart of Reagan's myth-making. The 1970s were the 'decade of neglect'.[12] America was not in decline but, as he proclaimed in the Inaugural Address, in the process of dynamic self-renewal. Supporters were told in 1980:

> ... for many years now, you and I have been shushed like children and told there are no simple answers to complex problems that are beyond our comprehension. Well, the truth is that there are simple answers – just no easy answers.[13]

The 'simple answers' were: free enterprise, deregulation, the ending of self-doubt, rearming in the face of Soviet aggression, and rejuvenation of the national democratic (and messianic) purpose. Reagan's speech-writers consciously immersed themselves in his characteristic themes and metaphors in order to produce speeches which radiated Reaganite authenticity.[14] The message was also eagerly taken up by Alexander Haig, the new Secretary of State, who told a television audience in April 1981 that 'Americans everywhere have a thirst to reinvigorate America's world mission'.[15] The 1970s was 'a decade when negotia-tions often seemed to be a substitute for strength', when 'the psychology of Vietnam and rising domestic resistance to military programs' had deflected America's purpose.[16]

The Committee on the Present Danger, to which Reagan himself belonged, supplied both personnel and themes to the new Administration. According to CPD publications, the Soviet threat outweighed all other considerations for US foreign policy. The Soviets had managed, partly by exploiting American eagerness for arms control, to achieve something like a first strike nuclear capability in the late 1970s. Coercive diplomacy (as in the 1962 Cuban missile crisis) was to be preferred to the preventive diplomacy adopted by the Carter Administration. Interdependence and the communications revolution summoned the US not to recognise limits, but to embrace a new globalism:

> In a world which is becoming smaller every day, the United States cannot protect its interests by drawing an arbitrary line around certain areas and ignoring the rest of the world. No region of the world can be excluded in advance from the agenda of our concern.[17]

Even more in line with Reaganite authenticity, the CPD declared in its *The 1980 Crisis and What We Should Do About It*:

> America is more than a superpower. The idea of the United States is a living part of Western Civilization, with a compelling and altogether special history which belongs to all who cherish human liberty.[18]

The new Administration's assertiveness and overriding concern with Soviet power was rooted in CPD attitudes. Haig could have been quoting from a CPD publication when he referred in his Senate confirmation hearings to the:

> ... central strategic phenomenon of the post-World War II era: the transformation of Soviet military power from a continental and largely defensive land army to a global offensive army, navy and air force, fully capable of supporting an imperial foreign policy ... .[19]

At Georgetown University in April 1982, Haig stated that 'first use' of tactical nuclear weapons was a viable military option.[20] CPD chairman

Eugene Rostow was named to head the Arms Control and Development Agency (ACDA), with CPD co-founder Paul Nitze as chief negotiator for European theatre nuclear forces. During the campaign against Carter's SALT II treaty, Nitze had argued against the acceptance of parity: 'To have the advantage at the utmost level of violence helps at every lesser level.'[21] At his confirmation hearings, Eugene Rostow was asked if he thought the US could either win or survive a nuclear war. He replied: 'Japan, after all, not only survived but flourished.'[22]

The new Administration's priorities for the developing world were free trade, anti-communism and control of terrorism. One of Reagan's favourite aphorisms was that governments do not solve problems; they subsidise them. Markets, not aid, would solve the problems of the developing world. In his first major speech on development issues, in Philadelphia in October 1981, Reagan asserted that 'no matter where you look … you will see that development depends on economic freedom.'[23] Radical free market views were more characteristic of rightist think tanks like the Heritage Foundation,[24] than of the more security-oriented Committee on the Present Danger. However, CPD perspectives were clearly evident in emerging Administration attitudes towards human rights. CPD activist Ernest Lefever was nominated as Assistant Secretary for Human Rights at the State Department. In 1979, he had proclaimed that the US 'should remove from the statute books all clauses that establish a human rights standard' for aid. At his confirmation hearings, Lefever partially disavowed the 1979 statement, but attacked Patricia Derian's record on human rights and declared his own disinclination to be seen as 'a saint or missionary.'[25] (Lefever's nomination was withdrawn in the face of Senate resistance.) Alexander Haig announced early in 1981 that control of terrorism would 'take the place of human rights in our concern because it is the ultimate abuse of human rights'.[26] Both the war against terrorism and the secondary concern for human rights were to be subsumed under the drive against communism in the Third World. Haig's testimony to the House Foreign Affairs Committee in March 1981 contained the assertion that all revolutionaries (except anti-communist ones) were terrorists. He warned the Committee of the 'terrorists' in Central America, 'most of whom have been through the schools in Eastern Europe and the Soviet Union, and all of whom are armed'.[27] Eliott Abrams, named to replace Lefever, was careful in his (successful) confirmation hearings to tie human rights to anti-communism: '… resistance to the expansion of communism is an essential part of human rights policy'.[28] The most celebrated discussion of Administration attitudes towards the Third World was provided by Jeane Kirkpatrick, Reagan's Ambassador to the United Nations. Kirkpatrick distinguished between 'totalitarian' (leftist) and 'authoritarian' (anti-communist) regimes. The former were seen as incapable of moving towards democratic forms; the latter were capable of such movement and could be supported.[29] (Like Eugene Rostow at ACDA, Kirkpatrick appeared thoroughly out of sympathy with the institution to which she was assigned. She described the UN General Assembly as 'a theater of the absurd', and assailed the Security Council as 'a Turkish bath: a place to let off steam rather than to resolve conflict'.)[30]

Though embodying attitudes commonly identified with the New Right, the CPD was not an accretion of the evangelical, fundamentalist, Sunbelt-oriented Republican right. For one thing, many CPD associates were neo-conservative Democrats. (Several of these, including Kirkpatrick, found their way into the Reagan Administration. Richard Perle, the increasingly influential Assistant for International Affairs at the Pentagon, had made his reputation on the staff of Democratic Senator Henry Jackson.) For another, and despite complex linkages between rightist configurations, the CPD essentially stood aside from the New Christian Right upsurge of the late 1970s and early 1980s. Dating back to the early Cold War years, the CPD represented an alliance of corporate and technocratic elites. It was internationalist in outlook, and constituted a strand within, rather than an assault upon, America's foreign policy establishment. Its principal target over the years was defence and foreign policy 'managerialism'. According to CPD pronouncements, 'policy' should reflect 'values' (defined primarily in terms of anti-communism).

There was a cleavage in Reagan's foreign policy team between 'true believers' (like Defence Secretary Caspar Weinberger and CIA Director William Casey) and 'pragmatists' (like George Shultz, the Administration's second Secretary of State). Yet very few even of the 'true believers' – at least those appointed to the regular departments, rather than to the White House staff – emanated from circles beyond those of internationalist defence and foreign policy elites. Weinberger had worked for Reagan in California, and William Casey had been Reagan's 1980 campaign director. Yet both men had served in the Nixon Administration, and both were members of the Council on Foreign Relations, the best known of all internationalist foreign policy elite organisations and parent to the Trilateral Commission. The Reagan departmental appointments did include a sprinkling of

Sunbelters with New Right antecedents ('cowboys' to offset the traditional 'Yankees').[31] European opinion, in particular, became distressed
at the apparent insularity of some of these 'cowboy' appointees. (At
his confirmation hearings as Undersecretary of State, William Clark –
Reagan's old staff chief from the California governorship – appeared
ignorant of any European opposition to nuclear weapons.) But
Reagan's top departmental foreign policy team consisted neither of tyro
'cowboys' nor doctrinaire New Right insurgents. Significantly, the
evangelical New Right was represented at Reagan's early Cabinet
tables not by foreign or defence specialist, but primarily by James Watt,
the Interior Secretary.

(b) Process

Reagan's foreign policy inexperience and lack of detailed expertise had
important consequences for the policy process. The President's relaxed
leadership style does have its defenders. Clearly, Reagan was not a
President likely to become overwhelmed by excessive workload or
over-immersion in enervating detail. George Shultz saw Reagan as able
'to get to the essence of the problems pretty well'.[32] According to Don
Regan, White House chief between 1985 and 1987, the President
'believed that large questions were easier to resolve than small ones'
and that 'the big answer usually contained all the smaller answers
within it'.[33] Unlike Eisenhower, with whom he is often compared,
Reagan's instincts were (despite his personal amiability) divisive rather
than consensual. He had a strong sense of 'the enemy' – both within
and outside the United States. Yet he clearly had a sympathetic feel for
what was concerning many Americans. Lou Cannon suggests that he
possessed a kind of sequential, story-telling (actor's) intelligence,
rather than an analytic 'logical-mathematical' intelligence.[34] What is
clear, however, is that Reagan's extremely relaxed leadership style had
severe implications for the cause of democratic foreign policy. At the
very least, as Don Regan writes, his failure to master a detailed foreign
policy brief 'gave some of his subordinates the idea that they had a
duty to save him from himself'.[35] At worst, what Richard Perle called
Reagan's extreme 'intellectual delegation of authority'[36] invited either
bureaucratic chaos, or the pushing of policy far into the regions of
unaccountability.

These tendencies became manifest in the Iran-*contra* revelations of
1986 and after. Yet signs of a distressed policy process were apparent

in the first term, notably in the antagonism between Secretary Haig and the National Security Council staff. At the outset of his Administration, Reagan promised that Haig would be the 'vicar' of foreign policy and that power would flow back to the State Department. Haig took this undertaking very seriously. Many observers, however, remembered that such promises had been made even by Nixon, and expected the organisational and political advantages of the NSC staff (especially the National Security Adviser (NSA)) again to work against the Secretary of State. Typically, Reagan's undertaking was actually a genuine one; but it was to be vitiated by his own virtual abdication of authority.

As journalist Dick Kirschten wrote in 1981, Reagan apparently made 'a conscious decision to lower the profile of the NSC' and to avoid 'the turf building' of a Kissinger or Brzezinski. Richard Allen, Reagan's first NSA, told his staff that theirs would be 'a true coordinating role, one that involves a low profile'.[37] In fact, none of Reagan's NSAs (Allen, William Clark, Robert McFarlane, John Poindexter, Frank Carlucci and Colin Powell) were especially powerful figures, at least beyond the confines of White House bureaucratic politics. None ever remotely approached the stature of Kissinger or Brzezinski. At least before Carlucci, little effort was apparently even made to recruit experienced personnel. According to Larry Speakes (White House press spokesman under Reagan), the 'President and his top aides' held the NSA in low esteem, paying 'little attention to those who held the post.'[38]

Reagan's early NSAs were essentially part of the 'cowboy', largely Californian, group of ideological right-wingers who dominated the White House in this period. Richard Allen, a rightist CPD activist, was brought in by Ed Meese, another associate of Reagan from California and member of the White House staff management 'troika' (of Meese, James Baker and Michael Deaver). Allen reported to the President only via Meese. According to Lou Cannon, much of Allen's time was 'spent vainly trying to shove decision documents and position papers' down the 'funnel-like management system that Meese had created to spare Reagan from decision-making'.[39] Allen's consequent frustrated assertiveness annoyed not only Secretary Haig, but also Michael Deaver, who engineered Allen's ouster in 1982.

To Haig, the White House looked like a Renaissance court running to insanity. In his memoir, *Caveat*, Haig was to complain bitterly about the incoherence of the Reagan NSC staff system, comparing it to a 'ghost ship': occasionally one 'glimpsed the crew on deck', but it was impossible to know 'which of the crew had the helm'.[40] To the White

House staffers, Haig was an object of intense suspicion. He was thought to covet the Presidential office to an indecent degree – a perception which Haig's histrionic reaction to the 1981 assassination attempt on Reagan did nothing to diminish. As an old Kissinger associate, Haig was also suspected of harbouring designs to restore detente. (Haig had been recommended to Reagan by ex-President Richard Nixon.) William Clark was apparently designated to succeed Richard Allen – Clark served concurrently as NSA and as Undersecretary of State – primarily to keep Haig in check. The Secretary's personality also upset Reagan. Michael Deaver records Reagan's adverse reaction to Haig's hysterical threat to turn Cuba into a 'parking lot'.[41] Amid extraordinary confusion, Reagan accepted Haig's resignation in June 1982, later remembering: 'He didn't even want me as the president to be involved in setting foreign policy – he regarded it as his turf.'[42]

The developing situation is well captured in the following description by John Spanier and Eric Uslaner:

> ... the president's lack of interest and competence in foreign policy meant that the conflicts that naturally erupt in any administration were usually not resolved. The result was that the secretary of state, secretary of defense, CIA director ... and others were continuously feuding. Instead of a battle between the secretary of state and NSA, the Reagan administration ended up with a confused mêlée.[43]

It was not merely a problem of Haig's personality. George Shultz also clashed frequently with what he regarded as the forces of narrow dogmatism, even quasi-isolationism, in other parts of the Administration. (He saw Weinberger, for example, as both inflexible and overly affected by post-Vietnam inhibitions on using force to achieve international aims.) But much of the thrust of Shultz's attack in his memoir, *Travail and Triumph* was – as with Haig – to be directed at White House bureaucratic politics. In Shultz's memorable phrase, it was 'worse than a university'. While reserving special venom for William Clark and displaying loyalty to Reagan, Shultz laid the blame at the Presidential door. Reagan 'frustrated' Shultz by 'his unwillingness to come to grips with the debilitating acrimony among his national security advisers', and by his 'over-reliance on his immediate staff'.[44]

Reagan's campaign promise to 'restore leadership to US foreign policy' was directed primarily at the supposedly rudderless Carter

Administration. Yet it also implied that Congress required firmer executive control.[45] Conventional promises about partnership and openness in executive – legislative relations were conspicuously not made. The Democratic leadership on Capitol Hill, concerned that the 1980 Presidential election did indeed signify a conservative revolution, appeared initially willing to accept Reagan's view that Presidential discretion in foreign affairs had become unduly fettered in the post-Vietnam years. (The Democratic party controlled the House of Representatives throughout the two Reagan Administrations. Between 1981 and 1986, the Senate had a Republican majority.) Republican Charles Percy, the new Senate Foreign Relations Committee chairman, spoke of the need for a new bi-partisanship and invoked the need for Presidential leadership.[46] Potentially controversial measures, such as the 'reprogramming' of funds to assist the government of El Salvador, were accepted with little Congressional protest. But even in 1981, the *annus mirabilis* in which the White House tax and domestic spending cuts were accepted by Congress, there were a few signs of legislative independence. The House rejected Reagan's plan to sell five Airborne Warning and Control System aircraft to Saudi Arabia. A year later, the House passed the first amendment successfully offered by Representative Edward Boland (Democrat from Massachusetts), disallowing covert US aid to the anti-government, *contra* forces in Nicaragua. Both the AWACs decision and the 1982 Boland amendment were killed in the Senate. (The Senate AWACs vote was actually trumpeted as a great Administration victory. Yet it was won only by adopting the high-risk strategy of invoking Presidential credibility in a highly publicised 'set-piece' vote.)

Outside Washington, evidence also began to mount of the reaction to Reagan's bellicose utterances. Peace campaigners (notably Randall Forsberg in Massachusetts) were organising a movement, rooted in an alliance between peace activists and middle class opponents of Reagan, to have Congress pass a resolution demanding a 'mutual and verifiable freeze' of US and Soviet nuclear weapons. The proposal was narrowly defeated in the House in August 1982; a Reagan-backed substitute, supporting the President's arms control efforts, passed 204–2. In May 1983, the House actually passed the proposal. The Administration's rattled response combined leaden attempts to co-opt the movement with clumsy accusations about its putative links with communism.[47] There was virtually no prospect of the resolution passing the Republican-controlled Senate. However, these various rumblings in the House presaged future problems for the Administration.

Reaganite attitudes towards the Central Intelligence Agency combined hostility to Congressional oversight with enthusiasm for covert operations. William Casey's closeness to the President, his elevation to Cabinet rank and the intensified Cold War atmosphere all contributed to a breaking of post-Vietnam inhibitions on the CIA. According to Bruce Berkowitz and Allen Goodman, Casey became the first CIA Director 'who can be said to have had effective control over the resources of the national intelligence community.'[48] The covert operations budget soared, much of it effectively invisible and beyond Congressional control. By 1986, at least five hundred million dollars annually were going to anti-Soviet covert operations in Afghanistan. Much of the US aid given to the government of El Salvador – over two billion dollars between 1980 and 1985 – came under the control of the CIA. Intelligence gathering was becoming ever more politicised. Casey almost certainly suppressed CIA reports with which he disagreed; for example, concerning the lack of evidence that Moscow was implicated in the 1981 assassination attempt on Pope John Paul II. Both specific and general reports on Soviet behaviour – on, for example, the shooting down of aircraft KAL 007 in 1983, and on the economic condition of the USSR – were finessed for political and polemical ends. As for Congressional oversight, even formerly staunch defenders of the CIA were driven to exasperation. In 1984, it became apparent that the CIA had overseen the mining of Nicaraguan harbours. Barry Goldwater, conservative Republican chairman of the Senate Intelligence Committee, was incredulous in the face of Casey's stonewalling. Congressman Norman Mineta of the House intelligence oversight panel declared in 1983 that Casey and the CIA 'keep us in the dark and feed us a lot of manure'.[49]

REARMING AMERICA

The Reagan rearmament represented the most rapid and extreme increase in defence spending authority in US peacetime history.[50] It was predicated, and sold to Congress, on the assertion that the Soviets had been allowed to race ahead in the post-Vietnam years. The later 1970s had seen, in Haig's extraordinary phrase, 'the Carter experiment in obsequiousness' towards the USSR, when the US had been a 'virtual spectator' (according to Reagan) in face of the Soviet arms surge.[51] William Clark announced that America had 'allowed its investment in defense to decline steadily in real terms throughout ... the 1970s'.[52]

Such claims were misleading. Following fiscal year 1975, annual defence budget authority grew in real terms at an average rate of two per cent. Clark's claim was based on budget *outlay* levels, which, because of long defence acquisition lead-times, inevitably lag behind budget authority figures. Important weapons systems (such as the Trident submarine and the M-2 Bradley fighting vehicle system) were acquired in the late 1970s, and indeed formed the basis of the Reagan modernisation programme. Al Haig actually acknowledged as much on French television in February 1981. In a tone which contrasted with his own Senate confirmation testimony, Haig described 'most of the experts' as accepting that the US–Soviet military balance was 'at a point of relative balance and equilibrium'.[53]

However dubious their assertions about the 'decade of neglect', Reagan's civilian appointees to the Pentagon – notably Defence Secretary Weinberger, Deputy Secretary Frank Carlucci and Assistant Secretary Richard Perle – encouraged a massive spending spurt. Between 1980 and 1985, defence budget authority increased in real terms by approximately 53 per cent. The Pentagon was permeated by a rejuvenated culture of conspicuous, prodigal and rapid acquisition. All were aware that Congressional and public support for the defence spending feast might not endure. (Already in the early 1980s, the 'military reform movement' was gathering strength in Congress, with its demands for enhanced accountability and a more disciplined procurement process.) Pentagon military and civilian interests, led by Weinberger, were also concerned to counter intra-Administration doubts about the economic wisdom of vastly accelerated spending. Budget Director David Stockman was urging Reagan to keep his commitment to a balanced budget, and urged in 1981 a 'slower growth alternative' for defence. Though even Stockman's proposal would have amounted to newly high peacetime spending levels, Weinberger's approach prevailed. Congress was warned not to 'temporize any longer in the face of the Soviet threat'.[54] Anxieties about abandonment of the balanced budget commitment were assuaged by hopes that deregulation at home would enhance economic activity (and hence tax revenues), and by the notion that, in the last analysis, security concerns were paramount. Weinberger, sometime host of a public affairs television programme in California, mobilised his considerable propagandistic and presentational skills in the cause of vastly increased spending. Simultaneous promises to extract efficiency gains from the defence budget – as Nixon's Budget Director, Weinberger had been known as

'Cap the Knife' – were effectively forgotten. The atmosphere of these early Reagan years was captured in remarks made by a Pentagon official involved in the 1981 budget:

> I was in the Office of the Secretary, working for the readiness accounts. Carter had given us a lot. The Weinberger team came in and said, 'Add more. Find room to add. Find places to put more money ...' .[55]

One military officer active in the Pentagon in this period estimated that 50 000 governmental defence contracts were being signed every day.[56] For the time being, Congress was unwilling seriously to question swollen defence appropriation requests, even acquiescing in the expansion of 'blank' defence programmes (where putatively sensitive details remained undisclosed even to the legislature). Many individual Members of Congress, of course, were only too anxious to attract defence funds into their constituencies. Built-in cost overruns, and virtually unmonitored complicity between arms contractors and the Pentagon, further exacerbated what David Stockman called the 'contracting idiocy'.[57]

The Reagan Administration's strategic doctrine involved enhancement of Carter's 'countervailing' strategy. As noted in Chapter 3, Jimmy Carter (in Presidential Directive 59) had embraced a strategy which – arguably – allowed for 'limited' nuclear war. The prime purpose of PD59, however, had, in Phil Williams' words, been 'to ensure that the Soviet leadership would not conclude that it could win a nuclear war'.[58] Weinberger clung to the concept of deterrence, but reserved 'escalation' as a possible last ditch response to Soviet nuclear attack. The Administration's 'Five-Year Defence Guidance', leaked in 1982, insisted that the US must have the ability to 'render ineffective the total Soviet military and political power structure.'[59] No doubt previous Administrations had indulged in extended private debate about 'limited' (usually European) nuclear war and about the 'winnability' of total nuclear war. Reagan and his team, however, seemed to treat these concepts almost as casual points of reference. Haig's increasingly alarming *obiter dicta* included the notion of firing a nuclear warning shot to keep the Soviets in line. At a 1981 press briefing, the President announced that he 'could see where you could have the exchange of tactical' nuclear weapons 'without it bringing either one of the major powers to pushing the button'.[60]

This cowboy-casual approach to nuclear issues incensed sections of European public opinion and further goaded the US nuclear freeze movement. Congress was notably far keener to endorse conventional arms hikes than to support the drive for enhanced nuclear capability. Environmentalist lobbying against nuclear power (civil as well as military) had an impact on Congress, as did worries about budget deficits. The Reagan Administration itself accepted that the Carter deployment plans for the MX were overly expensive. 'Dense pack' deployment, in fixed silos, was preferred to the rather exotic notion of mobile deployment on underground railways. Even so, the Administration's battle for MX funds was protracted and politically costly. In December 1982, Congress rejected MX funding: the first such vote against a major weapons system request since the Vietnam war. Though winning subsequent votes (notably in the House in March 1985), the Administration's MX programme still represented a decrease on the original Carter projections. In addition to MX, more Trident nuclear submarines were deployed and the B-1 bomber restored. (The B-1 was actually the only additional nuclear system deployed during the Reagan years.) The Administration also concurred in military advice that the despised SALT II levels were, at least for the time being, acceptable to the US and should not be breached.

The confusions and alarms of the rearmament agenda were transcended and re-ordered by Reagan's Strategic Defense Initiative ('Star Wars') speech of 23 March 1983. In *An American Life*, Reagan traced the origin of SDI to his own anxieties about nuclear war, and in particular about deterrence theory:

I came into office with a decided prejudice against our tacit agreement with the Soviet Union regarding nuclear missiles. I'm talking about the MAD policy – 'mutual assured destruction' – the idea of deterrence providing safety so long as each of us had the power to destroy the other with nuclear missiles if one of us launched a first strike. Somehow this didn't seem to me to be something that would send you to bed feeling safe. It was like having two westerners standing in a saloon aiming their guns at each other's head – permanently. There had to be a better way.[61]

The 'better way' was a strategic defence system, a high-tech shield which could intercept incoming nuclear missiles. Several commentators remembered that Reagan had starred in a 1940 Hollywood movie, *Murder In The Air*, as Brass Bancroft, keeper of plans for an American 'inertia projector', designed to intercept enemy aircraft. Reagan was also undoubtedly influenced by Edward Teller, who had long lobbied for strategic defence research. (Teller, leader of hydrogen bomb research, had associations with some of Reagan's Republican business support, notably the Coors beer interests.) Though it did, in a sense, emanate from the conservative Republican defence agenda, SDI also constituted a response to the nuclear freeze movement. In a bid for the moral high ground, Reagan offered to share SDI technology:

> I've had to tell the Soviet leaders a hundred times that the SDI was not a bargaining chip. I've told them I'd share it with others willing to give up their nuclear weapons.[62]

Reagan was presenting himself as – indeed, in a sense, he *was* – in J. Spanier and E. Uslaner's phrase, 'a populist utopian on nuclear matters'.[63] The President also clearly had an eye on future battles with Congress over long-range missile modernisation. In moving the debate into new areas, reruns of the December 1982 MX defeat might be avoided.

'Star Wars' represented a characteristically disarming (so to speak) Presidential response to certain emotional and political needs. Huge claims have been made concerning its intended and actual effect on Soviet conduct. (SDI's role in the winding down of the Cold War will be considered in Chapter 6.) Yet 'Star Wars' raised many problems. Most obviously, the difficulties were technical and technological. To the extent that 'Star Wars' operated at the declaratory and symbolic level, this did not necessarily matter all that much. A completely effective defensive 'astrodome', based on laser technology, was regarded as feasible (at least within any meaningful time scale) only by Reagan and a few enthusiasts. In any case, absolute safety could never be 'proved' in advance of an actual attack. This did not mean, however, that strategic defence technology research was not worth pursuing. It might have advantageous effects on Soviet behaviour. It might increase the *level* of effective American defences. It might lead in unexpectedly beneficial directions. However, the gap between the 'astrodome' concept and the feasible operationalisation of SDI was potentially damaging, as was the inevitable conceptual confusion about the programme's precise purpose.

Critics of SDI also contended that the initiative threatened to destabilise the regime of deterrence which had kept the nuclear peace for so
many years. From Moscow's viewpoint, SDI raised the spectre of the
US attaining a safe first-strike capability. The Soviets might respond by
increasing their offensive capability, as well as by embarking upon
their own defensive programme. The world would be faced by both
offensive and defensive arms races. SDI seemed also to run counter to
the Anti-Ballistic Missile (ABM) Treaty, negotiated by President Nixon
in 1972. Administration apologists argued for an expansive reading of
the ABM Treaty. (When the Democrats regained control of the Senate
after the 1986 elections, they managed to force a restrictionist reading
of the 1972 treaty on the Administration.) Reaganites like Weinberger
also argued that critics of SDI failed 'to appreciate the deterrent value
of missile defenses'.[64] These arguments failed to impress not only
Reagan's political opponents, but also 'Star Wars' doubters within the
Administration.

It was partially in order to circumvent bureaucratic doubt and caution
that Reagan had launched the SDI idea in so hasty and so almost
unprecedentally 'top-down' a manner. Peremptory efforts to gain the
approval of the Joint Chiefs of Staff were made only in February 1983.
The notion of sharing defensive technology with the Soviets, as a step
along the road to mutual renunciation of missiles made useless by the
new lasers, was a bureaucratic non-starter. Richard Perle declared
bluntly in 1985: 'If it were up to me, I would discourage scientific
exchange with the Soviet Union.'[65] During the second quarter of
Reagan's eight years' tenure in the White House, the prospects for SDI
appeared both exciting and ambivalent. The research agenda had been
shifted in an extraordinary manner. The money flow, impressive at first
though unpredictable for future years, seemed sure to create new,
vested interests. (Originally sold as a 26 billion dollar, five-year
research exercise, SDI achieved 1984 funding levels in Congress only
slightly below Reagan's request.) Above all, the effects on US–Soviet
relations could not be foreseen.

US–SOVIET RELATIONS: 1981–5

Reagan's military buildup demonstrated his faith in Theodore
Roosevelt's advice about carrying a big stick. But the fortieth President
certainly did not speak softly. The Soviet Union, the 'empire of evil',

was 'the focus of evil in the modern world'. The USSR was responsible for all the world's unrest: 'If they weren't engaged in this game of dominoes there wouldn't be any hot spots in the world.' The Soviet leaders 'reserve unto themselves the right to commit any crime, to lie, to cheat ...'.[66]

Some of these 'red meat' speeches were made in some emotional heat to right-wing audiences. The 'evil empire' speech, for example, was made in March 1983 to the US National Association of Evangelicals. That it was made in the same month as the SDI speech says much for Reagan's ability to internalise apparently contradictory symbolic images. The SDI speech seemed to presume a degree of rationality in Moscow. Could an 'evil empire' really be expected rationally to appreciate the benefits to all of the new technology, and abandon the arms race? Reagan's first-term rhetoric also contained contradictions concerning the perceived strength of the Soviet Union. On the one hand there was this 'focus of evil': armed to the teeth, vicious, expansionist, racing ahead (because of America's post-Vietnam self-doubts) in crucial areas of military strength. Deriving from Reagan's conservative roots and from the 1980 campaign, this rhetorical thrust was perpetuated to some extent as a means of generating public and legislative support for swollen defence spending. Yet it sat uneasily with another strain in Reagan's first-term account of Soviet power: the view that communism was on the ropes, and that the world was actually witnessing a Leninist *Gotterdammerung*. During the election campaign, he told *Washington Post* editors that excessive Soviet military spending meant that the leadership 'can't provide for the consumer needs'. Strikes were breaking out 'because people aren't getting enough to eat'.[67] At the first Presidential press conference, where he made his remarks about Soviet leaders reserving the right to lie and cheat, Reagan described communism as 'a sad, bizarre chapter in human history whose last pages are now being written'.[68] At a June 1981 press conference, he referred optimistically to Russia's 'younger generation': 'I think we are seeing the first, beginning cracks, the beginning of the end.'[69] A year later, he told the British Parliament that in 'an ironic sense Karl Marx was right'; ideological systems which defied the logic of history would crumble. It was, of course, the Soviet Union – not the US – which bucked 'against the tide of history'. The USSR was 'in deep economic difficulty'. A country 'which employs one-fifth of its population in agriculture' was 'unable to feed its own people'.[70]

Reagan's invocations of Soviet weakness now seem extraordinarily prescient. After all, many academic specialists on the Soviet Union were arguing that, despite its problems, there was no immediate danger of collapse. This was also essentially the view of the CIA, who in 1982 predicted continued – if slow – Soviet economic growth. A widely cited piece in *Foreign Affairs* in 1982 held that Reagan's approach was 'based on illusions about the weakness of the Soviet system'. Reaganite policies offered the post-Brezhnev leadership 'only confrontation or capitulation'. (Four years later, the same authors – Bialer and Afferica – concluded that the Soviet 'economic system cannot deliver the sustained expansion without which Soviet power will falter'. According to key tests of productivity and technological progress, 'capitalism has virtually won'.)[71]

How perspicacious and coherent was Reagan's understanding of Soviet weakness? As was evident in the 1980 remarks to the *Washington Post* editorial board, Reagan did seem to think in terms of forcing the Soviets (through military buildup) either to over-stretch or to admit defeat. How well-judged was this strategy? Was this, in fact, the story of the Cold War's end? How well crafted and effective was Reagan's policy of negotiating from strength? Answers to these questions will be offered in Chapter 6. For the moment, it is simply the intention to note the rhetorical inconsistencies of Reagan's first term, and to trace the rather faltering evolution of policy.

Reagan's containment policies had a more overtly ideological edge than those of his predecessors. Headed by the President's friend, Charles Wick, the International Communication Agency resumed its former name, the US Information Agency. American public diplomacy became far more obviously propagandistic, especially in its treatment of Eastern Europe. This reversion to the ways of the 1950s appeared to reflect the influence of 'hard-liners' within the Administration. Figures like Richard Perle and Richard Pipes (on the NSC staff in the early Reagan period), sought the destruction of Soviet power, primarily through economic warfare and the heightened arms race. Perle, in particular, became identified (along with his boss, Weinberger) with this 'squeeze' strategy: pressuring the Soviet regime through the denial of Western technology and by increasing US defence spending.

On the other hand, 'soft-liners' within the Administration appeared to favour the search for moderation in Soviet behaviour, especially in Eastern Europe and the developing world. Among some in the Administration – essentially those people who still regarded the commitment to South Vietnam as a mistake – the notion of 'selective containment' became fashionable: the view that the US should concentrate on resisting Soviet expansionism in areas of the world that were particularly vital to American interest. The Gulf, Western Europe, neighbouring regions in the Caribbean and Central America, and South Africa – with its important mineral deposits – seemed to qualify.[72]

Also important to the 'softer' elements within the Reagan Administration was the revival of 'linkage'. When martial law was proclaimed in Poland in December 1981, and the Soviets widely blamed for the deteriorating situation, economic sanctions were applied. The following year, Charles Meissner, economic specialist at the State Department, emphasised that the USSR could not 'expect to continue business-as-usual with us in the economic realm' if it attempted 'to solve political problems in other sovereign countries by force or encourage violations of human rights'.[73] But if sanctions could be used to influence Soviet behaviour, then so could incentives. Along this road lay the diplomacy of 'carrot and stick' (or, to use the terminology applied by the Reagan Administration, 'olive branch and cattle-prod') rather than of 'squeeze'. (Though, even in Meissner's formulation, it was possible for hard-liners to define communist expansionism in terms so broad as to exclude any prospect of 'business-as-usual' this side of Soviet collapse. Reagan's own campaign remarks, about the Soviet 'game of dominoes' lying at the root of the world's problems, seemed to point in this direction.)

During the early Reagan years, the litmus test of 'hard' or 'soft' position-taking tended to revolve around arms control. First term hard-liners, especially in the Pentagon, had no interest in arms control whatsoever. Most Reaganite soft-liners tended to see arms control as a 'carrot' in the context of 'linkage'. Few wished (as Cyrus Vance had under Jimmy Carter) to pursue arms control for its own sake. Alexander Haig later explained:

One may argue that nuclear arms control (and reduction) are such imperatives that linkage of negotiations in this field to Soviet behaviour in other spheres ought to be irrelevant. But any such argument is likely to be dashed against the hard rock of reality ... Moscow's international behaviour is such that linkage cannot be dismissed, whether or not a given Administration declares a policy on the subject.[74]

Haig's views put him to the left on the Administration spectrum. A former Carter staffer interviewed in 1981 put it as follows: 'to us

Democrats and moderate-to-liberals, Haig is the white knight, Weinberger is the rogue elephant'.[75] Haig's subordinates at the State Department – notably Richard Burt – tended to argue that, if the US were sufficiently tough-minded, a satisfactory arms deal could be struck with the Soviets. (An early victory for Burt's line was the qualified commitment to observe the SALT II levels.)

The most significant feature regarding arms control in Reagan's first Administration was the fact that talks were going on at all. These years were marked by constant American complaints (many fully justified) about Soviet violations of previous arms treaties. (After 1983, Reagan actually used the Soviet untrustworthiness as an argument for privileging SDI over conventional arms control. Addressing the nation on 'Star Wars' in 1985, the President declared that the Soviets had 'never accepted any meaningful and verifiable reductions in offensive nuclear arms. None.').[76] The Administration also alleged, in 1981, that apparent Soviet willingness to talk amounted only to an attempt to postpone the NATO deployment (according to Carter's December 1979 agreement) of cruise and Pershing II missiles in Western Europe. Yet Reagan always maintained that he was interested in arms negotiations. He insisted, for example, that the Congress should approve the MX 'not only for force modernisation' but also 'to keep the Soviets moving at the negotiation tables'.[77] Consummate juggler of conflicting rhetoric that he was, Reagan even contrived at times to sound as if he subscribed to the Cyrus Vance view of arms control. In a November 1981 speech, conspicuously lacking the intense anti-Soviet tone to which listeners had become accustomed, Reagan announced that the US would participate in intermediate range arms control talks in Geneva: 'to negotiate in good faith ... willing to listen and consider the proposals of our Soviet counterparts'. [78]

At Geneva, the American negotiators presented the 'zero option': no new cruise or Pershings in Europe if the Soviets would withdraw their SS-20s, along with some other missiles. The 'zero option' represented a bureaucratic victory for Perle and Weinberger. According to Reagan, Weinberger supported the 'zero option' as a way of getting 'the arms control talks moving on a realistic basis and putting the Soviets on the defensive in the European propaganda war'.[79] Soviet rejection was virtually assured, given that the American offer failed to include European allied missiles targeted on the USSR. Soviet Foreign Minister Andrei Gromyko told George Shultz in September, 1982, that the 'zero option' was nothing less than a call for the Russians to disarm unilaterally.[80]

A certain disingenuousness distinguished US attitudes towards both intermediate and long-range missile control. America's failure to address the issue of the allied missiles was a familiar sticking point in the intermediate talks. (The US insisted that the question of British and French nuclear forces be handled in separate, bi-lateral talks with Moscow. A State Department official remarked: 'It isn't our fault that the Soviets have too many enemies'.)[81] The 'zero option' is explicable, in fact, almost entirely in terms of an attempt to placate European opinion in advance of the new missile deployments. In relation to the long-range missiles, Reagan made a speech at Eureka College (his old college in Illinois) in May 1982, proposing equal cuts in the US and Soviet land-based intercontinental missiles. Again, the offer was absurd. With the Soviet strategic weapons concentrated on land, and the American equivalents dispersed between land, sea and air, it was bound to come to nothing. (Lou Cannon suggests that the Eureka offer derived not so much from a disingenuous public relations policy, but from the President's ignorance about the Soviet nuclear disposition.)[82] Great hopes for intermediate arms control were raised in May 1982, with Paul Nitze's famous walk in the Geneva woods with his Soviet arms negotiator counterpart. Yet the informal compromise (involving mutual SS-20 and cruise cuts) was rejected both in Washington and Moscow. The latter months of 1983 witnessed a series of events which further contributed to the breakdown in superpower relations: the shooting down of the Korean airliner by Soviet air defences (September); the award of the Nobel Peace Prize to Polish Solidarity leader Lech Walesa on October 6; the Middle East US troop alert following the bombing of US marine barracks in the Lebanon, and the US invasion of Grenada (both late October); NATO's nuclear exercise 'Able Archer' (November); and the eventual deployment of the new missiles in Europe. The latter development provided the cue for Soviet negotiators, in December 1983, to quit both the intermediate and long-range sets of arms control talks.

Despite all the ideological firepower, Reagan's attitude towards economic relations with the USSR was – economic sanctions over Poland apart – 'business-as-usual'. Carter's embargo on grain sales was lifted, and a new five-year deal on grain agreed with the USSR in 1982. Reagan contended that the embargo had been ineffectual in any case; although, in fact, the Soviets had had a poor harvest and continuation of the embargo would obviously have been in line with Richard Perle's 'squeeze' strategy. However, this was a Republican Administration, with strong desires both to conciliate the US farm vote and to ease its balance-of-payments problems. By 1983, the US was exporting one and a half billion dollars worth of agricultural products annually to the Soviet Union. Haig reminded journalists of Reagan's legislative priorities; failure to lift the grain embargo would, declared Haig, have left Reagan's 'farm bill and even his economic program ... in jeopardy'.[83] The sanctions applied in December 1981, in connection with the imposition of martial law in Poland, pointedly affected technology transfers and Soviet civil aircraft access to the US, rather than grain sales. Reagan's rhetorical support for, especially, Jewish dissidents inside the Soviet Union also did not disrupt 'business-as-usual'. By the end of its first term – especially after the lifting of martial law in Poland in the Summer of 1983 – the Administration was encouraging a wide range of trade, including high-tech transfers, with the Soviet Union.

In a way familiar to students of the Cold War, the first Reagan Administration's relations with Moscow seemed to serve domestic needs as much as international priorities: the needs of the conservative agenda, the need both to mould and respond to public and Congressional opinion, the perceived needs of the US economy, continuing electoral needs (such as those relating to the Polish-American vote, which had generally supported Reagan in 1980). Coral Bell has noted the 'almost total absence ... of true crises between Washington and Moscow' during the Reagan years.[84] Yet the first Reagan term was, especially for Europeans living on the likely site of 'limited' nuclear war, a frightening time. The events of, in particular, late 1983 – with the superpowers apparently talking across each other – engendered a sense of general crisis unknown since 1962. The US Administration no doubt felt that the infirm and uncertain state of the Kremlin leadership (under Brezhnev, Andropov and Chernenko) severely inhibited the prospect for diplomatic progress. Nevertheless, Reagan's failure to establish any personal top-level diplomacy, even neglecting to attend any of the proliferating Soviet leadership funerals between 1982 and 1985, was unnecessary and alarming. (Reagan did not meet a Soviet leader until he encountered Mikhail Gorbachev at the summit of November, 1985.) To Reagan's credit, the door to negotiation was never slammed entirely shut. Indeed, following the alarms of late 1983, Reagan adopted a far more conciliatory tone in the early part of 1984. Yet the overwhelming impression of Reagan's first term is of a policy of muddle, bluster, spectacular but disingenuous gesture and bureaucratic disorder. No Reaganite 'grand plan' shines through this fog. Even as George Shultz (and even, in his way, Reagan) attempted to revive arms control in 1984 and early 1985, National Security Adviser Robert McFarlane declared that the US had no interest in any such agreement.[85] The effect of these confusions on allied opinion was not such as to inspire confidence.

REAGAN AND THE ALLIES

The Reagan Administration did not share the Trilateral Commission's assumption that interdependence necessitated a newly cooperative sharing of power with the allies. Rhetorically wedded to policies of liberal free trade, the Administration's instinctive nationalism underpinned disputes with the allies in both the political and economic spheres. Richard Perle later accused European leaders of being 'woefully ignorant' of the 'unrelenting buildup of Soviet military power'.[86] In the economic arena, America's growing trade deficit (approaching 160 billion dollars by 1986) and economic nationalism in Congress conspired to produce high levels of protectionism. Significantly increased protection for US manufacturers was legislated by Congress in Reagan's first term. The Omnibus Trade and Competitiveness Act of 1988 required the executive to retaliate unilaterally against any country adopting 'a consistent pattern of import barriers and market distorting practices'.[87] Against this background, significant clashes developed between the US and Western Europe: over the Siberian pipeline and Polish sanctions, and over defence priorities.

Representing the largest ever commercial agreement between East and West, the Siberian natural gas pipeline was expected by 1984 to supply five Western European nations with one-third of their gas needs. Originally agreed in the late 1970s, the project embodied a recognition of economic interdependence and a commitment to the revival of detente. In 1981, the Administration adopted measures designed to prevent construction of the pipeline: US technology transfers were banned and sanctions levied on European companies involved. European and Japanese leaders (who were involved in their own gas project with the USSR) protested; even Mrs Thatcher, Reagan's closest European ally, condemned the American injunction to break pre-existing contracts. A compromise, which allowed the pipeline to go ahead and which represented the first major diplomatic success of the Secretaryship of George Shultz, was achieved in late 1982.[88] Acrimony over the pipeline in 1981 was compounded by the reluctance of the

European Community to participate in anything but a symbolic way in the Polish sanctions.

Virtually every aspect of US military thinking in the early Reagan years caused consternation and opposition in some, sometimes in all, sections of Western European opinion. Both public and elite opinion tended to resent the implication that Europeans were naive in their understanding of Soviet intentions. Reagan himself became the object of almost unprecedentedly intense public derision in Europe. The 1983 European missile deployments awakened extensive anti-nuclear protest in the UK and West Germany, and found expression in policy positions adopted by the British Labour Party and (after its 1983 defeat) the German Social Democrats. In France, the Socialist government of François Mitterrand seemed more solidly Atlanticist than its predecessors. The early 1980s revival of moves towards European military cooperation, in the Western European Union, did to a degree reflect US–American tensions; but it also represented a French response to fears of German drift away from NATO. Yet, despite Mitterrand's Atlanticism, French Foreign Minister Claude Cheysson urged his country in 1982 not to 'kneel' before the US, and proclaimed that Reagan's policies were inciting 'progressive divorce' between America and its European allies.[89] For their part, American defence and foreign policy elites were disturbed by anti-nuclear and anti-American public protests in Europe. They were also dismayed at what they saw as the crass populism of leaders like Cheysson, and exasperated by the perceived reluctance of European governments to pay their way in NATO. Defence analyst Stanley Kober presented the following summary in 1983:

> The opposition to the deployment of the Euromissiles has been based on the belief that in the event of war, these weapons would be the object of Soviet nuclear strikes ... some Europeans believe there is no reason for Western Europe to assume this risk, that the United States will assume all the risk of nuclear war because it has to, allowing the European NATO members to enjoy the benefits of the American nuclear umbrella.
>
> The point must be made bluntly: if this is an accurate assessment of the European interest in NATO, there is nothing in the alliance for the United States.[90]

Reasoning such as this found expression in an important US Senate debate on the commitment to Europe in June 1984. A proposal substantially to reduce US troops in Europe, if NATO allies failed to meet increased spending targets, was defeated by a 55–41 vote.

Fears of US conventional and nuclear 'decoupling' from NATO were prominent in the concerns of the pro-nuclear and pro-American governments of the large Western European nations. European leaders had countenanced the 'zero option' primarily, as Margaret Thatcher put it, 'in the hope that the Soviets would never accept'.[91] The Strategic Defence Initiative was interpreted in Europe as a means of absolving the US from expensive NATO commitments. It was at the Reykjavik summit of 1986 – ironically derailed by Reagan's attachment to SDI – that tensions within NATO assumed extreme form. In offering to elim- inate nuclear weapons in Europe, Reagan seemed to be bargaining away European security without even observing the courtesy of con- sulting with his allies. European leaders protested the threat to the concept of extended deterrence and the laying open of Western Europe to (in Margaret Thatcher's words) Russia's 'huge superiority of con- ventional forces, chemical weapons and short-range missiles'.[92] Mrs Thatcher hurried off to Camp David to make common cause with the Joint Chiefs of Staff in dissuading Reagan from repeating the offers made at Reykjavik. Meanwhile, leftist opinion in Europe assailed Reagan for squandering the hopes for disarmament because of his obsession with 'Star Wars'.

The breakthroughs of the second Reagan Administration, including the 1987 Intermediate Nuclear Forces Treaty, were supported by European governments as part of their commitment to the thawing of the Cold War. Yet European anxieties about the undermining of NATO's strategy of 'flexible response' remained, causing alliance ten- sions in 1988 and in the early Bush years. The European alliance was severely strained during the Reagan years. US policy in Central America and the Middle East, and the 1986 US bombing raid on Libya, caused further rifts. Among European leaders, only Prime Minister Thatcher gave full, public backing to the 1986 raid, which largely emanated from US bases in Britain. Thatcher and Reagan agreed on most things. From London's point of view, some progress was even made in these years on the difficult issue of having wanted Irish repub- licans extradited from the US. Yet a major rift opened in 1983, over Washington's failure to consult London prior to the 1983 invasion of Grenada (the Caribbean island which had achieved full independence within the British Commonwealth in 1974), as well as over the Reykjavik summit. Significantly, however, the US stepped back from what would have been by far the biggest breach to Anglo–American relations of modern times, and indeed a major threat to the entire NATO alliance: the adoption of a neutralist, or even quietly pro-Argentinian position, during the 1982 Falklands war. Such a position was urged, in the interest of hemispheric solidarity and support for the anti-communist military regime in Buenos Aires, by Jeane Kirkpatrick and Thomas Enders (Undersecretary for Latin America at the State Department). It was effectively opposed by Secretaries Haig and Weinberger, who succeeded in tilting US influence (decisively as far as the outcome of the war was concerned) towards Britain.

Economic relations with Europe were marked by disputes over Europe's Common Agricultural Policy, over the putative overvaluation of the dollar and over US interest rate policy. In the later 1980s, attention turned to the need to contain the international economic impact of the 1987 Wall Street crash. Little headway was made on the Japanese trade surplus. The US strategy was 'to use a continuing series of action-forcing events to put the spotlight on Japanese restrictions on trade and to get these restrictions reduced'.[93] At a speech given at Princeton in 1985, George Shultz argued that both the Japanese and the Americans needed to alter their attitudes towards savings and domestic consumption: the US needed to appreciate more the virtues of the former, Japan should prioritise the latter. Modest increases in Japanese defence spending were agreed in the early 1980s. (Though less than one per cent of Gross National Product, Japan's aggregate defence spending was still the fifth highest in the alliance.) Premier Nakasone also agreed to share military technology with the US. Japanese leaders insisted that their economic strategy and attitudes were not to blame for the trade imbalance. Reagan's budget deficit, with its associated high interest rates, lay at the root of America's economic problem. And indeed, as the Reagan years ran their course, it became apparent that the fortieth President's abiding legacy would not necessarily reside in the triumphs of negotiation from strength. An alternative legacy, of accelerated national decline associated with the budget and trading deficits, appeared as an unwelcome guest at the party to celebrate America's victory in the Cold War.

5　The Reagan Doctrine: War and Coercive Diplomacy

On 29 April 1985, Secretary Shultz gave a speech at the State Department to mark the tenth anniversary of the fall of Saigon. Against the advice of Dick Childress, NSC staff specialist on Vietnam, Shultz offered the most sustainedly upbeat account of the recent war yet attempted by a senior figure in the Reagan Administration. While admitting that 'mistakes' were made in 'how the war was fought', Shultz declared that there could now be no question as to the morality of US intervention. America's 'sacrifice was in the service of noble ideals – to save innocent people from brutal tyranny'. The Secretary of State emphasised that this interpretation of the war inevitably 'affects our conduct in the present, and thus, in part, determines our future'. Reagan himself added that US troops in Vietnam had been 'fed into the meatgrinder' by leaders who had no 'intention of allowing victory'. He agreed with Richard Nixon that 1973 was actually an American victory. The US withdrew in that year only after making pledges of support to the viable non-communist regime in Saigon. The cause was lost, according to Nixon and Reagan, not in 1973 but in 1975 when, in President Reagan's words:

> ... the North Vietnamese did violate the agreement [of 1973] and the blitz started ... and then the [Ford] administration in Washington asked the Congress for the appropriations to keep our word, the Congress refused. We broke our pledge ... .[1]

As the Reagan Administration wore on, such reinterpretations of the Vietnam legacy became increasingly confident and unqualified by the caution and hesitation on this issue shown during the 1980 Presidential campaign. Revisionist interpretations of the war tended to support key Administration concerns: negotiating from strength, restoring confidence, exorcising 'Vietnam syndrome' doubts about military intervention, and the denial to Congress of anything approaching partnership status in the making of foreign policy. Nevertheless, the 'Vietnam syndrome' persisted throughout the Reagan years. Its most eminent guardian was Caspar Weinberger, the truest of Reaganite true believers. In his memoir, *Fighting For Peace*, Weinberger recalls telling Reagan that 'one of the principal lessons' to be learned from 'the whole Vietnam experience was that we could not suddenly explode upon the American people a full-fledged war and expect to have their support'. National Security Adviser Robert McFarlane and 'the "wilder members"' of the President's staff had not learned this lesson.[2] Weinberger codified these views in a speech delivered (as 'the Weinberger Doctrine') to the National Press Club in November 1984.

The major troop commitment of the Reagan era – the Lebanese peacekeeping force of 1982–4 – produced humiliation for the Administration and was beset by intense Congressional, media and public fears of 'another Vietnam'. The Grenada invasion of 1983 did represent a decisive, though controversial, use of military force to attain a limited and well defined objective. However, in Central America, the obsessive heart of the Administration's Third World concerns, covert military involvement was the order of the day.

The Reagan Doctrine combined vigorous opposition to communism in the developing world with a recognition that foreign policy could not simply be returned to the *status quo ante* Vietnam. From Afghanistan to Nicaragua, the Reagan Doctrine represented a commitment to a rather uncertain form of coercive diplomacy. In some parts of the globe, this coercive diplomacy was highly ideological, and always threatened to collapse into pure militarism; elsewhere, the policy was more pragmatic. Formulated by sympathetic journalists and bureaucrats in the mid-1980s, the Reagan Doctrine attempted to force a marriage between the approach inherited from John Foster Dulles in the Eisenhower Administration, and post-Vietnam realities: 'a synthesis' – in Richard Melanson's phrase – 'of rollback and the Nixon Doctrine'[3] (which committed the US both to the use of anti-communist surrogates and to recognising limits on its own power). At one level, the Reagan Doctrine offered American sponsorship to all enemies of communism in the developing world. In his 1985 State of the Union Address, Reagan declared:

> We must stand by our democratic allies. And we must not break faith with those who are risking their lives ... to defy Soviet-sponsored aggression and secure rights which have been ours from birth.[4]

The echoes of 'rollback' appealed to Republican conservatives. Yet even Dulles had been forced to temper anti-communist liberationism with a more pragmatic commitment to containment. Reagan, in his turn, was offering not a full-scale liberationist crusade, but a kind of pragmatic messianism appropriate to the 1980s. The perceived Soviet over-extension of the late 1970s would be exploited. The Doctrine was bound to recognise limits as well as opportunities. As it developed, the Reagan Doctrine also embraced those 1981 orientations towards regional conflicts and the developing world which had been outlined by Alexander Haig: the preoccupation with terrorism rather than human rights; the identification of 'development' with 'free markets'; and the overarching concern for Cold War geopolitical configurations.

THE MIDDLE EAST AND STATE TERRORISM

(a) Lebanon and the Middle East

Reagan Administration officials oriented their understanding of the problems of the Middle East within a framework provided by containment theory and geopolitical security considerations. 'Strategic consensus' for the region was the declared goal. Richard Burt of the State Department told the House Foreign Affairs Committee in March 1981 that the new Administration:

> ... viewed the Middle East, including the Persian Gulf, as part of a larger politico-strategic theater, the region bounded by Turkey, Pakistan and the Horn of Africa and we view it as a strategic entity requiring comprehensive treatment to insure a favorable balance of power.[5]

Containment of Soviet power, seen to be operating in the region through its Syrian surrogate, represented the cornerstone of Reagan's reaffirmation of the Carter Doctrine (and of additional commitments – the 'Reagan Corollary' – to Saudi Arabia). It provided the basis for US involvement in the Lebanese conflict. Speaking on 25 October 1983, two days after 241 US military personnel had been killed in an explosion at the marine headquarters in Beirut, Reagan enquired: 'Can the US ... stand by and see the Middle East incorporated into the Soviet bloc?.'[6]

Containment theory was insufficiently flexible to provide the Administration with a reliable guide to the developing crisis in Lebanon. Here, the Arab–Israeli conflict merged into the internal Christian–Muslim war. Especially before Haig's resignation (which itself was prompted by the opening by the White House of channels to the Palestinian Liberation Organization), the Reagan Administration was itself damagingly divided. Haig's objective was the removal of the PLO and its Syrian allies from the Lebanon. This would be achieved by maximising pressure on the PLO. Haig's ambivalence toward Israeli military action in the Lebanon put him at odds with Weinberger and George Bush. Both the Defence Secretary and the Vice-President expressed concern about the dangers of alienating the conservative Arab states. The early Reagan years saw, on the one hand, the AWACs sales to Saudi Arabia and expressions of disapproval by Washington when Israel voted to extend its law to the Golan Heights in December 1981. On the other hand, the Israeli invasion of the Lebanon in June 1982 took place alongside an understanding by Israeli Defence Minister Ariel Sharon that (in Weinberger's words) his 'line of argument had a certain amount of appeal to Al [Haig] and others who tended to view the Palestinian–Israeli problem as a subset of the Cold War'.[7]

Shultz and roving Washington envoy Philip Habib worked out an arrangement whereby the PLO would leave Beirut, with security being guaranteed by a multinational force. With Weinberger and US General Jack Vessey unsuccessfully opposing US participation in this force, the PLO evacuated Beirut in August 1982 and the force withdrew. In September, Reagan and Shultz announced a new 'land for peace' proposal: Israel would achieve security through the transfer of the West Bank to joint Palestinian–Jordanian control. The plan sank amid mutual mistrust and the prospects of imminent disintegration of the Lebanon's Christian government. With the Israelis occupying Muslim West Beirut and the slaughtering of Palestinian refugees by Christian militias, the multinational force returned to Lebanon. The US Administration was in no doubt about Israeli complicity in the Palestinian slaughters. Shultz contacted Jimmy Carter who advised: 'You have to throw the book at Begin.' Reagan agreed that 'Israel must realize it had gotten itself into a terrible swamp and the sooner it got out of Lebanon, the better'.[8]

The multinational force (wherein US marines were joined by French and Italian troops) found itself drawn into a conflict of bizarre complexity. Reagan told Congress that it was 'not possible to predict the duration of the presence of these forces in Lebanon'.[9] He attempted to side-step the 1973 War Powers Resolution, whereby deployment of troops for more than 90 days without Congressional approval was disallowed. Clarence Long of Maryland, chairman of the House Foreign Operations Appropriations Subcommittee described the marines on 8 September 1983 as 'sitting duck targets in an undeclared war'.[10] Towards the end of September 1983, Congress cleared a compromise measure invoking the War Powers Act, but allowing Reagan to keep troops in the Lebanon for 18 months. In February 1984, American troops were withdrawn.

Throughout 1983, the Administration had attempted to push forward with some kind of 'land for peace' deal. In February 1983, the US even promised to act as guarantor of Israel's Northern borders in the event of an Israeli withdrawal. The US–Israeli relationship was complicated by a number of cross-cutting factors. Shultz found himself increasingly exasperated not only by Israel's intransigence but also by the potency of pro-Israeli forces in Congress. In December 1982, Congress had voted to *increase* military aid to Israel. The fall in world oil prices also took some ground from under those who argued the unwisdom of offending the conservative Arab states. The Administration's own *volte-face* on Israeli settlements further complicated matters. (Following the arguments of Eugene Rostow, the Reagan Administration dropped Carter's insistence that such settlements in the occupied territories were illegal.) In May 1983, Shultz achieved a flimsy Lebanese–Israeli agreement on a PLO, Syrian and Israeli withdrawal. On 5 May 1984, the Lebanese government, under Syrian influence, cancelled the agreement.[11] The Reagan policy in the Middle East had reached impasse.

Efforts to re-float 'land for peace' and to induce Jordan to sponsor an international conference on terms acceptable to the US and Israel continued to founder. The Palestinian *intifada* of 1987–8 (the anti-Israeli uprising in the West Bank and Gaza) prompted Shultz to a repackaging of the Camp David Accords: Shultz proposed an 'interlock' between transitional and 'final status' negotiations for the West Bank and Gaza.[12] A combination of Israeli recalcitrance and Jordanian reluctance to act as a spokesman for Palestinian interests drove the US towards more direct contact with the PLO. Freed from electoral constraints, the Administration announced in December 1988 that a 'dialogue' with PLO leader Yasser Arafat would be opened. Concessions regarding the legitimacy of Israel and his own attitude towards terrorism were extracted from Arafat. Though manifestly a response to the *intifada*, this US–PLO 'dialogue' did present opportunities to the incoming Bush

Administration and go at least some way to redeeming the Administration's record of failure in the Middle East.

(b) State Terrorism, Libya and the First Gulf War

The debate within the Reagan Administration over the use of American military power was conducted largely in the context of the issue of state-sponsored terrorism. To George Shultz, the Weinberger Doctrine (that force should only be applied 'wholeheartedly', with clear objectives and overwhelming public support, and as a 'last resort') was 'a counsel of inaction bordering on paralysis'.[13] It seemed to codify American decline and to invite terroristic nations to test America's will. Cap Weinberger's formula became known to its bureaucratic enemies as 'the Capgun Doctrine'.

Syria, Libya, Iran and Cuba (besides the USSR itself) were the states most frequently cited as sponsoring terrorism. The official Reagan line was that America would never make concessions to terrorists. In April 1984, the Administration proposed four 'anti-terrorism' bills in Congress. One contained a section empowering the Secretary of State simply to designate certain countries as 'terroristic', thereby banning US citizens from extending anything that might be construed as 'support' for these pariahs. The Administration moved also, notably at the 1986 Tokyo Economic Summit, to encourage the allies to foreswear all accessions to terrorist demands.

The Iran-*contra* affair, which erupted on to the public stage after the 1986 Congressional elections, illustrated the inconsistency between the Administration's words and deeds. Even before 1986, some of the difficulties inherent in absolutist approaches to the problem of how to respond to terrorism had become apparent. The hijacking of TWA flight 847 in June 1985, for example, eventually caused the Administration to negotiate directly with President Hafez Assad, leader of the Syrian 'pariah'. The TWA 847 episode exposed deep rifts between the NSC staff and the State Department. The *Wall Street Journal* carried an editorial, criticising the uncertain Administration response, under the heading, 'Jimmy Reagan'.[14]

The major use of force to combat 'state terrorism' came in April 1986, with the raid on Libya. Before this, aircraft from the American Sixth Fleet had – in October 1985 – forced hijackers of the cruise ship *Achille Lauro* to land in Italy. Libya was blamed for this and other acts of terrorism associated with Palestinian extremists. Following attacks on Rome and Vienna airports, and the bombing of a Berlin nightclub frequented by US service personnel, economic ties with Libya were suspended. Clashes in the Gulf of Sidra culminated in the air raid of April 1986. Weinberger had initially counselled caution, but announced at a 14 April press conference that the bombing would 'send an unmistakable signal' which would 'go very far toward deterring future acts' by Libya and others.[15]

Libya's leader, Muammar al Qaddafi, apparently the raid's principal target, escaped. Members of his family, as well as Libyan civilians were killed. The raid made a nonsense of requirements in war powers legislation that the President should 'consult' with Congress before taking military action. Reagan 'consulted' with fifteen Members of Congress, after the planes had left their bases in Britain. Both Senate Minority Leader R.C. Byrd (Democrat of West Virginia) and Sam Nunn (Senate Armed Services Committee chairman: Democrat from Georgia) dismissed this 'consultation' as merely 'notification'.[16] By force of circumstance, Reagan was obliged to consult the British Prime Minister to a far greater degree than his own Congress. Despite some doubts, Mrs Thatcher gave permission to use British air space (' ... the cost to Britain of not backing American action was unthinkable'). In retrospect, she felt the raid – which was popular in the US, but unpopular in Europe – provoked 'a marked decline in Libyan-sponsored terrorism' in succeeding years.[17]

The Administration's early promise to exalt the fight against terrorism over that for human rights presaged some stark reversals from the Carter period. Undersecretary of State James Buckley depicted the new Administration as reversing its predecessor's 'escape from reality'.[18] The Reagan State Department urged immediate restoration of military aid to Chile, Guatemala, Uruguay and Argentina. Yet, as the years passed, Administration pronouncements on human rights softened in tone. Human rights, it was argued, were best promoted by anti-communism, 'quiet diplomacy' and the identification of 'targets of opportunity' (notably Chile, Haiti, the Philippines and South Korea). Elliot Abrams, who served as Assistant Secretary for Human Rights at the State Department in the early Reagan years, argued that human rights should be at the centre of the Administration's agenda. Largely because of the efforts of Congressional Democrats to keep Carter's human rights focus alive, studies of foreign aid in this period do not show quite the stark contrast between the Carter and Reagan Administrations which their competing rhetorics would suggest.[19] Many Reagan officials undoubtedly saw 'human rights' primarily as an anti-Soviet weapon, at least in the first (pre-Gorbachev) term. Nevertheless, where possible – as with Chile after 1983 – the Administration also attempted to stem Congressional opposition to its Central American policy by edging away from some of the more notorious rightist human rights abusers. Yet proponents of this strategy had always to contend with the President's prejudices. Elliot Abrams later recalled that Reagan objected to 'constant criticism of people who for the most part were pro-American'. At one stage, General Vernon Walters, Ambassador to the United Nations, threatened to complain directly to Reagan about what he saw as excessive State Department criticism of General Pinochet's regime in Chile. Secretary Shultz had forcefully to dissuade Reagan from personally inviting Pinochet to Washington.[20] Throughout the 1980s, the Administration continued to define 'human rights' so as to exclude economic rights and to downgrade 'integrity of the person'.[21]

Human rights activists on Capitol Hill joined with the pro-Israeli lobby to protest the Administration's 'tilt' towards Iraq in the first Gulf War (1980–8, between Iraq and Iran). Efforts to obviate a victory by anti-Western, fundamentalist Iran were supported by Arabists in the State Department and by Weinberger. (A counter-policy, of attempting to 'win back' Iran was being promoted by an intra-Administration alliance which included William Casey and NSC personnel like Robert McFarlane and John Poindexter.[22] This shadow policy erupted eventually into the Iran-*contra* scandal, discussed in the next chapter.) As part of the official pro-Iraqi policy, Saddam Hussein's Baghdad government was removed in 1982 from an official State Department list of nations furthering state terrorism. In November 1984, full diplomatic relations – broken off in 1967 – were restored with Baghdad. US trade with Iraq, including high technology transfers, rose to a value of over three and a half billion dollars by 1989.

Administration attitudes towards Iraq appeared to contravene its policies on state terrorism. In 1982, Representative Jonathan Bingham (Democrat from New York) protested the dropping of export controls to Iraq, Syria and South Yemen:

> I think it's a shocking example of the hypocrisy involved in their claim that they're really putting terrorism as a matter of top priority. I think in this case, they're putting profits for business first.[23]

Later Congressional investigations exposed the extent to which the US was, at various times, actually proferring military and security assistance to both sides in the first Gulf War. US satellite photographs of Iranian targets were transmitted to Baghdad, with the CIA at one point establishing a direct secret intelligence link between Washington and the Iraqi capital.[24] The 'tilt' towards Iraq became clear after 1984. Eric Hooglund noted that between 1981 and 1987 the US went from a policy of 'ignoring Iran to secretly wooing Iran to directly confronting Iran'.[25] The confusion of US policy reflected the factionalism in Washington and an uncertain and reactive approach to the attainment of key US objectives: protecting oil flows; countering Soviet influence in Baghdad; resisting the spread of anti-Western Islamic fundamentalism (or, alternatively, using it as a lever against the Soviets); and securing a rough power balance – between Iran, Iraq and the Gulf countries – in the region.

Major Congressional protests attended Reagan's 1987 decision to protect Kuwaiti oil tankers in the Persian Gulf. (Kuwait was allied with Iraq in the first Gulf War. The tankers were allowed to sail under the US flag in order to deter Iranian attacks.) A lawsuit brought by over one hundred Representatives tried, without success, to trigger the war powers legislation. In May 1987, an Iraqi fighter attacked the US destroyer, *Stark*, apparently misidentifying it as an Iranian ship. In July 1988, aircraft from the *USS Vincennes* shot down an Iranian passenger plane; Reagan offered his 'deep regret' and compensation for the victims. The August Gulf ceasefire, traceable to Iranian exhaustion rather than to US influence, rescued a confused and erratic American policy. In September 1988, the US Senate voted to cut off all American aid to Iraq, following Saddam's use of chemical weapons against Kurdish rebels.

CENTRAL AMERICA AND THE CARIBBEAN

As we have seen, Reagan Administration policies in the Middle East were driven by an alarmist and unrealistic assessment of Soviet intentions. Moscow was preoccupied with the conflict in Afghanistan rather than with a bid to overrun the Gulf oil fields. US involvement in Central America was similarly rooted in some extraordinary judgements concerning Soviet expansionism. It also, even more than policy in the Near East, revived debates emanating from the Vietnam era.

The Reaganite conservative analysis of the communist threat to Central America was emotional and so lacking in factual support that it invited accusations of disingenuousness. The 1980 Republican platform drew on views propounded by the conservative Council for Inter-American Security (Committee of Santa Fe) which in 1980 proclaimed that the Caribbean was 'becoming a Marxist-Leninist lake'.[26] The 1980 platform denounced 'the Marxist takeover of Nicaragua' as part of Carter's failed legacy.[27] A February 1981 State Department White Paper referred to 'definitive evidence of the clandestine military support given by the Soviet Union, Cuba, and their communist allies to Marxist-Leninist guerrillas in El Salvador.[28] Secretary Haig discerned an 'externally managed and orchestrated interventionism'.[29] In 1983, Reagan told the Organization of American States that world communism had 'established footholds on American soil for the expansion of its colonialist ambitions'.[30] In March 1986, he exhorted Members of Congress to support aid to the Nicaraguan *contras* if they did not 'want to see the map of Central America covered in a sea of red, eventually lapping at our own borders ... '.[31]

To some extent, such rhetoric was the product of the intense lobbying of Congress for *contra* funding. New bureaucratic and propagandistic factors were created by the Administration to press this cause. It is unsurprising that statements emanating from such sources (notably the Outreach Working Group on Central America and the State Department's Office of Public Diplomacy for Latin America and the Caribbean) should incline to extremism. Some Administration spokesmen did emphasise – in an implied attempt to distance this issue from Vietnam – that real and immediate US interests were involved. Assistant Secretary for Inter-American Affairs Thomas Enders testified to a House Appropriations subcommittee in 1982:

> If, after Nicaragua, El Salvador is captured by a violent minority, who in Central America would not live in fear? How long would it be before major strategic US interests – the Canal, sea lanes, oil supplies – were at risk?[32]

George Shultz told the Senate Finance Committee that 'the Caribbean is now a seven billion dollar market'.[33] Yet emotionalism was never far away. To Reagan, any 'communist' advance in the Americas flew in the face of manifest destiny. It attacked 'freedom' in its very stronghold. In March 1986, he announced that only if it voted for *contra* aid would the current membership of Congress be able to assert: 'We left America safe, we left America secure, we left America free ... .'[34] In a television broadcast in May 1984, he described Sandinista rule in Nicaragua as 'a communist reign of terror'. Not content merely to 'brutalize their own land', the Sandinistas sought to 'export their terror' across the Americas: those 'two great continents ... placed here – you can call it mystical if you want – ... to be found by people who had a love for freedom ...'.[35] Shultz testified in 1986 that one of the 'striking characteristics of Sandinista communism is its messianic impulse to violence'.[36] Soviet communism was using Nicaragua as a 'stepping stone'.[37]

Invoking memories of Vietnam, conservative columnist William Safire in 1981 hailed the opportunity to purge memories of defeat: 'Let's win one in El Salvador!'[38] The Administration was keen to point out not only that US interests in Central America were more immediate than they had been in Indochina, but also that Nicaragua did not have a China on its borders and that the Salvadoran rebels lacked the solidarity of the Vietnamese communists. Reagan insisted in 1983 that there was 'no comparison with Vietnam. There isn't going to be anything like that ...'.[39] Opponents of the policy like Clarence Long (Democratic Congressman from Maryland) disagreed:

> ... the similarity of Vietnam is so close it is almost uncanny. There is the unwillingness of people to fight, incompetent, corrupt leadership, and calling everyone a Communist.[40]

Mike Hatfield, the Republican Senator from Oregon who had opposed the Vietnam war, responded in 1986: 'Here we go again, old men creating a monster for young men to destroy.'[41]

(a) Nicaragua and El Salvador

To a large degree, the entire Reagan strategy towards the developing world turned on events in these two small countries. In 1987, Viron Vaky, Assistant Secretary of State for Inter-American Affairs under Jimmy Carter, wrote that 'the Reagan Doctrine grew out of U.S. *contra* support as a kind of *ex post facto* rationalization' of efforts to reverse Soviet gains in the Third World. Nicaragua became 'the premier example': 'If the rollback promise could not be realized there, where could it be realized?'[42]

The Administration's case rested on assertions that the Sandinistas were instruments of Soviet/Cuban expansionism, that the *contras* were a potentially effective (and 'democratic') force, and that a *contra* victory could be attained without unacceptable levels of US military intervention. In seeking to advance this case, the Reagan Administration was able to exploit high levels of public ignorance of the region's affairs. In 1983, a survey indicated that only eight per cent of respondents knew that Washington supported the government of El Salvador against rebel guerrillas, but supported anti-government rebels in Nicaragua. Yet the public clearly did not accept Reagan's view that there was no danger of replaying Vietnam. US public opinion consistently appeared to oppose any incremental intervention which could conceivably be portrayed as presaging 'another Vietnam'. This acted as a major constraint on the Administration. Gallup polling between 1981 and 1983 showed, typically, that 68 per cent of those aware of the situation in El Salvador felt that it 'could turn into a situation like Vietnam'. CBS and *New York Times* polls between 1983 and 1985 showed majority opposition to military intervention against the Sandinistas, even if there were to be evidence of Soviet missiles in Nicaragua. Opposition to intervention rose to over 70 per cent after 1986, when the extent of illegal *contra* funding came to light. Public disapproval of various *contra* aid packages remained above 54 per cent between April 1983 and April 1986. Despite the lack of detailed public knowledge, polls showed that public criticism of Reagan's foreign policy was especially intense with regard to Central America.[43]

White House statements and policies in the region provoked a grass-roots reaction which did, indeed, evoke memories of the early stages of the Vietnam involvement. Central American solidarity groups (notably church groups, incensed by the murders of Nicaraguan Archbishop Oscar Romero and of four North American churchwomen in El Salvador in 1980, and the California-based Committee in Solidarity with the People of El Salvador) condemned US aggression and advertised the democratic credentials of the Sandinistas.[44] Such groups found it a relatively simple task to expose the paucity of evidence connecting Managua and Moscow. In particular, the 1981 State Department White Paper incited criticisms so devastating that even one of its authors was forced to admit that it was 'misleading' and 'over-embellished'.[45]

Many Members of Congress found the Administration's arguments unconvincing. The attempt to portray the *contras* as Jeffersonian 'freedom fighters' was particularly ludicrous. As Viron Vaky explained:

Both the United States and the *contras* have been trapped by the way in which the *contras* were founded in 1981 – they were organized and sponsored by the CIA – and by the vested interests thus created within the *contra* movement and the U.S. government. The 1981 presidential finding authorizing the CIA to undertake covert paramilitary activity against the Sandinistas was in effect a decision to reconstitute the violent Right to challenge the Sandinista revolution rather than to trust centrist opposition elements within Nicaragua.[46]

It was not difficult to establish that some links between Managua, Havana and Moscow existed. The 1981 White Paper famously and ludicrously offered the evidence of an air ticket to the USSR in a captured Salvadoran rebel's trousers. The Sandinistas did suppress press freedoms and were guilty of some human rights violations (for example, in regard to Miskitu Indians). Yet, as Piero Gleijeses of Johns Hopkins University wrote in 1984, 'despite their incompetence and their arrogance', Daniel Ortega and his Sandinista colleagues were 'the first Nicaraguan leaders who have sought to improve the lot of the people'.[47] The Soviet Union did supply arms and money to Managua. Yet factions within the Sandinista leadership, aware of the price paid by Havana for Moscow's support, were alert to the dangers of their own revolution becoming 'Sovietised'. During the mid-1980s, over 60 per cent of Nicaragua's economy remained privately owned. Moscow itself appeared less than keen again to test the Monroe Doctrine by recruiting 'another Cuba'. Any such action threatened to provoke the US and to drain the Soviet economy. (Cuban aid in this period was costing Moscow perhaps as much as nine billion dollars annually.) Certainly, Castro's regime in Havana did see the Nicaraguan revolution as a victory for its style of anti-Yanqui socialism, and sought to extend and radicalise it. Both Cuba and Nicaragua were concerned to promote their cause in Moscow. Sandinista leader Daniel Ortega had continually to weigh the possibility of securing valuable Soviet aid and protection against the danger of alienating the US Congress. (His 1985 visit to Moscow was, in House Speaker Jim Wright's view, especially 'maladroit' in this regard.) An American observer noted in 1990: 'Perhaps we need also to speak, coining a deliberate paradox, of Cuban and Nicaraguan subversion in Moscow.'[48]

In El Salvador, Administration strategy centred on support for various Christian Democratic governments against leftist guerrillas. In the 1984 Salvadoran Presidential election, the US also extended substantial financial backing to Christian Democrat leader Jose Napolean Duarte against the extreme-right ARENA party led by Roberto D'Aubuisson. (Though D'Aubuisson's party was closely associated with the Salvadoran 'death squads', Duarte's Christian Democratic Administrations – which nominally controlled El Salvador during much of the Reagan era – were either unwilling or unable to control the excesses of the military.) At various times, Congress voted significant sums in aid to El Salvador. Slightly desperate attempts were made to distinguish 'lethal' from 'non-lethal' aid. Much of the American aid, however, was effectively disbursed beyond the control of Congress. Between 1980 and 1985, over two billion dollars went to the government of tiny El Salvador; much of this total derived from 'reprogrammed' funds of highly dubious legality and from a virtually uncontrolled and unaccountable CIA budget.[49]

In both El Salvador and in Guatemala, US policy proceeded without concern for human rights. The Rios Montt regime in Guatemala (1982–3), for example, was backed by US funds – many technically 'reprogrammed' to evade legislative bans on aid to human rights violators – which it used to massacre thousands of 'disloyal' peasants. Despite Reagan's undertaking not to 'Americanize' the war in El Salvador, CIA personnel and US troops (operating from Honduras) took part in the conflict. The extent of governmental and military repression in El Salvador was denied by the State Department in a spirit of bad faith which yet again recalled the Vietnam war era.[50] Congressional efforts to restrict the number of US 'advisers' in El Salvador were easily circumvented. A 1985 report by a Congressional investigating team concluded that, despite a legislative ban on such activities, 'US personnel are selecting targeting sites for bombing and maintaining equipment.'[51] Salvadoran villagers were assailed by fragmentation bombs, napalm and white phosphorous. In 1987, a CIA agent was killed in a guerrilla attack on the military base in El Paraiso. In 1988, the extreme right again won control of El Salvador's National Assembly.

Throughout Latin America, the Reagan Administration was engaged in a diplomacy of 'double messages'.[52] Ostensibly defending 'democracy' and 'centrists' like Duarte, the US was also in effect keeping open the possibility of an extremist rightist 'solution' to the advances on the left. Such a 'solution' was actually imposed on Guatemala and for long periods in El Salvador, as well as in large South American countries like Argentina before the Falklands war. As late as 1988, George Shultz's diplomacy in Guatemala – attempting to shift the government of Mario Vinicio Cerezo away from its policy of 'active neutrality' towards the Nicaraguan war – was encouraging the extreme right in that country. Robert Pastor offered his verdict in 1992 on the Reagan military assistance programme in El Salvador:

> One could argue that the Salvadoran military became more mobile and professional, but its war against the left moved no closer to success because Washington opposed land reform, stymied negotiations with the left, and failed to exert sufficient pressure on the military to stop the death squads.[53]

Pro-American forces did survive in San Salvador during the Reagan era: at a massive cost in lives, human rights, dollars, and erosion of democratic controls on US foreign policy.

Reagan's March 1981 'Presidential finding' (which authorised CIA recruitment of the Nicaraguan *contras*) inaugurated the illegal American proxy war in Nicaragua. In June 1986, the International Court of Justice in The Hague voted (12–3) that:

> ... the United States of America, by training, arming, equipping, financing and supplying the *contra* forces or otherwise encouraging, supporting and aiding military and paramilitary activities in and against Nicaragua, has acted, against the Republic of Nicaragua, in breach of its obligations under customary international law not to intervene in the affairs of another State.[54]

The proxy war also appeared to violate the United Nations charter, the charter of the Organization of American States, and various US domestic laws: notably war powers legislation, various appropriations laws and the 1982 and 1984 Boland amendments (effectively prohibiting the CIA and Defence Department assistance to the *contras*). The Administration's case focused, firstly, on the degree to which its policy represented assistance to the threatened OAS ally in San Salvador; and, secondly, on the implausible assertion that the *contras* did not actually intend to overthrow the Managua government. (The earliest version of the Boland amendment expressly banned funds designed to 'overthrow' Sandinistas.)

The Administration's desire to see the Sandinista regime overthrown was transparent. Some Reagan officials were, it is true, prepared to 'acknowledge' the revolution in Nicaragua. Thomas Enders advised Constantine Menges of the NSC staff that 'there is no chance for democracy in Nicaragua'.[55] Enders was joined in promoting the policy of 'coercive diplomacy' – designed to pressure Managua into accepting reforms and bowing to US security interests, rather than to achieve an immediate change of regime – by Shultz and special negotiators Harry Shlaudeman and Philip Habib. Administration hardliners (like William Casey, William Clark, Jeane Kirkpatrick and NSC staff irregular Oliver North) took the opposing view: that a mediated settlement between Washington and Managua was impossible. As Kenneth Roberts explains: 'hardliners effectively nullified coercive diplomacy by vetoing ... attempts to offer positive inducements to the Sandinistas or negotiate a mutual accommodation'.[56] Nancy Reagan later recalled the common Washington perception that Alexander Haig (who 'alarmed Ronnie') wanted a precipitate invasion of Nicaragua.[57] US negotiators either offered impossibly humiliating terms to Managua, or found their efforts sabotaged by bureaucratic opponents in Washington.[58] The Administration failed to support the peace diplomacy of the Contadora Group (Colombia, Panama, Mexico and Venezuela) after 1983, preferring to back the Central American Defence Council (CONDECA) as a proxy military force. Huge US pressure was exerted on Costa Rica to abandon its traditional neutrality. The Costa Rican 1987 peace strategy was rejected in 1987, despite attracting the active sponsorship of House speaker Jim Wright. In August 1987, five Central American Presidents requested an end to all outside sponsorship of the insurgencies. Costa Rican leader Oscar Arias responded to Reagan:

> We agree on the ends but we disagree on the means. You want democracy in Central America by imposing it with bullets. I want democracy by imposing it with votes.[59]

The annual battle for funding the war dominated Presidential–Congressional relations. These disputes provoked a major and extended debate on the fundamental principles of American foreign policy. According to Congressman James Shannon (Democrat from Massachusetts) in 1984, what was at stake here was 'not what we think about the Nicaraguans, but rather what we think about the United States and the role that we are going to play in the world'.[60] In April 1984, it became known that the CIA had mined Nicaraguan harbours and bombed oil storage facilities. (These bombing and mining decisions were apparently taken by the CIA, with Presidential approval, while Secretary Shultz was in Europe.) The ensuing Congressional furore coincided with the preliminary ruling of the World Court that the US should halt activities which jeopardised Nicaragua's sovereignty. The 1984 minings and bombings caused Barry Goldwater, Republican chairman of the Senate intelligence oversight committee and formerly a staunch ally of the CIA, to lose patience: 'The President has asked us to back his foreign policy,' declared Goldwater. 'Bill [Casey], how can we ... when we don't know what the hell he is doing?'[61] In January 1985, the US Administration announced that it was boycotting the World Court proceedings. House Judiciary Committee chairman Peter Rodino, a central actor in the Watergate affair during the previous decade, linked these events to the earlier crisis:

> On the weekend that President Reagan vowed to uphold the Constitution for his second term in office, his administration decided to flout international law by walking out of the World Court proceedings in Nicaragua's suit ... . In the 39-year history of the World Court, only three other nations have ever walked out on a case ... Iran, Iceland and Albania.
>
> Only ... eleven years ago, we prevented the unraveling of our system by a President who tried to place himself above the law. Let us hope that history will not record our withdrawal from the World Court as the first sign of a new arrogance of power.[62]

In 1986, Democratic Senator Alan Cranston from California declared his opposition to the 'idea that US military force should be used indiscriminately to make foreign governments in our own image'.[63] The Administration responded to criticism with a mixture of threat and entreaty, with Shultz in 1985 arguing that, without *contra* aid, 'we will be faced with an agonizing choice about the use of American combat troops'.[64] The main Administration success – remembered by Shultz in his memoirs as 'a moment of triumph'[65] – occurred in the summer of 1986. Congress confirmed Reagan's request for one hundred million dollars in *contra* aid, as well as three hundred million in support to Costa Rica, Honduras, Guatemala and El Salvador. Only after the exposure of the Iran-*contra* scandal, and the Democratic capture of the

Senate in the 1986 mid-term elections, did Congress again turn firmly against the war. Reagan insisted that the Sandinistas would only negotiate if the *contras* were being supported by Washington. US helicopters, with American pilots, were actually shot down over Nicaragua while Congress was investigating Iran-*contra*. Secretary Shultz involved himself in complex manoeuvres to co-opt or de-rail the peace initiatives promoted by Oscar Arias and Jim Wright.[66] In March 1988, with *contra* aid officially suspended by Congress, the Arias initiative achieved a Nicaraguan ceasefire.

The proxy war cost perhaps as many as 30 000 Nicaraguan lives. (In El Salvador, one estimate puts the loss of civilian life at the hands of governmental and associated forces at 70 000.)[67] Within the US, public opinion and the 'Vietnam syndrome' prevented the open commitment of troops. Vietnam-era divisions reappeared. For Reagan, the *contras* were 'counterrevolutionary, and God bless them … it makes me a *contra* too'.[68] To Stansfield Turner, Carter's CIA Director, the *contras* were engaged in what the Reagan Administration affected most to despise: 'State-sponsored terrorism.'[69] Yet again, and now in the final phase of the Cold War, the US was aligning itself with the forces of reaction in the developing world.

(b) The Kissinger Commission, Grenada and Panama

Administration spokesmen tried to present Reagan's Central American policy as a 'dual strategy'. In 1983, Secretary Shultz described the US as being concerned to provide 'military assistance' but not to 'seek a military solution'.[70] The non-military branch of the 'dual strategy' was to consist of democracy-promotion, diplomacy and economic assistance. Colonel J.C. Waghelstein, commander of the El Salvador US Military Advisory Group, declared in 1985 that the 'only territory' he wanted to hold was 'the six inches between the ears of the *campesino*'.[71] To so many observers, all this raised the ghosts of Vietnam-era 'nation-building' and the battle for 'hearts and minds'. Reagan declared in a 1983 speech, which – apparently unwittingly – echoed Lyndon Johnson's 1965 Johns Hopkins address on Vietnam:

Of all the words I've spoken today, let me underline these especially: America's emphasis in Central America is on economic and social progress, not on a purely military solution. But to give democracy

and development a chance to work ... we are providing a shield of
military training and assistance ... .[72]

Aid totals reflected Reagan's 'shield' rather than the commitment to
'economic and social progress'. The Reagan Administration inherited a
Central American aid budget roughly equally divided between 'pure'
economic aid on the one hand, and a combination of 'military' and
'economic support' aid on the other. The first Reagan term saw a huge
shift away from 'pure' economic aid, with non-military programmes
being cut by approximately 180 billion dollars. In order to lend credibility to the 'dual strategy', the Administration created in 1983 a
Bipartisan Presidential Commission on Central America, chaired by
Henry Kissinger. The move was designed to build on the Caribbean
Basin Initiative, announced by Reagan in 1982, and to build a consensus behind *contra* aid. The Caribbean Basin Initiative involved long
tangles in Congress over proposals to relax Caribbean import duties.
Some 350 million dollars were voted for the programme in 1982.[73]

Kissinger's Commission acknowledged that the Sandinistas had
made 'significant gains against illiteracy and disease' and actually
stated that 'indigenous reform, even indigenous revolution' was not 'a
security threat to the United States'. Yet Central America had witnessed, according to the Commission's majority, 'the intrusion of
aggressive outside powers' intent on presenting a 'serious threat' to US
and hemispheric security. The report was far from uncritical of previous public and private US dealings with Central America. It called for
an extra eight billion dollars in US governmental aid over the next five
years; (about four billion was provided for this ostensibly 'non-
military' budget by Congress). It advocated an expansion of private US
investment and commended America's erection of a strong military
'shield' behind which development could take place.[74]

In delivering his report, Kissinger was careful to point out that he
favoured far more than a token commitment to Central American economic regeneration. In fact, 'doing nothing' would, according to
Kissinger, be better than 'doing too little'. The Reagan Administration's emphasis on military aid to the *contras* and to the government
of El Salvador ensured that the whole commitment to a 'dual strategy'
remained unconvincing. The view through much of Latin America was
that economic initiatives and invocations of the Soviet threat were
essentially attempts to obscure the reimposition of US hegemony. The

Reagan years saw a clear – albeit temporary – reversal of the secular trend away from US military domination of Latin America.[75] Reagan's only outright use of military power in the hemisphere, the 1983 invasion of Grenada, represented the first US overthrow of a Latin American government since Lyndon Johnson's 1965 incursion into the Dominican Republic.

Reagan's National Security Decision Directive, ordering the invasion of the tiny Caribbean island of Grenada, apparently mentioned three overarching objectives: the protection of US citizens; the restoration of democracy; and the cessation of Cuban involvement on the island. As R.J. Beck put it: 'The second and third objectives reflected core Reagan administration values.'[76] Though Cuban military involvement in the Western hemisphere was actually declining between 1982 and 1984, curtailment of such involvement was a major Administration goal. Substantial energy was expended in an effort to increase Cuba's political isolation and to tighten the economic blockade. Cuba's close links with Moscow effectively precluded an invasion of that particular Caribbean island, but the assault on Grenada was clearly designed to deliver a strong message to Havana. Cuba's inability to deter the invasion would also not go unnoticed by the Nicaraguan Sandinistas. The background to the Grenada invasion involved the accession to power on the island of Maurice Bishop's leftist/nationalist New Jewel Movement in 1979. Between 1979 and 1983, Bishop's regime drew close to Cuba and stimulated US hostility. Washington condemned the arms buildup on the island. (Documents seized during the invasion indicated that this buildup was designed to secure the revolution from internal and external threats, rather than to support incursions into neighbouring islands.) Immediately prior to the October 1983 invasion, Bishop was deposed and murdered by a New Jewel faction led by General Hudson Austin. Reagan swiftly launched the invasion, described as a 'rescue mission' aimed at US medical students on the island. There ensued three days of conflict (25–27 October 1983) against government and Cuban forces. A 'democratic' administration, under British Governor General Paul Scoon, was installed.[77]

Some Congressional Democratic leaders initially condemned the invasion as precipitate, and claimed that legislative consultation had been inadequate under the provisions of war powers legislation. In fact, the invasion's basis in international law was even flimsier. The Administration's legal case shifted between equally unconvincing appeals to the danger posed to US citizens, and to members of the

Organization of East Caribbean States, by the Grenada government. Nevertheless, the various Commonwealth Caribbean leaders (including those in Jamaica and Barbados – both, like the US, non-OECS members) were willing to back the invasion. From Washington's viewpoint, the whole adventure was a triumph. Observing the invasion from the Pentagon, Major General Colin Powell considered it 'a sloppy success'.[78] US public opinion, enthusiastically backing an invasion which occurred only two days after the Beirut massacre, drowned out doubts.

American denunciations of 'undemocratic' regimes in New Jewel Movement Grenada, Cuba and Nicaragua were to some degree undercut by US tolerance towards the rightist regional dictatorships. As noted above, awareness of this problem combined with Congressional pressure to cause the second Reagan Administration to distance itself from some of these regimes. In 1986, the younger Duvalier quitted Haiti aboard a US aircraft bound for France. The Administration expressed support for a transfer of power from General Stroessner's fascist clique in Paraguay. In Panama, the close US attachment to General Manual Noriega was broken.

Noriega had come to power in Panama in 1984 as the strongman behind President Barletta's National Democratic Union. He was distrusted by the State Department, especially by Elliot Abrams. George Shultz's opinion was that Noriega could not be bought: 'you can only rent him'.[79] Initially, Noriega was valued by the Pentagon and by the Drug Enforcement Agency. The Pentagon's Southern Command headquarters was in Panama, and the DEA actually extended a special commendation to Noriega for his help in drug interdiction. The Panamanian leader was also on the CIA's payroll until the early part of 1988. Noriega's support in Washington was undermined to some degree by developments within Panama. Opponents accused Noriega of murdering former Panamanian leader Omar Torrijos. Governmental human rights abuses grew more extensive, while Noriega attempted for a time to identify himself with the anti-Americanism of the opposition. More important, however, were the ramifications of Iran-*contra* and the unconcealable evidence that Noriega was himself an enthusiastic drugs trafficker. With the breaking of the Iran-*contra* scandal in 1986, Noriega became a liability. Before 1986, Panama appeared the ideal base for an invasion of Nicaragua. From November 1986, however, the Administration was engaged in damage limitation rather than invasion plans. Both CIA Director Casey and National Security Council staff aide Oliver North disowned the General. With drug trafficking indictments pending, Noriega's position in Washington became bureaucratically unsustainable.[80] Economic sanctions were applied after Noriega refused to leave Panama. In January 1989, George Bush – who, as CIA Director in 1976, had presided over the original recruitment of Noriega – was faced in Panama with a leader operating in open defiance of the United States.

ASIA, AFRICA AND REGIONAL DISPUTES

(a) Afghanistan and Pakistan

Outside Central America, the main application of the Reagan Doctrine occurred in relation to the war in Afghanistan. Throughout the Reagan years, it was felt that a Soviet withdrawal from Afghanistan could be achieved, and that such a withdrawal would represent a historic breach in the practice of Soviet foreign policy. When Secretary Shultz was informed by Soviet Foreign Minister Eduard Shevardnadze in 1987 that the withdrawal was imminent, Shultz hailed 'the first-ever retreat by Soviet forces from a territory or country they dominated'.[81] When it came in April 1988, Gorbachev's Tashkent announcement of the withdrawal did not even make the retreat conditional on ending US aid to the Afghan resistance.

To some extent, the Soviet retreat was the product of Mikhail Gorbachev's 'new thinking' and of internal Soviet pressures. Shevardnadze later testified that the entire reorientation in Soviet foreign policy flowed from the decision to quit Afghanistan.[82] The Soviets had failed to exploit divisions between the Afghan *mujahadin* resistance, Pakistan and the US. The 1986 replacement of Babrak Karmal by Mohammad Najibullah simply increased the factionalism in Afghanistan's government. The *mujahadin* success was, of course, made possible by international support. (Besides receiving US aid, the *mujahadin* were also armed by China, Saudi Arabia, Iran and Egypt.) American support for the resistance found broad backing in Congress, despite the virtually unaccountable manner with which the CIA managed this assistance. George Shultz recalled: 'The CIA was running the war.'[83] At first sight, the lack of oppositional overspill from the Congressional debate on Central America seems remarkable. However, it should be remembered that Congressional control of CIA operations even in Central America was ineffective – more 'afterview' than 'oversight'. In areas of less immediate legislative concern, or where US geopolitical interests seemed more clearly drawn, the Administration faced relatively little difficulty in obtaining Congressional acquiescence in its covert operations. Apart from Afghanistan, covert action was funded in Angola, especially after 1985, and in Kampuchea (Cambodia). (Here, US aid to the anti-Vietnamese guerrillas put Washington in the invidious position of helping to arm the mass-murderous Khmer Rouge.) In the mid-1980s, Congress actually *increased* the CIA's covert action budget for Afghanistan. From 1985, as a result of battlefield research undertaken by the State Department's Intelligence and Research Bureau, the US began supplying the Afghan resistance with highly effective Stinger missiles for use against Soviet helicopter gunships.[84]

American desire to aid the *mujahadin* brought Washington into close alliance with Zia ul-Haq's regime in Pakistan. As Craig Baxter writes, 'Zia ... presents a textbook example of a tyrant whose many failings ... were glossed over' in the cause of anti-Sovietism.[85] Pakistani 'failings' extended to human rights abuses, opium export and the clandestine development of nuclear weapons. In 1981 and 1986, Congress voted major aid packages to Pakistan, effectively suspending legislative bans (notably the 1976 Symington amendment) on aid which might enhance nuclear proliferation. Some forty F-16 advanced aircraft were sold to Pakistan over India's objections.

(b) The Philippines

During his 1984 Presidential campaign debate with Walter Mondale, Reagan announced that the only alternative to the dictatorship of Ferdinand Marcos in the Philippines was 'a large Communist movement' poised 'to take over'.[86] During his first term, Reagan moved closer to the Filipino dictator than had any American President since Lyndon Johnson. To Reagan, Marcos was a force for anti-communist stability and a guarantor of American military presence in his country. US intelligence in this period was none the less wary of Marcos. A US Embassy telegram from Manila noted in 1982 that 'foreign support' for the anti-Marcos insurgency was 'a negligible factor'.[87] A leaked 1984 National Security Council Study Directive announced:

> While President Marcos ... is part of the problem he is also necessar-
> ily part of the solution. We need to be able to work with him and to
> try to influence him through a well-orchestrated policy of incentives

and disincentives to set the stage for a peaceful and eventual transition to a successor ... Marcos, for his part, will try to use us to remain in power indefinitely.[88]

The 1983 murder of oppositionist Ninoy Aquino provoked a crisis which peaked when Marcos fraudulently claimed victory in the 1986 Presidential elections. Important interests in Washington began to press the agenda outlined in the 1984 NSC Study Directive. (These interests included influential Members of Congress – notably Stephen Solarz, chairman of the House Subcommittee on Asian and Pacific Affairs – as well as bureaucratic actors such as Ambassador and Undersecretary of State Michael Armacost, and Richard Armitage, Pacific specialist at the Pentagon.) It was impressed upon Reagan that to persist with Marcos might actually turn the Philippines – to use Reagan's own phrase from the 1984 debate with Mondale – into 'another Nicaragua'. Reagan personally requested the dictator to make way for Corazon Aquino, who assumed the Presidency of the Philippines in February 1986.[89]

(c) China and Asian Economic Transformation

A 1984 article in the journal, *Foreign Policy*, described the 'current state of US-China ties' as 'Reagan's single foreign success' – a 'triumph of pragmatism over ideology'.[90] The early Reagan period saw important developments in China's 'strategic partnership' with the US, springing from the normalisation process inaugurated by Carter. A 1982 joint communiqué limited US arms sales to Taiwan, despite the strong historical attachment of the Republican right to defending the nationalists' stronghold. US textile interests failed to halt important new Sino–US trade deals.

With up to a quarter of Soviet ground forces tied down on China's border, even Republican dogmatists had come to appreciate the opportunities provided by the Sino–Soviet rivalry (and, indeed, by the sight in Southeast Asia since the late 1970s of communists fighting communists). China was clearly emerging as a modernising economic power with a developing nuclear capacity. To some Chinese strategists, however, the 'strategic partnership' looked too much like strategic exploitation. The Chinese Politburo in 1982 announced a new 'independent foreign policy' of 'relative equidistance' from Moscow and Washington. China began to criticise the manner of US resistance to Soviet expansionism in Central

America, Africa and the Middle East. By the later 1980s – especially in the wake of Gorbachev's decisions to restrain Russia's Vietnamese ally and to remove SS-20 missiles from Asia – China's relations with Moscow dramatically improved. By this time, however, the waning of the Cold War had raised for Beijing in newly acute form the need to achieve a new balance between revolution and modernisation.[91]

The US continued to play its part in the liberalisation of China's economy. The number of students from the People's Republic in US higher education reached 40 000 by the late 1980s. From Washington's viewpoint, Sino–American relations became almost subsumed into the wider agenda of accommodating to Asia's economic transformation. Asia's percentage share in global export trade grew from 15 in 1980 to almost 25 by 1988. With huge advances in the four 'tiger' economies (South Korea, Taiwan, Hong Kong and Singapore) as well as in Malaysia, Thailand and Indonesia, it was no longer obvious that Japan would hold ultimate economic sway. During the 1980s, US trade with the Asian-Pacific region overtook European trade in value and volume. To George Shultz, these changes were traceable to the 'American security umbrella' and 'our willingness to keep our own large and expanding market open'.[92] Both Shultz and Reagan spoke optimistically of an upcoming Pacific Age: an era in which the US could participate in an interdependent, dynamic Pacific economy. However, in 1987 the US bought 105 billion dollars more in goods from Asia than it exported there (about 61 per cent of America's entire trade deficit). Such statistics rapidly became a staple in the intense debate over US decline.[93]

(d) Southern Africa

Reagan's 1980 election was enthusiastically welcomed by the South African government. Radio South Africa welcomed the 'mighty victory' in November.[94] In March 1981, Reagan responded as follows to a question concerning the possibility of applying sanctions on South Africa:

> Can we abandon a country that has stood by us in every war we've ever fought, a country that strategically is essential to the free world in its production of minerals we all must have and so forth?[95]

Reagan's own criticisms of *apartheid* were usually hedged by warnings about communist influence in the African National Congress. His major address of July 1986, following years of township insurrection, showed more concern for white security 'in this country they love',[96] than for racial justice. Reagan's emphases were distressing to many Administration members, including Shultz and Chester Crocker, the Assistant Secretary of State for African Affairs. Crocker recalled in his memoirs the President's discomfort in criticising Pretoria:

> ... the President tended to discredit his case by sounding so much like the government from which he was so reluctant to distance himself.[97]

Compared with Central America, however, South Africa was not a front-burner issue for the Reagan Administration. Only during the post-1985 Congressional debate over sanctions was policy in South Africa dominated by the White House rather than Crocker's State Department Africa Bureau. Crocker's approach was pragmatic and regionalist. He successfully opposed conservative Reaganite efforts to supply covert military support to the rightist RENAMO guerrillas in Mozambique. He continued Carter's policy of non-hostility towards Robert Mugabe's government in Zimbabwe.[98] The expected rush to back the Mobutu regime in Zaire did not occur until after 1984. Regarding South Africa, Crocker held that Washington's leverage in Pretoria was insufficient to force a lifting of *apartheid*. (A special Advisory Committee reported a similar conclusion to Secretary Shultz in 1987.)[99] Crocker's central policy, which united the various State bureaus with the CIA and Pentagon, was 'constructive engagement'. Punitive sanctions, disinvestment and disengagement were condemned as 'ostrich' policies. 'Constructive engagement' would utilise quiet diplomacy, facilitate 'institution building' and encourage 'black empowerment' by funding training programmes. It would support 'those advocates of constructive change in South Africa of all races in and out of government'.[100]

Above all, 'constructive engagement' was a regionalist policy. As Crocker wrote later, it made 'no sense *except* as a regional strategy'.[101] Again, Crocker's approach was pragmatic. He told the Senate Judiciary Subcommittee on Security and Terrorism in 1982:

> We proceed on the basis that the Soviet Union does not have a grand strategy design for southern Africa, but that it is, in fact, taking

advantage of targets of opportunity that present themselves ... . The Soviet Union, alone, has a vested interest in keeping the region in turmoil.[102]

Though unconcerned about governments (such as those in Zimbabwe and Mozambique) which proclaimed Marxism for 'their own practical purposes',[103] Crocker sought to deny the USSR its 'targets of opportunity'. He aimed at a comprehensive regional settlement, involving the end to South African domination of Namibia and the removal from Angola of the 50 000 or so Cuban troops who had been stationed there since the mid-1970s. Crocker initially opposed the CIA's plans to restore Angolan covert operations in support of Jonas Savimbi's Pretoria-backed UNITA guerrillas. As initially conceived, 'constructive engagement' was to be the framework under which Namibia would achieve independence, and Angola become de-Sovietised. South African power was to become an 'anvil' of US diplomacy.[104]

By the end of Reagan's first term, it was clear that 'constructive engagement' was not performing as intended. Difficulties were traceable to the intransigence and opportunism of P.W. Botha's Pretoria regime, and to Washington's uncertain application of the 'constructive' side of its engagement. South Africa's military raids into Botswana, Lesotho, Zimbabwe, Zambia and Mozambique amounted to a policy of regional destabilisation, at odds with Crocker's strategy. The Botha government's response to the township uprisings was repressive rather than reformist. P.W. Botha's 1985 'Rubicon' speech – originally heralded as a major move to positive reform – was a disappointment to Washington. Crocker later described Botha as 'falling into, instead of crossing, the Rubicon'.[105] For its part, Washington was timid in its application of 'constructive engagement'. Few channels were opened to the African National Congress. Like Carter, Reagan opposed legislation making the Sullivan fair employment code mandatory for US firms in South Africa. Such 'constructive' moves as were made tended to be undermined by Reagan's intemperate statements, as well as by Pretoria's network of contacts with the Administration's right wing. (In his memoirs, Crocker acknowledges that there was substantial cooperation between the CIA and South African military intelligence.)[106]

By the start of Reagan's second term, it was clear that events were running ahead of the Administration's policy. Domestic anti-*apartheid* groups like TransAfrica were mounting effective campaigns on Capitol

Hill. Even Congressional Republicans were questioning 'constructive engagement' (Richard Lugar, Indiana Republican and chairman of the Senate Foreign Relations Committee before 1987, later wrote that he had no 'reasonable confidence' in Reagan's understanding of the South African situation.)[107] Crocker pointed to important interim agreements reached in 1984 in Angola and Mozambique (the Lusaka and Nkomati Accords). He also promised a more activist pursuance of 'constructive engagement' with more contacts with leading oppositionists. (In 1986, Washington sent a black ambassador, Edward Perkins, to Pretoria to pursue 'activist constructive engagement'. In 1987, Shultz met African National Congress Leader Oliver Tambo.)

Again, however, the Administration was failing to keep abreast of events. US firms were responding to domestic pressure, and to the uncertain situation in South Africa, by withdrawing. During 1985, the Administration was able to exploit divisions between proponents of 'selective' and of 'comprehensive' sanctions.[108] It argued the case – denied by the ANC – that sanctions would only hurt black South Africans. During 1985, the Administration also secured the repeal in Congress of the 1976 Clark amendment, barring US covert operations in Angola. In 1986, however, Congress passed the Comprehensive Anti-Apartheid Act; it included a ban on all new investment and on private loans to the South African government. Reagan's veto of the Act was overridden: 317–83 in the House and 78–21 in the Senate.

For Crocker, it was Congress which was destroying policy coherence, reducing Washington's messages to a 'high-decibel garble'.[109] In reality, the sanctions legislation represented more a justified response to failed policy, than a misconceived derailing of a policy which was succeeding. Despite all this, Crocker managed to keep his 'activist' version of 'constructive engagement' afloat. Congressional attempts to legislate punitive, comprehensive sanctions (the Dellums bill) failed in 1987 and 1988. More spectacularly, on 22 December 1988, Crocker achieved apparently lasting accords in Namibia and Angola. Cuba, South Africa and the Angolan government agreed to a deal whereby Namibian independence would be recognised, and foreign troops begin a phased withdrawal from Angola. Crocker's Southern African triumph was real, and an important achievement for Reaganite pragmatism. It represented an indication of what might be achieved in the new era of melting Cold War. Yet the accords were signed only after the post-Clark amendment resumption of direct US military assistance to UNITA; this involved not only the reversal of Crocker's original strategy,[110] but also an incursion into Angola's civil war more redolent of the 'high' Cold War than of this new era. Crocker's accords did not bring peace to Angola. Nor did they compensate for the inadequacies of 'constructive engagement' as a formula for encouraging South African democracy.

(e) The Horn of Africa

The pragmatism evident in Administration policy towards Southern Africa was even more pronounced with regard to Somalia and Ethiopia. The new Administration's policy review for the Horn was not even completed until Spring 1982. The review's recommendations – aid to Sudan and Kenya, cautious arming of Somalia, the maintenance of a dialogue with the Soviet-backed Mengistu regime in Ethiopia – embodied a natural bureaucratic growth from the Carter years.[111] White House attention was directed to the Horn during the Somalia–Ethiopia conflicts of 1982, with the result that Somalia now received substantial aid. The House of Representatives Foreign Affairs Subcommittee on Africa emerged in this period as an important critic of Administration policy, of the Somali human rights record, and of Somali ambitions in the disputed Ogaden territories. Pentagon strategists indicated the desirability of secure US bases along the Gulf of Aden, particularly in view of the possibility of conflict in the Persian Gulf. It was far from clear, however, if stability would be enhanced by backing Somalia. Yet it was public and Congressional responses to the widely publicised Ethiopian famines of the mid-1980s which occasioned the most clear breach of Reaganite dogma. As Peter Schraeder writes, in 1985 'the staunchest anti-communist administration' in US history became 'the largest official donor to the most doctrinaire Marxist country on the African continent'.[112] Relief aid was given with no political strings beyond rhetorical condemnation of Mengistu's human rights record. With policy still being made largely at State Department bureau and aid agency level, the Administration refrained from involving itself with the various Ethiopian secessionist movements. The savage intensification of Somalia's civil war in 1988 again stimulated a debate on US policy in the Horn. Here, as elsewhere, the waning of the Cold War was provoking intense questioning of American globalism.

6   Reagan: The Waning of the Cold War and Iran-Contra

The previous chapter illustrated the continuing power of the Vietnam legacy during the Reagan years. This chapter will consider the development of this book's three other major themes during the second Reagan term. The Reagan–Gorbachev dialogue constituted the crucial moment in the demise of the Cold War. This and the following chapter will examine and seek to explain the manner in which the international system which had held primacy since the late 1940s began to disintegrate. It will discuss the making of foreign policy under Reagan and the implications of the Iran-*contra* scandal for democratic foreign policy. Finally, in the context of an evaluation of Reagan's foreign policy, we consider again the debate over American decline.

US–SOVIET RELATIONS: 1985–9

In March 1985, Mikhail Gorbachev succeeded Konstantin Chernenko as leader of the Soviet Union. Widely regarded as a proponent of 'forward thinking', Gorbachev was seen – in the words of Raymond Garthoff – as a 'forward-looking, active younger version' of Chernenko's predecessor, Yuri Andropov. In 1984, Gorbachev had signalled his attachment to Andropov's legacy by proclaiming the need 'to bolster and augment everything new and progressive that has recently become part of our societal life'.[1] Gorbachev represented forces within Soviet communism which advocated reform as the condition for systemic survival. By 1987, Gorbachev was urging his country to 'get out of the quagmire of conservatism, and to break the inertia of stagnation'.[2] *Perestroika* (economic restructuring) and *glasnost* (political openness and reform) were to provide the key. Seeking to lead reform from above, Gorbachev instead found himself presiding over forces which were rapidly escaping control. The Soviet system, so long fixed in Stalinist glaciation, appeared by the late 1980s incapable of rejuvenative reform. Like its Tsarist predecessor, Soviet communism engendered not reformist renewal, but its own revolutionary annihilation.

Throughout Reagan's second term (and, indeed, during the early phase of George Bush's Presidency), Washington was divided and uncertain as to what exactly was happening in the USSR. The CIA initially dismissed Gorbachev as, in George Shultz's account, '"just talk", just another ... attempt to deceive us'.[3] To many leading figures in the Reagan Administration, Gorbachev's talk of 'peaceful coexistence'[4] represented a familiar Soviet ploy, designed to destroy NATO and to buy time in which to rearm. The departure from the Administration before the Washington Summit (December 1987) of Secretary Weinberger and Richard Perle lessened the bureaucratic prominence of such views. (Nevertheless, the notion that Gorbachev was about to be replaced by a new hardline leadership in the Kremlin continued to dominate Pentagon thinking into the Bush years.) By 1987, the CIA had developed the line that Gorbachev was serious about reform, but that he would be defeated by vested interests. After all, as CIA Deputy Director Robert Gates put it in 1986: 'The Soviet Union is a despotism that works.'[5] Reagan was frequently reminded by his associates of Andrei Gromyko's remark that behind Gorbachev's smile there were 'iron teeth'.[6] The President continued to receive conflicting advice about the nature of Soviet power. Before the 1985 Geneva Summit, White House chief Don Regan advised his boss that 'Gorbachev was driven by his economic problems' and would accede to an American hard line.[7] The senior US official who was most obviously impressed by Gorbachev was Secretary Shultz. In 1979, Shultz had declared in a speech at Stanford University that the 'Soviet system' was 'incompetent and cannot survive'. At Chernenko's funeral, Shultz recognised Gorbachev as a leader who appreciated that the old Stalinist system was not working. Canadian Prime Minister Brian Mulroney asked Shultz when he thought 'serious change' would begin in the Soviet Union. The Secretary of State replied in one word: 'today'.[8]

While he shared the common suspicions of Gorbachev, Reagan himself exhibited a clear second term commitment to personal diplomacy with Moscow. The journalist Don Oberdorfer recalled the President's evident belief that 'if he could just get a Soviet leader into a room for a private talk, he could convince him' of the error of Moscow's ways.[9] Reagan's approach to the new era of opportunities was uncertain; it was also by turns naive, direct, obscure and effective. At the 1985 Geneva Summit, the President startled Gorbachev by announcing that their work would be facilitated 'if there was a threat to this world from some other species, from another planet'. Americans and Russians would then 'find out once and for all that we really are all human beings on this Earth together'.[10] In early 1987, Reagan told news reporters that he had 'a new hobby': collecting jokes about Soviet communism. At the Washington Summit in that year, he interrupted Gorbachev's serious account of conditions in his country to tell an ancient and inappropriate anti-Soviet joke.[11]

Despite the occasionally offensive tone of Reagan's folksiness, the personal summitry of the late 1980s achieved an extraordinary degree of success. The hopes engendered by the long, informal dialogue between Reagan and Gorbachev at Geneva in November, 1985, established a dynamic which survived apparently ominous setbacks: the April 1986 Chernobyl nuclear disaster; the Libyan air raid; the arrest in Moscow of US journalist Nicholas Daniloff in September, 1986; and, most importantly, the failure of the Reykjavik Summit in October, 1986. By the time of Reykjavik, it had become apparent not only that both leaders had made a major political commitment to the process, but that each was prepared to think and act in unprecedentedly radical ways. In January 1986, Gorbachev effectively accepted the 'zero option' for Europe (with the elimination of NATO intermediate and of Soviet SS-20 missiles). Not only was Moscow now prepared to accept the 'zero option', disingenuously offered by Richard Perle in Reagan's first term; Gorbachev also raised the prospect of a world free of nuclear weapons by the century's end, contingent on the elimination of the Strategic Defense Initiative. Reagan responded with sweeping disarmament proposals, but with an unswerving commitment to SDI.

The Reykjavik Summit collapsed amid assertions by Reagan that he had 'promised the American people that I will not give up SDI'.[12] Despite its failure, the summit stands as one of the most breathtaking and bizarre events of modern history. The date of Reagan's departure for Iceland was set according to guidance offered by Nancy Reagan's San Francisco astrologer.[13] The Presidential performance at the summit convinced, to quote Jane Mayer and Doyle McManus, 'Washington's policy professionals that his untutored optimism may have reached dangerous proportions.'[14] Ex-President Richard Nixon judged that no 'summit since Yalta has threatened Western interests so much as the two days at Reykjavik'.[15] Both Gorbachev and Reagan later described Reykjavik as *the* turning point in US–Soviet relations; Shultz considered it 'the most remarkable superpower meeting ever held'.[16] To former Defence Secretary James Schlesinger, it was a 'near disaster':

In Western strategy the nuclear deterrent remains the ultimate and indispensable reality. Yet at Reykjavik the President was prepared to negotiate it away almost heedlessly. By contrast, the Strategic Defense Initiative was treated and continues to be treated as if it were a reality ... instead of a collection of technical experiments and distant hopes.[17]

At this extraordinary meeting in Iceland, the world's most powerful leaders, in the words of Michael Mandelbaum and Strobe Talbott, 'engaged in a bout of feverish one-upmanship'; each attempted 'to outdo the other in demonstrating his devotion to the dream of a nuclear-free world'.[18] On the American side at least, the summit had been poorly prepared. According to Weinberger, Reagan had been 'pushed very hard by a number of people who thought the only way to improve relationships was to have meetings'. (Weinberger later described Reykjavik as an 'unstructured poker game' in which Gorbachev seemed to be trying to get the maximum amount of favourable world publicity.)[19] At Reykjavik, Gorbachev's initial bid was breathtaking: not just acceptance of the 'zero option'; but also 50 per cent cuts in Soviet and US strategic weapons and agreement not to include French and British nuclear weapons in the calculations. He insisted, however, upon a ten-year strict enforcement of the 1972 Anti-ballistic Missile Treaty, effectively freezing SDI. The American response was to suggest the removal of all ballistic missiles within ten years, with the right to develop strategic defences after that time against remaining bomber and cruise missile forces. (The Zero Ballistic Missiles notion had, in fact, long been nurtured in sections of the Pentagon. Undersecretary Fred Ikle had advocated it, seeing the high speed of intercontinental missiles as the greatest threat to US security. In June 1986, Weinberger became converted to the idea that the US could only gain from elimination of 'fast-flying' ballistic missiles.) Gorbachev now raised the ante, suggesting the abolition of *all* nuclear weapons by 1996. Reagan's response was ecstatic: '*All* nuclear weapons? Well, Mikhail, that's exactly what I've been talking about all along.'[20] The stumbling block, of course, was SDI. At one level, the issue dividing the leaders – whether or not laboratory testing for SDI could continue – seemed small. The 1972 treaty actually allowed for a degree of laboratory testing. Clearly, however, SDI had acquired by this time a symbolic importance for both leaderships, quite out of proportion to any prospects the system possessed for successful deployment.

The breakdown at Reykjavik left international arms control in a state of confusion. World opinion looked to a compromise whereby 'Star Wars' would be deprioritised in return for progress on a strategic arms reduction (START) treaty. Following Reykjavik, the US abandoned its voluntary adherence to the (unratified) SALT II arms limits. US and NATO military doctrine conspicuously failed to keep pace with momentous changes on the Soviet side. In May 1987, a Warsaw Pact statement unveiled a new Soviet doctrine. This now included the objective of preventing war; the termination of conflict – rather than victory – should war break out; and proposals for joint NATO–Warsaw Pact consultations on military doctrine.[21]

The way forward proved to be agreement on intermediate-range nuclear forces (INF). A key negotiating relationship had been established between Secretary Shultz and Soviet Foreign Minister Eduard Shevardnadze. (Andrei Gromyko's May 1985 replacement by Shevardnadze had been an important advance for Gorbachovian 'new thinking', and had reaped benefits in terms of Western public opinion.) The INF breakthrough was achieved with Moscow's espousal of the 'double zero': NATO would remove Pershing I, II and cruise; the Soviets would eliminate SS-20s from the western regions of the USSR, SS-20s targeted on China, as well as the shorter-range SS-12s and SS-23s. The INF treaty was signed at the Washington Summit of December 1987. An entire class of missiles was to be eliminated within three years, with US and Soviet observers actually witnessing the dismantling and destruction of enemy missiles. The verification and information exchange provisions in the 1987 treaty were comprehensive and unprecedented. An important aspect of the process was the 'Gorbymania' which affected US public opinion. The Washington walkabouts by the General Secretary of the Soviet Communist Party brought home the extent to which the Cold War was indeed coming to an end. During 1988, Gorbachev's opinion poll popularity ratings in the US rose to levels comparable to those of Reagan himself; in Western Europe, the Soviet leader's popularity was higher than Reagan's.[22]

The accelerating superpower arms control dynamic produced significant bureaucratic casualties in Washington. Weinberger resigned on 5 November 1987, immediately after the announcement of the date for the Washington Summit, and was replaced by the more pragmatic Frank Carlucci. (General Colin Powell replaced Carlucci as National Security Adviser.) The Defence Secretary had long been the most conspicuous Administration critic of the entire Reagan-Gorbachev dialogue. He sought to temper Reagan's utopian tendencies either by appealing to the President's anti-Sovietism or, in the case of SDI, harnessing the utopianism to the cause of undermining the dialogue with Gorbachev. Just before the 1985 Geneva Summit, the Pentagon leaked a letter from Weinberger, advising Reagan against cutting any arms deals with Moscow. (On being asked if he intended to fire Weinberger, Reagan responded: 'Do you want a two-word answer or one?' The reporter wanted two words. Reagan replied: 'Hell, no.')[23] Weinberger's annual reports to President and Congress painted a bleak picture of Soviet intentions. In 1986, he argued for accelerated US military buildup:

> ... all the evidence we have suggests that preparing to deter an attack only by assembling forces adequate to deter us under similar conditions could provide too little to deter the Soviets.

Only now, in 1986, was the US 'beginning to deal from strength'.[24] Weinberger's 1987 report completely ignored the new Soviet military doctrine, despite US access to it. He continued to cite Lenin's commitment to world communist revolution, rather than Gorbachev's Geneva statement that nuclear war was unwinnable.[25] In February 1987, Weinberger requested immediate Presidential approval to begin deploying aspects of SDI. Shultz and Admiral William Crowe (Chairman of the Joint Chiefs of Staff) succeeded in dissuading Reagan from immediately approving Weinberger's suggestion. (The President's initial response to the suggestion that Moscow should be consulted on the implications for the 1972 Anti-ballistic Missile Treaty was: 'Don't ask the Soviets – tell them.')[26]

A comprehensive START treaty was not achieved under Reagan. The INF treaty was accepted by the Senate in May, 1988 (93–5). (Weinberger attempted to sabotage the process by raising the question of whether 'futuristic' weapons like lasers and particle beams were to be covered in the treaty.) Before the Moscow Summit (May 1988) some modest progress was made in START and other areas: on intercontinental and submarine-launched ballistic missile subceilings; and on chemical weapons, with the Soviets agreeing unilaterally to halt manufacture and to begin to destroy stocks. Verification arrangements for 50 per cent START reductions proved impossible to finalise before the meeting in Moscow.

The summit in Russia's capital was primarily a media event. Even America's actor President remarked on the theatricality of the exercise. Ideas of an 'evil empire' now belonged, in Reagan's words, to 'another time, another place'.[27] Gorbachev took up this remark of Reagan's on his farewell public address at the summit. The US used the occasion to probe the limits of Soviet tolerance on human rights issues, with Reagan meeting a group of dissidents. Soviet efforts to step up conventional force reductions in Europe, and to defuse a number of regional conflict issues, were rebuffed; (this, despite the 1987 decision to withdraw from Afghanistan). For Gorbachev, the process was moving too slowly – 'more slowly', as he said in his address, 'than is called for by the real situation in both our countries and the world'.[28] For Reagan, however, the summit was a symbolic cap on the achievements of his second-term personal diplomacy. At a speech given at London's Guildhall on his way home from Russia, Reagan mused:

> Imagine the President of the United States and the General Secretary of the Soviet Union walking together in Red Square, talking about a growing personal friendship, and meeting together average citizens, realizing how much our people have in common ... quite possibly, we're beginning to take down the barriers of the postwar era ... .[29]

The final meeting between the two leaders occurred on the occasion, in December 1988, of Gorbachev's address to the UN General Assembly in New York. Addressing the Assembly as Soviet President as well as General Secretary, Gorbachev called for the 'deideolization' of superpower relations. Extraordinarily, he spoke of 'the compelling necessity of the principle of freedom of choice' as a 'universal principle'.[30] Western commentators could not imagine how near was the day when these promises would come to the test in Eastern Europe, much less in the constituent republics of the USSR. Gorbachev also announced a unilateral reduction of 10 per cent in Soviet armed forces, with major and swift cuts in European conventional deployments. As Raymond Garthoff comments, this initiative amounted to nothing less than a commitment 'to break down the political divisions of Europe'.[31] The meeting between the two Presidents on Governor's Island represented a coda to their historic dialogue. Reagan seemed instinctively to grasp the significance of what was occurring by echoing his call of 1987 for the Soviets to tear down the Berlin wall. He expressed his hope to 'see the day' when the peoples of Eastern Europe could 'enjoy the freedom, democracy, and self-determination' that they 'have long awaited'.[32]

REAGAN AND THE WANING OF THE COLD WAR

Speaking in 1990, Ronald Reagan ascribed the breakthrough in US–Soviet relations which took place under his watch to 'mutual interest'. Gorbachev had been forced to make accommodations due to economic crisis at home – a crisis caused largely by swollen defence spending. The US interest lay in transforming 'a world so heavily armed that one misstep could trigger a great war'.[33] The Cold War did not come to an end during Reagan's Presidency. Its ending cannot be assessed without consideration of the East European revolutions of 1989 or the disintegration of Soviet power in 1990–1. Some general theoretical arguments about the course, nature and termination of the Cold War will therefore be postponed until the next chapter. However, it seems appropriate at this point to examine the familiar, and superficially persuasive, assertion that the late 1980s witnessed the vindication of the Reaganite analysis of Soviet power: the triumph of the 'squeeze' strategy and of negotiation from strength.

Reagan's comment about 'mutual interest' pointed up the role of his own instinctual anti-nuclearism. In the unfolding dialogue with Gorbachev, this was indeed important. As Daniel Deudney and G.J. Ikenberry point out, 'Reagan's anomalous anti-nuclearism' signalled to Gorbachev 'that bold initiatives would be reciprocated rather than exploited'.[34] It is possible to trace on the Soviet side a growing awareness that Reagan's anti-nuclearism was genuine, and that it could extend beyond a commitment to strategic defence. Reagan's personal unpopularity in liberal and leftist circles, especially in Western Europe, made it difficult for many commentators to acknowledge this, or to extend due credit for his second term flexibility.[35] Reagan's desire to be a second term peacemaker was actually extremely important. The force of this point should not be diminished by the realisation that, in a sense, he was fulfilling the predictions of academic 'roles' theory, in a way peculiarly appropriate for someone of his professional background. After 1984, Reagan seemed almost to be following a preordained role as the second term President concerned to avoid being recorded in history as a warmonger. In all this, there was also a strong element of 'Nixon goes to China'. As Dan Oberdorfer has argued, Reagan's right-wing background made it easier for him to come to terms with Moscow than for 'a centrist or liberal president'.[36] Shultz's part in the drama also needs constant emphasis. The Secretary of State provided an invaluable counter to ideologues, cowboys and true-believers in the White House and Pentagon. To quote Deudney and Ikenberry once more, Shultz 'picked up on Reagan's strong convictions and deftly side-stepped hard-line opposition to agreements'.[37]

Yet the pro-Reagan interpretation of the waning of the Cold War claims far more than credit for Reagan's unexpected flexibility and Shultz's pragmatism. In January 1988, Vice President Bush declared that Gorbachev's policies were the result of 'our strength' and 'our resolve'.[38] In August of the same year, Robert McFarlane published an article entitled, 'Reagan: Architect of Perestroika'.[39] Conservative journalists and academics in the early 1990s offered a 'Reagan victory' interpretation of the late twentieth century. Moscow had been forced to compromise by Reagan's 'revitalised containment', by 'squeeze', toughness and SDI. In *Victory: The Reagan Administration's Secret Strategy that Hastened the Collapse of the Soviet Union*, Peter Schweizer applauded the 'squeeze' strategy and its presiding genius, William Casey.[40] To some extent, the 'Reagan victory' school of the late 1980s and early 1990s constituted an attempt to recapture the legacy of Reaganism for the cause of conservative anti-Sovietism. Many members and supporters of the Reagan Administration were actually extremely anxious about the implications of the Reagan–Gorbachev dialogue. Arms negotiator Paul Nitze wrote as late as 1988 that the US needed always to base its 'security policies on Soviet capabilities rather than hoped or expected intentions'.[41] On 23 June 1988, a group of prominent conservatives – including Robert Bork and Norman Podhoretz – appended their names to a *New York Times* cartoon showing a bear attacking a man wearing a business suit. Implicitly very critical of Reagan's policies, the cartoon's caption announced that the US could 'ill afford to assume that the bear has been tamed'. In the same month, conservative columnist George Will announced that, for conservatives, Reagan's foreign policy had 'produced much surprise but little delight'.[42]

Whatever its provenance, the 'Reagan victory' arguments deserve to be taken seriously. As noted in the previous chapter, some of Reagan's early 1980s remarks about Soviet *weakness* appeared, a few years later, extraordinarily acute. There are, however, major problems with the 'Reagan victory' analysis. The first of these relates to the inconsistency, contradictions and oftentimes bureaucratic anarchy which characterised the Reagan strategy. As Stephen Ambrose noted in 1992, 'with regard to Reagan's policies, it was the contradictions that stood out'.[43] Certainly up to the inception of the Reagan–Gorbachev dialogue – and to some extent even in the later years – the policies were driven by competing and contradictory perceptions of Soviet power. There were elements of appreciation that the Soviet empire might be crumbling; there was also a genuine fear about the extent to which Soviet power had grown under the cover of detente; yet there was considerable disingenuous exaggeration of the extent of the Soviet threat, especially in Central America. (In 1983, a bipartisan commission chaired by Brent Scowcroft concluded that the 'window of vulnerability', so important to Reagan's 1980 campaign, had never been open.)[44] The 'squeeze' strategy was never applied consistently. Confusion in Washington and the attitude of America's European allies ensured that the economic aspects of detente were never entirely dismantled. There is little evidence that the Soviet economy was damaged by the dismantling which did occur. To quote Michael Cox:

> What hurt the Soviet Union after 1980 was not US economic pressure so much as the drop in the price of oil, the devaluation of the dollar, and the economic decision by western bankers not to lend any more money to Moscow's indebted East European allies. Indeed, the accident at Chernobyl probably cost the USSR more than any American embargo.[45]

The US nuclear freeze and Western European peace movements also complicated the messages being received in Moscow.

The muddle and confusion attending the 'squeeze' strategy clearly point away from any notion that Reaganism gave birth to *perestroika*. What the effects of a concerted 'squeeze' *would* have been is impossible to gauge. However, it is worth remembering that the initial Soviet reaction to Reaganite rhetoric and to the arms buildup was a relatively hardline one. Above all, Soviet reform was manifestly rooted in internal Soviet dynamics: in structural economic difficulties, in generational changes and intra-Communist Party cleavages. Of course, it was also connected to international events and processes – (such as the cost of aid to Soviet allies in the Third World and the debilitating Afghan war)[46] – over which the Reagan Administration exerted some influence. But there was nothing like a direct reaction to Reaganite 'squeeze'. Gorbachev's 'new thinking' on foreign policy was far more a response to global interdependence. 'New thinkers', like Georgi Shakhnarazov, were influenced by Western detente intellectuals and spoke the language of interdependency theory.[47] (The Soviet delegation to a 1988 Virginia conference on Eastern Europe framed their analysis in terms of 'today's era of growing interdependence', where 'no region' should be 'the arena of interstate rivalry ... of the two great powers'.)[48] Reaganism in the early 1980s probably hindered rather than furthered the cause of Soviet reform. It gave Russian hard-liners the opportunity to invoke the 'American threat'. It can also reasonably be argued – as it is by German *Ostpolitik* intellectuals – that, in the words of Neal Ascherson, '1989 was only possible because "Europe" managed to prevent Reagan and Thatcher riding their anti-Communism into full confrontation.'[49] In this analysis, it was precisely the degree to which detente was *not* dismantled which emboldened the new Soviet leadership to begin to disarm. Apparently successful economies in Western Germany, Sweden and Japan – along with economic reform in Eastern Europe (especially Hungary) – also spurred Soviet economic liberalisation.

The important breakthroughs for 'negotiation from strength' came only after Gorbachev's accession to power. One detailed study of the INF treaty concludes that the treaty's content and timing 'has to be explained in terms of domestic coalition-building dynamics, particularly in Western Europe and in the Soviet Union' rather than in terms of US bargaining strategies.[50] It may be objected that this analysis ignores 'Star Wars' and the operation of the 'squeeze' in relation to Soviet defence spending. Did not Moscow simply perceive the scale of the US arms buildup and, after a brief attempt to act tough, surrender to the inevitable? There is no question that Soviet leaders took the Strategic Defence Initiative very seriously. As Francis Fukuyama puts it, SDI 'threatened to make obsolete an entire generation of Soviet nuclear weapons', as well as shifting 'the superpower competition into areas like microelectronics and other innovative technologies' where the Soviets had major disadvantages.[51] Moscow correctly interpreted SDI as a conscious, and illegal, effort to undermine the 1972 Anti-ballistic Missile Treaty. Soviet leaders were reluctant to gamble that SDI was mere comic-strip fantasy. The prospect of an unexpected technological advance shifting the terms of superpower relations had disturbed both sides throughout the Cold War. The US reaction to the 1957 Sputnik launch exemplified such worries, as did Khrushchev's observation in his memoirs about 'these "rotten" capitalists' who keep 'coming up with things that make our jaw drop in surprise'.[52] Back in 1946, George Kennan's 'long telegram' from Moscow had invoked the long-standing Russian anxiety about Western technological competence. Soviet defector Arkady Shevchenko in 1985 described the 'man in the Kremlin' as 'absorbed by questions of America's political, military and economic power, and awed by its technological capacity'.[53] It seems certain that reaction to Western technology was a key factor in launching the 'defensive modernisation' that constituted the early phase of *perestroika*. Moscow's 'new thinkers' were alarmed by spiralling arms costs. By the mid-1980s, almost one quarter of Soviet GNP was being taken up in defence spending. Yet, as Mike Bowker suggests, there are some indications that defence costs did not dominate Gorbachev's thinking.[54] Defence cuts began to affect Soviet budgets only in 1989. Moscow's defence spending levels remained fairly constant throughout the period of Reagan's Presidency. In fact, during the entire Cold War, it has proved exceedingly difficult to demonstrate any direct correlation between US and Soviet defence spending shifts. On *both* sides, pressures to increase spending appear to have operated almost independently of the changing nature of the objective 'threat'.[55] Moreover, although the Soviets were clearly worried by SDI, it strains credulity to imagine that they were unaware of the highly uncertain nature of its operationalisation. Rather than SDI as such, it was possibly the cost of extended intercontinental ballistic missile deployment, needed to counter a new US strategic defence, which daunted Moscow. Lastly, much has been made of the way in which 'Star Wars' destroyed the Reykjavik agreement. But, as Bowker again points out, Moscow *never* received any US commitment on the abandonment or even downgrading of SDI; this 'suggests that the system may not have been the pivotal reason for Gorbachev's reassessment of foreign and defence policy'.[56] At the very least, it seems likely that Moscow's concern with SDI decreased considerably after 1986.

The point of this discussion is not entirely to deny the importance of SDI, nor to argue that Soviet concern for defence cuts was not crucial to the Reagan–Gorbachev dialogue. Rather, the intention is to illustrate the complexity of these events; to emphasise that *perestroika* was not a direct response to any concerted US 'squeeze'; and to contend that the early phase of Reaganism did little to help the cause of Soviet reform. Raymond Garthoff concludes that there 'was no consideration whatsoever by the Soviet leadership of any actions that the American military buildup deterred'.[57] Arms control concessions by Moscow after 1984 were causally unrelated to the reckless military spending of Reagan's first term. Retrenchment in the face of Russian imperial decline was Moscow's main priority.

If the Reagan years did not see a remorseless working out of any coherent 'squeeze' strategy, why did an apparently bellicose Washington leadership turn eventually to the ways of peace? Some answers to this question have already been noted: Reagan's second term self-image; the role of Shultz; bureaucratic defeat for Perle and Weinberger; Gorbachev's central role as initiator of the process; public unease or ambivalence about aspects of the Reaganite hard line. Also important were the increasing difficulties faced by the Reagan Administration in convincing both America and the world of the potency of the 'Soviet threat'.[58] The idea that Western liberal democracy was imperilled by the Sandinista regime in Nicaragua was absurd. Second term peace-making represented, at one level, an accommodation to those forces – most obviously in Western Europe, but also in the US – which simply remained unconvinced by such rhetoric. It is also worth recalling that Reagan's second term dialogue with Gorbachev was as much the product of political weakness and vulnerability, as it was of 'strength'. During 1986, the Reagan Administration was faced not only by midterm election defeats, but also by the most damaging scandal to hit an American Presidency since the days of Richard Nixon.

IRAN-CONTRA: THE NEGATION OF DEMOCRATIC FOREIGN POLICY

Though ferociously complex, Iran-*contra* had at its heart a simple scheme: to trade US arms to Iran for the release of American hostages held by Tehran's allies in the Middle East, with proceeds from the secret sales being diverted to the Nicaraguan *contras*. The illegal operation, mounted by Reagan's National Security Council staff, implicitly denied the constitutional right of Congress to monitor arms sales, to deny (in the Boland amendments) funds to the *contras* and – in effect – to exercise any control whatsoever on executive foreign policy. It was rooted in the Administration's obsession with Nicaragua, its genuine desire to secure hostage releases (and to avoid the mistakes of the Carter Administration), and in the possibility of re-establishing close ties with Iran. It violated stated Administration aims, notably on Middle Eastern policy and on the dangers of dealing with terrorists. Commissioned and operationalised outside regular bureaucratic channels, it demonstrated all that was damaging and corrupt in the Administration's penchant for cowboy diplomacy.

In July 1987, Fawn Hall, secretary to Oliver North and the most glamourous player in the scandal, informed the joint Congressional investigating committee that there were some 'considerations', regarding national security, which were above the law.[59] Fawn Hall's opinion accurately reflected the views of more senior figures. North at his trial defended lies he had told to the House Select Intelligence Committee in August 1986. 'I was raised,' declared North, 'to know the difference between right and wrong.' He knew 'it wasn't right not to tell the truth, but he didn't think it was unlawful'.[60] In May 1986, Admiral John Poindexter, who had succeeded Robert McFarlane as National Security Adviser five months previously, told his deputy Don Fortier that Congressional authority to appropriate funds should not be allowed 'to restrict what the President can do in foreign policy'.[61] Private, unappropriated money could be utilised to circumvent the Boland amendment on Nicaragua. In the same message, Poindexter revealed Reagan's attitude. Discussing *contra* aid, the President was reported as saying: 'If we can't move the contra package before June 9, I want to figure out a way to take action unilaterally.'[62] In June 1984, James Baker, representing the 'pragmatic' wing of the White House, had given his opinion that such circumventions of Congress constituted an 'impeachable offense'.[63] His view was overruled by Vice President Bush and Attorney General Ed Meese. Warned by Weinberger about the legal implications of the emerging 'arms for hostages' policy towards Iran, Reagan replied: 'Well, the American people will never forgive me if I fail to get these hostages out over this legal question.'[64]

The attitudes of North, Poindexter and Reagan were potentially destructive of constitutional democracy. They recalled the cynicism and constitutional insouciance of the Watergate era. As with Watergate, the farcical and headline-grabbing elements of the unfolding story tended to mask the scandal's profound seriousness. The story was unheroic. It was first broken, not by crusading Washington journalists or by Congressional investigators, but by an obscure, pro-Tehran, Lebanese newspaper, *Al Shiraa*. The Democratic leadership in Congress appeared reluctant to revive the agony of Watergate in the last phase of Reagan's Presidency, and failed to push enthusiastically for impeachment. To some degree this reflected the problems of clearly establishing Presidential complicity in the misdeeds. (Between 1972 and 1974, the US had been preoccupied by the question of how much Richard Nixon knew about the crimes commit-ted in his name. In 1987–8, Reagan's proferred memory lapses provoked the question: 'Who knew what, and when did he forget it?)'[65] It has also been suggested that Democrats were less than eager to contest the 1992 elections against an incumbent President Bush. In any event, the Iran-*contra* affair raised serious questions about the practical efficacy of the Constitution's impeachment provision.

Throughout Iran-*contra*, farce was never far from the surface. The November 1985 'arms for hostages' shipment to Iran was attended by inter-agency bungling on a scale reminiscent of the Keystone Cops. When eighty HAWK missiles finally reached Tehran on 25 November, many were rejected because – due to Robert McFarlane's use of Israeli intermediaries – they were inscribed with the Star of David. In May 1986, McFarlane secretly visited Tehran, equipped with a Bible and a cake in the shape of a key. In October 1986, North and his irregular associate Richard Secord entrusted negotiations with the Iranians in Frankfurt to Secord's business partner, Albert Hakim. Lou Cannon commented later:

> The initiative that was supposed to chart the course of U.S.–Iranian relations had been put in the hands of a private citizen who had lived most of his life in Iran, lacked any background in diplomatic negotia-tion and stood, by his own estimate, to make 'many millions' of dollars from the agreements he was negotiating.[66]

When Reagan sacked Oliver North from the National Security Council staff in November 1986, it was amid Presidential assurances that North was an 'American patriot' and a 'national hero'.[67] In 1987, the Fawn Hall and Oliver North testimonies to the Congressional investigating committees became national spectator events, inspiring 'Ollie mania' and bumper-sticker philosophising. North boasted of the NSC's 'shred-ding party', designed to throw Congress and the press off the scent. The Lieutenant Colonel's bravado was to be extended in his 'no regrets' memoir,[68] and into his political adventures during the Bush and Clinton Administrations.

The roots of Iran-*contra* lay in an unconcern for Congressional authority and for constitutional restraint which infected large sections of the Reagan Administration. According to Louis Fisher, here was 'a stunning collapse of democratic government'.[69] Poindexter explained in July, 1987: 'I simply did not want any outside interference'.[70]

Weinberger initially counselled against the adventure, yet became progressively implicated in it. Theodore Draper puts it thus:

> Instead of resigning, Weinberger gave up the struggle against the operation. He made himself an accessory by legalistically preferring one way of getting the missiles to Iran to another ... he became a hostage to a policy that he says he detested ... .[71]

On 10 December 1985, Weinberger made a note: 'President – worried about hostages – but Israelis go ahead with arms sales ... .'[72] Shultz did offer to resign in August, 1986 on a range of issues ranging from the Philippines to Iranian arms sales, but primarily over 'constant sniping' from the NSC staff. Reagan assured his Secretary of State that both men '*were* on the same wavelength', and Shultz decided to 'slug it out' and battle to rescue his boss from Casey and the NSC staff.[73] For Shultz, Iran-*contra* was the nadir of cowboy-Reaganism. In his memoir, *Turmoil and Triumph*, he made little effort to offer excuses. (In contrast, Ed Meese's memoir, *With Reagan*, argued unconvincingly that 'arms for hostages' was justified by the fact that the Administration was dealing with 'third parties' in Tehran and with intermediaries like Manucher Ghorbanifar, rather than 'directly' with the Lebanese and Palestinian hostage takers.)[74] George Bush's defence, that he was 'out of the loop' on Iran-*contra*, was far from entirely persuasive. Like Shultz, he was an underinformed onlooker rather than a complete innocent. Release of the Vice Presidential diary for the period, November 1986 to January 1987, revealed his feelings of ambivalence about jumping 'into the fray' of Iran-*contra*. On 21 November, he was informed of a meeting attended by Meese, Don Regan, Poindexter and the President, 'excluding me'. Bush's response was uncertain:

> I am the one guy that can give the President objective advice and I have felt a twinge as to why the hell they didn't include me, but, on the other hand, you wind up not dragged into the mess. The other hand to that is you can't give the President proper advice.[75]

As for Reagan, the best indication of his attitude was his cynical issuance of a retrospective 'Finding', in December 1985, designed to absolve the CIA (under the terms of the 1980 Intelligence Oversight

Act) from charges of illegal involvement in the November arms ship-ments.[76] In June 1993, Theodore Draper concluded that there was 'no longer a mystery about who was responsible for the arms-for-hostages deals'. It was 'the President of the United States'.[77]

The concrete results achieved by Iran-*contra* were minor. The adventure did not revive the pre-1979 closeness in US–Iranian re-lations. The Nicaraguan rebels probably received about four million dollars from the diversions. Hostage taking in Lebanon continued. (The US hostage, Father Lawrence Jenco, was released in Beirut after McFarlane's May 1986 trip to Tehran. Yet, later in 1986, three more American hostages were taken, and another murdered.) The true significance of Iran-*contra* lay rather in its implications for democracy and constitutional government.

It was precisely the underlying constitutional issue which received shallow and inadequate treatment in the three main Iran-*contra* investi-gations:[78] the Tower Commission, the Congressional inquiries led by Senator Daniel Inouye (Democrat of Hawaii) and Representative Lee Hamilton (Democrat of Indiana), and the special prosecution led by Lawrence Walsh. The commission chaired by former Texan Republican Senator John Tower included Brent Scowcroft (National Security Adviser in the Ford Administration) and Carter's former Secretary of State, Edmund Muskie. The Commission concluded that 'significant questions of law do not appear to have been adequately addressed'. Reagan 'did not seem to be aware of the way in which the operation was implemented and the full consequences of U.S. participation'.[79] The freewheeling style of the NSC operators and of Casey's CIA were criti-cised. The Congressional investigation revealed the extent to which the NSC staffers had deliberately sought to escape legislative control. (Ironically, North and Poindexter later claimed successfully that they had been promised immunity from criminal prosecution in return for their cooperation with the Congressional investigating committees.) Lawrence Walsh's final report was not published until December, 1993. Walsh's work was continually hampered: by the precise mandate given him by the US Court of Appeals; by the reluctance of agencies and indi-viduals to cooperate; by the Congressional grant of immunity to key players; and by delays in accessing Swiss bank records. Most damaging to his work, however, were the 'midnight' pardons issued by President Bush in his last days in the White House. Weinberger's pardon undercut much of Walsh's labour. The former Secretary of Defence had been indicated following the discovery of his diary notes on key Iran-*contra* meetings. Besides Weinberger, in December 1992 Bush also pardoned McFarlane and Elliot Abrams, as well as relatively minor figures like Duane Claridge and Alan Fiers. Walsh concluded that Iran-*contra* was 'the product of two foreign policy directives by President Reagan which skirted the law and which were executed by NSC staff with the knowledge and support of high officials in the CIA, State and Defense Departments'.[80] (Surprises in Walsh's report were few, and related largely to the scale of the profits made by Secord and Hakim. In 1994, the US government began litigation in Switzerland to recover the money from the two irregular arms-dealer-diplomats.) As for Bush's pardons, Samuel Dash, former Chief Counsel to the Senate Watergate committee, commented that – especially in view of the fact that they were made after the 1992 elections, when Bush had lost the popular mandate – they were improper. Indeed, the 'pardons and the campaign to discredit Walsh may very well have been the final acts of coverup of the Iran-*contra* affair'.[81]

EVALUATING REAGAN'S FOREIGN POLICY: PRESIDENT REAGAN AND AMERICAN DECLINE

Iran-*contra* may not exactly have been Ronald Reagan's Watergate. Iran-*contra* seems to have had no equivalent to the 'smoking gun' tape recordings which the Supreme Court ordered Richard Nixon to release in August 1974. Reagan did not face a serious impeachment challenge. Larry Speakes, Reagan's press officer, called Iran-*contra* rather the Administration's 'Bay of Pigs': a serious and damaging misjudgement, more than redeemed by success elsewhere.[82] Such an analysis holds its attractions in view of the achievements of the dialogue with Gorbachev. It has already been acknowledged that Reagan deserves credit for the degree to which he was able to free himself from the narrow anti-communism of the first term. (In the opinion of Colin Powell, Reagan was 'probably the most pliable man in the administration'.)[83] In a January 1993 survey of the Republican Presidential years, David Broder of the *Washington Post* concluded that Iran-*contra* was not of overwhelming significance. He commended Reagan for supporting 'the people whose values and aspirations came closest to our own ... '.[84] In this view, the ending of the Cold War was a triumph for those American liberal democratic values which the Reagan Administration – though excoriated by liberal opinion at the time – somehow embodied.

In fact, the case against Reagan is very strong. The values which underlay Iran-*contra*, notwithstanding the genuine desire to secure release of the hostages, were undemocratic. The Administration's anti-communism led it to support groups whose purpose was also frequently undemocratic and destructive of human rights. Reagan's personal casualness in regard to such issues was a source of embarrassment to the more responsible and punctilious of his associates. The Administration's policy toward Central America in particular was indefensible. The conduct of policy was often incompetent and confused, despite the good efforts of Secretary Shultz. (During the first term in particular, incompetence and confusion had the unintended benefit of mitigating the effects of overblown dogma.) Reagan himself was ill-informed and often negligent, with elements in the Administration continually threatening to convert policy into a sequence of semi-private, unaccountable escapades.

Reagan was elected in 1980 to reverse American decline and the perception of decline. As we have seen, he neither restored consensus nor expunged the legacy of Vietnam. For a time his Administration did contribute to a blurring of perceptions of decline. The policies pursued by the Reagan Administration were domestically divisive. Yet clearly, especially among the more affluent sections of the population – those Americans most likely to vote – Reaganism did appear a potent force against the spectre of decline. First term assertions about restoring American greatness and the appearance of economic recovery obviously did influence the national mood. Reviewing the Reagan record in 1989, Robert Tucker concluded that the Reagan Presidency radiated facile optimism. The fortieth President had 'visibly failed' in his 'responsibility to tell the public what it does not want to hear but should hear'. Nevertheless, for a time, Reagan did 'restore the conviction that America was a force for good in the world'.[85]

The early Reagan boom was achieved at the cost of massive borrowing and importation of foreign capital. Investment was sacrificed to consumption. Savings rates in the 1980s fell to less than half their level in the period 1950–79.[86] The strategy followed by Federal Reserve chairman Paul Volcker amounted, in David Calleo's phrase, to 'loose fiscal policy combined with tight monetary policy'.[87] High interest rates failed to stimulate saving and an overvalued dollar harmed US trade; 1984 saw a trade deficit of some 110 billion dollars. By 1985, Volcker himself was explaining to Congress: 'We are in a real sense living on borrowed money and time.'[88] Though prepared to compromise its free market commitments, the Administration attempted nothing in the way of an industrial policy designed to bolster America's problems of economic competitiveness. When James Baker moved in 1985 to the Treasury, he tried to institute a more pragmatic approach than that associated with his predecessor, Don Regan. Yet Baker's strategy for international economic cooperation and attempts to engineer a 'soft-landing' for the US economy and for the dollar had only partial success. The virtual breakdown of the Louvre Accords (the 1987 monetary agreement negotiated between the seven leading industrialised nations in 1987) preceded the Wall Street crash of October 1987. By the end of the 1980s, the US was again slipping into recession.

It also seems appropriate here to draw attention to two further features of the Reagan legacy, both of considerable importance to the debate on US decline: structural debt and neglect of America's social fabric.

Second term pragmatism, various Congressional readjustment measures and an end to the military spending explosion all failed to solve the budget crisis. Structural problems within the federal budget had been apparent since the early 1960s, but were immensely exacerbated by the policies of the Reagan Administration.[89] (In the late 1980s, Samuel Huntington went so far as to argue that American decline, far from being deep-seated and multi-faceted, related entirely to the Reagan budget and trade deficits. As a direct consequence of one Administration's errors, this 'decline' could easily be reversed.)[90] Tax cuts in the early 1980s did not stimulate the expected gains in economic performance. Fiscal year 1983 saw the first two hundred billion dollar deficit in American history. The national debt tripled during the Reagan era. Debt service costs, as a percentage of federal spending, rose from almost 9 in 1980 to nearly 15 per cent in 1990. In 1981, Reagan assumed the Presidency of the world's leading creditor nation. In 1985, the US became a debtor nation, rapidly becoming the world's largest. All this 'plunder in the name of patriotism' (to use Haynes Johnson's phrase)[91] inevitably damaged America's public services, its social fabric and its social capital. Welfare and other domestic spending was cut in a vain attempt both to satisfy dogma and to compensate for tax cuts and high defence expenditures. Iwan Morgan has summarised the results as follows:

> Investment in new buildings and equipment as well as in new social programs was ... needed to deal with a failing school system, rundown inner cities, and violent drug-filled ghettoes. Dire as these

social problems were in human terms, they also blighted economic productivity by preventing individuals from maximising their talents and fulfilling their potential.[92]

The urban crisis inherited by George Bush threw sharp and critical light on Reaganite aspirations to national renewal.

7 President Bush: American Democracy and the End of the Cold War

What people mean, when they say we worry about a Vietnam, is they don't want to put this nation through a long drawn-out inconclusive experience that had military action that just ended up with a kind of totally unsatisfactory answer .... I will not, as commander-in-chief, ever put somebody into a military situation that we do not win – ever. And there's not going to be any long drawn-out agony of Vietnam.[1]

President Bush's remark to a Gulf crisis press conference in November 1990, indicated that the legacy of Vietnam remained strong even as the US prepared to face a world transformed. The collapse of Soviet communism bequeathed to George Bush the opportunity to make American foreign policy anew. Writing a year after the disintegration of Soviet power in Eastern Europe, Michael Mandelbaum described the events of 1989 as 'the greatest geopolitical windfall in the history of American foreign policy'.[2] Bush's ability to shape a new policy – if not precisely for an era of peace, certainly for a world changed utterly – was not only constrained by circumstance; by long-standing traditions and assumptions within US foreign policy; by America's own economic problems; and by the Bush Administration's conception of America's proper place in the world and of the role of Presidential leadership. It was affected also by George Bush's often rather uneasy commitment to develop and sustain the legacy of Ronald Reagan.

The positive aspects of Reagan's legacy – improved Soviet relations, economic optimism even in the face of recession – carried Bush to victory in 1988. Democratic candidate Michael Dukakis's efforts to raise the spectre of Bush involvement in Iran-*contra* failed to impress voters. The Republican campaign embodied a kind of Reaganism without Reagan. Bush raised racial fears and divisions, proclaimed his allegiance to the flag, and committed himself to a strong defence.[3] The new President's Inaugural Address (written by Peggy Noonan, who had just composed Reagan's farewell speech) proclaimed that communist totalitarianism was dying, 'its old ideas blown away like leaves from an ancient lifeless tree'.[4]

In many respects, George Bush was a loyal disciple of Ronald Reagan and the new Administration seemed poised to constitute – in a familiar phrase from the period – not so much a changing of the guard, but a guardian of the (Reagan Administration's) changes. Like the outgoing regime, the Bush Presidency seemed sure to face problems from the Democratic Congress. (Echoing Bush's inaugural hopes for America, Secretary of State James Baker called during his nomination hearings for 'a kinder, gentler Congress'.)[5] The case for Reagan–Bush continuity seemed strengthened by the rather unexpected ease with which Reagan had worked with his Vice-President. The latter's condemnation of Reagan's 'voodoo economics' in the 1980 Republican nomination race remained a staple of journalistic comment on the relationship. Yet Bush had grown into a loyal, if rather low profile, Vice-President.[6] He had been prepared, in the early 1980s in particular, to describe Soviet power in terms which jarred with his reputation for pragmatism. In 1983, for example, he attacked Russia as a brutal country whose values were not in the 'European tradition'.[7]

Despite Bush's loyalty, his new Administration bore the stamp of Shultzian pragmatism rather than Reaganite true belief. As Bert Rockman put it in 1991, the new President surrounded himself with 'people much like himself – pragmatic, sceptical, experienced and political'.[8] Bush's *curriculum vitae* was impressive. Before 1980, he had served as a Congressman, representative to the United Nations, chief of mission to Beijing, and CIA head. The Connecticut patrician in the White House – the first Ivy League President since Kennedy – made much of his Texan residence and associations. He even railed, like a Carter or a Reagan, against 'insider' politics inside the Washington DC Beltway. All this could not disguise the extent to which Bush headed an 'insider' Administration. His appointments reflected Bush's own conservative public service ideals and capitalised, in a way which had been impossible for either Carter or Reagan, on his network of 'insider' contacts. An old associate, James Baker had been Bush's closest ally in Reagan's White House, and exemplified the Bush style (described by Maureen Dowd and M.L. Friedman as 'steel with an overlay of tennis').[9] The nomination of Texas Senator John Tower to head the Pentagon was politically damaging. The Senate considered that Tower's personal conduct rendered him unsuitable, and rejected the nomination. However, other major foreign policy appointments – Brent Scowcroft as National Security Adviser, Richard Cheney as second choice Defence Secretary – reflected Bush's sureness of touch. Together with Baker and Joint Chiefs of Staff chairman Colin Powell, Cheney and Scowcroft made up a competent team. Splits did occur, but were neither as deep-seated nor as damaging as those which affected their Carter and Reagan Administration counterparts.

Bush's early strategy combined an apparent determination to affirm Reagan's legacy with a practical and judicious distancing from the old order. Visiting Washington in 1989, British Prime Minister Margaret Thatcher discerned that Bush 'felt the need to distance himself from his predecessor'. (According to Mrs Thatcher, such distancing involved 'turning his back fairly publicly on the special position I had enjoyed in the Reagan Administration'.)[10] To the job of re-setting the compass of American foreign policy, Bush brought the cautious, unReaganite conservatism of an 'American tory'.[11] Quite unlike his predecessor, Bush also brought great energy, commitment and concern for operational efficiency – rather than for the 'vision thing'. To Walter Dean Burnham, Bush was a President who 'conceived of his role essentially in terms of management and administration'.[12] Good planning, avoidance of new commitments, close personal diplomacy: these were the hallmarks of Bush's approach.[13] The President's fondness for energetic personal diplomacy, invariably conducted at the end of a telephone, led commentators to speak of his 'Rolodex diplomacy'.

In quitting the Vice-Presidency, Bush undoubtedly felt, in his own phrase, 'a certain liberation'.[14] Ultimately, his sceptical toryism put Bush at odds with Reagan's legacy. Seeds of tension were evident in the Inaugural Address, even as it proclaimed the Reagan–Bush continuity. Peggy Noonan's speech set forth Bush's understanding of the vanity of human wishes in a way which was uncharacteristic of Reagan:

> Some see leadership as high drama, and the sound of trumpets calling. And sometimes it is that. But I see history as a book with many pages, and each day we fill a page ... the new breeze blows, a page turns, the story unfolds.[15]

What remained to be seen was whether a conception of leadership without 'the sound of trumpets calling' would prove adequate to the challenges of this particular unfolding story.

BUSH AND THE AMERICAS

The unfolding story of the Bush Presidency was to be dominated by Soviet collapse and by the Gulf War. At its outset, the Administration had little or no inkling of this. The previous Administration's obsessive preoccupation with Central America continued to affect the new leadership in Washington. More clearly than under Reagan, that leadership was now committed to the need to eradicate the 'Vietnam syndrome' and its inhibitions on US military action, especially in America's own hemisphere. Bush's Inaugural Address called for a 'statute of limitations' on all inhibitions and divisions deriving from the Indochina war.[16] Part of Bush's sceptical toryism involved a commitment to the idea that the judicious and measured use of force was a legitimate and indispensable tool of foreign policy. As it turned out, Bush was able only to limit, rather than expunge, the lingering effects of the war in Vietnam. To this end, the 1989 invasion of Panama was, in the President's own phrase, 'a warm-up'.[17]

(a) The Panama Invasion

George Bush inherited Reagan's policy of economic sanctions against General Manual Noriega in Panama. The fact that Bush had been CIA chief when Noriega was recruited as a US intelligence 'asset' in the mid-1970s added poignancy to the situation. The sanctions were very damaging to Panama's brittle economy, yet Noriega clung to power. He took up increasingly anti-American stances. Elections held in May 1989 were won by oppositionist Guillermo Endara, but 'voided' by Noriega, who installed his own President. In August, Deputy Secretary of State Lawrence Eagleburger declared that if the Noriega regime was not removed by 1 September, 'civilised nations' would have to consider what action to take against an illegal government.[18]

In October, a US-backed coup failed to unseat Noriega. Bush called on the Panamanian military to depose him. An Organisation of American States (OAS) mediation effort failed. On 15 December, the Panamanian National Assembly named Noriega as head of government and declared a 'state of war' with the US. A series of attacks on US military personnel culminated in the firing on a car carrying four American officers on 16 December. The US invasion was launched on 20 December. The eventual deployment of over 25 000 US troops made this the largest US military operation since the Vietnam War.

Combat continued until 26 December, involving high – and hotly contested – estimates of civilian casualties. Twenty-six American soldiers
were killed. Noriega was eventually driven from his place of refuge in
the Papal Nunciature, and transported to the US to face drug-dealing
charges. A new government, under Guillermo Endara, was established.

The invasion was widely interpreted in Latin America as a violation
of both the OAS and United Nations charters. Bush, on 20 December,
outlined four goals of the invasion: 'to safeguard the lives of
Americans, to defend democracy in Panama, to combat drug trafficking
and to protect the integrity of the Panama Canal treaty'.[19] Writing in
Foreign Policy, Charles Maechling, former professor of international
law and State Department employee, declared: 'Of the four reasons
cited by Bush to justify the invasion, two find no support in international law and indeed run directly counter to it.'[20] The defence of
Panamanian democracy – itself a curious concept in the light of that
country's undemocratic history – had no legal basis. That Noriega was
involved in drug trafficking – sometimes supporting anti-drugs initiatives, sometimes taking profits from the trade – is not in question. But,
as Maechling wrote, Noriega's 'civil arrest ... after surrender' was
'questionable enough'; to make his arrest 'a principal justification of
the invasion' was 'to defy the most elementary principles of state sovereignty'.[21] Any threat to American citizens or to the Canal was hardly
proportionate to an invasion of a quarter of a million US troops. The
invasion also proceeded without any real Congressional involvement
under the war powers legislation. Californian Democratic Congressman
Don Edwards called the invasion a 'trigger-happy act of gunboat diplomacy'. New York Democrat Charles Rangel, chairman of the House
Select Committee on Narcotics Abuse, wondered aloud what the
purpose of the war-making powers of Congress might be, if the
President 'can do it unilaterally'.[22] As with Grenada in 1983, although
with a much higher casualty rate, Operation Just Cause in Panama was
generally backed in Congress and by the American public. As Robert
Pastor later put it, 'the invasion liberated George Bush as much as it did
Panama'.[23] Only 7 per cent of US poll respondents in January 1990
thought the US was wrong to have invaded. A CBS poll also found that
most Panamanians approved of the invasion, although they probably
anticipated that the invasion would be followed by higher aid levels
than actually transpired.[24]

The invasion was attractive to Bush for disparate reasons: the desire
to terminate the 'Vietnam syndrome'; the need to be seen to be acting

against drugs – described by the President in September, 1989, as America's 'gravest domestic threat';[25] the impulse to serve notice that Jimmy Carter's Canal treaty did not mean that the US would allow control of the Canal to fall into hostile hands; the chance to show that beneath Bush's patrician exterior there was a will to fight. Noriega's own open defiance of his former American paymasters had also become increasingly irksome to Bush, who complained in October of feeling 'boxed in' and having his hands tied.[26] (When the invasion took place, Democratic Congressman Les Aspin of Wisconsin warned that the operation had become excessively personalised: 'We have to be careful not to define the success of this operation as the capture of Noriega.' America needed to ask: 'Have we disrupted the drug trade ... have we established democracy?')[27]

Aspin's comments raised important issues surrounding the use of American military force in the post-Cold War order. In a sense, Operation Just Cause was simply a familiar operationalisation of the 1823 Monroe Doctrine and the 1904 (Theodore) Roosevelt Corollary. Hemispheric domination was the irreducible essence of American foreign policy. Panama was also, however, the first intervention since World War II which was unrelated to anti-communism. Moscow made muted comments in early 1990 to the effect that the death of the Brezhnev Doctrine in Eastern Europe was clearly not being matched by any relaxation of the Monroe Doctrine in Latin America. The reality was that the waning of the Cold War had – at least temporarily – reduced international constraints on US action. What was unclear was exactly what the purpose of such action should be.

(b) Democracy Drugs, Debt – and Free Trade

Upon embarking on a tour of South America in December 1990, Bush announced the possibility of achieving 'the first fully democratic hemisphere in the history of mankind'.[28] These remarks were made in connection with Jean-Bertrand Aristide's victory in elections in Haiti. Although Aristide was supplanted in a military coup in 1991, there were important signs that hemispheric tides were turning in a democratic direction. Most of the South American military dictatorships established in the 1970s had now given way to democratic or quasi- democratic successors. Globally, it was estimated in 1992 that over thirty countries were in the process of embracing some mixture of democracy, constitutionalism and economic liberalisation.[29] Bush even put a brave face on the apparent determination in Cuba to buck the trend. He announced in December, 1991:

> I've got a pretty pessimistic prospect ... for Fidel Castro down there in Cuba, very pessimistic for him, because it is so hard to be the only one that still thinks communism is a good idea. And ... the Soviets – the Republics will be, if not cutting him off entirely, cutting him back considerably.[30]

Washington's elation at the progress of democracy tended to ignore the fact that the South American military regimes had oftentimes received American support as agents of anti-communism. Inevitably, however, special joy was reserved for the transitions in Central America.

One tangential motive for invading Panama had been to issue a warning to Managua. At one level, there was considerable continuity in the Bush Administration's policies toward the Sandinistas in Nicaragua. CIA involvement in Central America remained high. Yet Bush's pragmatism was evident in the attempt to achieve bipartisan consensus. A working accord between Speaker Jim Wright and Secretary James Baker was agreed in March, 1989. Some fifty million dollars were voted (in 'humanitarian' aid) to the *contras*, while Bush also announced his support for the Arias peace plan. The Sandinistas responded by announcing that free elections would be held in February 1990 if the US agreed not to resume military aid to the *contras*. For his part, Bush seemed willing, in the new superpower atmosphere, to run the risk of a Sandinista victory. Despite the refusal of visas to an official US monitoring delegation, the presence of several hundred outside observers of the election made it difficult for Washington to develop early signs that only an anti-Sandinista result would be recognised. The most prominent US observer, former President Carter, described the February poll as 'the most heavily monitored election in the history of the world'.[31] As for Soviet involvement, James Baker was excoriating Moscow for interfering in Central America as late as the December 1989 Malta summit. However, Soviet arms shipments and economic subsidies to Managua had been curtailed by early 1990. The Administration later claimed that an understanding on Soviet non-interference had been agreed prior to the elections.[32]

The election result was a surprise to world opinion. Violetta Chamorro, heading an anti-Sandinista coalition, gained over half the vote. Her election effort had been backed by Washington, with nine million dollars in overt aid having been authorised by Congress in October 1989. Chamorro's victory, however, was probably attributable more to the war-weariness of the Nicaraguan people than to US support. Bush declared that this was yet another indication that 'given the choice ... people all around the world are opting for democracy'.[33] A Fund for Democracy was launched by Bush, to a less than rapturous Congressional response, in April 1990. Washington's relations with the Chamorro regime rapidly cooled, as Chamorro moved to disarm the *contras* and to accommodate Sandinista influence in the unions and the military. By the end of Bush's term, a new Nicaraguan coalition government, which included Sandinistas, was in power. Washington's insouciance revealed the degree to which the ending of the Cold War had defused tensions. In El Salvador, the conflict was re-conceptualised by Washington as a civil war, rather than as a crusade against communism. United Nations mediation achieved an agreement between the Salvadoran government and the FMLN guerrillas in January, 1992.[34]

The post-Cold War intertwining of domestic and foreign policy agendas was foreshadowed in the action taken against Noriega's drugs trafficking. In Bolivia and Peru, US aid was linked to undertakings to destroy profitable coca crops. Such deals – especially where, as in Bolivia, they involved some role for the US military – caused difficulty and embarrassment for local leaders. Bush clashed with the Colombian government over the propriety and advisability of having local drugs gangsters stand trial in the US. In Peru President Fujimori's government (which had been cooperating in Washington's coca eradication programme) suspended the constitution in 1992, thereby indicating that the road to Latin American democracy was far from secure. Inter-American frustrations found expression when President Cesar Gaviria visited Washington in 1991. 'Each one of you,' declared the Colombian leader, 'has to realise that those who consume cocaine in the streets of Washington are as guilty as those terrorists who press the trigger in the streets of Medellin.'[35]

Divisions between Washington and Latin America over post-Cold War strategies for aid and development were revealed at the 1992 UN Earth Summit in Brazil.[36] For Latin America, the paramount issue was chronic indebtedness, not drugs. In 1989, Treasury Secretary Nicholas Brady, building on James Baker's initiatives under Reagan, offered a partial amnesty on the huge debts inherited from the 1980s, with Washington offering a degree of compensation to the lending agencies.

The Baker-Brady Plan was killed in Congress amid worries about US recession. A new Bush approach, essentially 'trade, not aid', emerged in the form of the Enterprise for the Americas initiative of June 1990. This combined an apparent commitment to US leadership of a post-Cold War regional bloc, with encouragement of economic and political liberalisation as the key to solving the debt crisis. Significant progress was achieved. Moses Naim, former Venezuelan industry minister, wrote in 1993 that, despite major problems of adjusting to the free market, Latin America had 'gone from being the fuse of the debt bomb ... to being a powerful magnet for global capital'.[37] Part of the Reagan–Bush strategy towards Latin American debt was divide-and-rule. Mexico, in particular, was singled out for generous treatment – partly as a means of preventing the formation of a hemispheric debtors' cartel. Bush formed a close alliance with the Harvard-educated Presidential technocrat, Carlos Salinas. Priority was given to the negotiation of the US–Mexico North American Free Trade Agreement. NAFTA, whose ratification by Congress was to become a major issue in the Clinton Presidency, was grafted on to an earlier US–Canadian Free Trade Agreement, signed in 1988. By the end of Bush's term, NAFTA had become the centrepiece of the Administration's strategy to enhance international US competitiveness and to reverse America's relative economic decline.

SOVIET COLLAPSE

(a) 1989

Bush's new pragmatists seemed more cautious than Reagan's outgoing team about Soviet intentions. Foreign policy commentator Arnold Horelick noted in 1990 that 'some Soviet officials were expressing nostalgia for the good old days of Reagan and Shultz'.[38] By the late 1980s, 'squeezers' in the Reagan team had mostly either left or had followed their boss and transformed themselves into 'dealers' with Moscow. An exception was Robert Gates, deputy CIA head (1986–9). (Reagan had originally nominated Gates to the CIA directorship after William Casey became incapacitated by brain cancer. Apparent complicity in Iran-*contra* caused the nomination to be withdrawn.) Under Bush, Robert Gates became deputy to Brent Scowcroft on the NSC staff and eventually succeeded William Webster as CIA chief in late 1991. During the

Bush Administration, Gates became the most complete sceptic regarding Soviet intentions.[39] Gates's influence seemed plain in remarks made by Scowcroft shortly before the inauguration. The National Security adviser suggested that Gorbachev's real goal might be the emasculation of NATO.[40] This view was echoed by Defence Secretary Richard Cheney, who told Congress in April 1989 that 'the perception of a reduced threat with respect to our allies makes it more difficult for us to maintain ... cohesion and unity within the Alliance'.[41] On 4 April 1989, Cheney told reporters that Gorbachev was 'serious' about reform.[42] Various statements made by Cheney and others in the early months of Bush's Presidency, however, raised a host of doubts and questions. Could alliance deterrence policies be maintained, especially in West Germany? If reform did succeed in the Soviet Union, would this not simply make the old enemy stronger? Doubts related not only to Gorbachev's intentions, but also to his survivability. On 29 April 1989, Cheney told a television audience that he thought Gorbachev's reforms would 'ultimately fail' and that someone 'far more hostile' to the West would come to power.[43] On this analysis, there was little point in helping *perestroika*. Rather, the US should practice benign neglect, awaiting the return of hard-line leadership. Above all, the US should keep its powder dry. The worst policy of all would be to rush into premature defence cutting. As late as September 1990, a year after the collapse of Soviet power in Eastern Europe, we find Cheney arguing that current Soviet intentions were insufficiently clear 'to support dramatic changes in our level of preparedness'.[44]

Secretary of State James Baker was keen to reject any inference that Washington did not fully endorse *perestroika*. Angrily responding to Cheney's 29 April remarks, Baker called the White House, urging Scowcroft to 'dump on Dick with all possible alacrity'. White House spokesman Fitzwater declared that Cheney's 'personal observations' on Gorbachev did not reflect Administration policy. In Vienna in early March, Baker assured Eduard Shevardnadze that the US did genuinely want *perestroika* to succeed. Bush's public statements throughout 1989 reiterated the importance he attached to making 'the Soviet Union understand that we want their *perestroika* to succeed and see them move forward'.[45] Yet his statements were tortuous in their hesitancy:

> Let's take our time now ... ; formulate the policy and then get out front – here's the US policy ... . If someone says Cold War to me,

that doesn't properly give credit to the advances that have taken place in the relationship. But if it is used in context do we still have problems; are there still uncertainties; are we still unsure in our predictions on Soviet intentions? I'd have to say, yes, we should be cautious.[46]

Extreme caution stood at the heart of three major early incarnations of the Bush approach: the 1989 foreign policy review; a series of speeches made by the President in April to May 1989, outlining the policy of Soviet 'integration'; and the 1989 defence budget proposals.

In February, 1989, Bush announced a 'pause' in negotiations with Moscow, pending a formal review of policy. Gorbachev vented his frustration during a visit to London in April. He felt that the review was being used as a 'braking mechanism' and persuaded Margaret Thatcher to convey his anxieties to Washington.[47] Ronald Reagan told Californian friends that Bush was moving too slowly. The policy review concluded that Gorbachev probably would remain in power, at least in the medium term. The American Administration should not concern itself with internal Soviet issues so much as with clear efforts to promote US interests in the arms control arena. Brent Scowcroft advanced the view that some of the Reagan positions on arms control were potentially damaging to the US (especially regarding land-based missiles) and needed to be re-examined. The 'status quo plus' doctrine of the foreign policy review was amplified in a series of Presidential addresses. Informing this whole process was the notion of 'testing' Gorbachev's good faith. (The policy of 'testing' the new thinking in Moscow had been advanced in 1988 by Harvard academic Graham Allison and had, ironically, found its way into the campaign positions of Michael Dukakis in 1988.)[48] On 17 April, Bush announced his firm support for change in Eastern Europe, but emphasised that any American aid would be conditional on the region adopting sound free market structures. At Texas A. and M. University on 12 May, Bush announced the 'integration' policy. Moving 'beyond containment', Washington was said now to be seeking 'the integration of the Soviet Union into the community of nations'. Soviet good intentions would be assessed in several ways: human rights progress inside the USSR; cooperation with the West over regional questions and global issues like drugs trafficking; force reduction in Europe; and consent to the liberalisation process in Eastern Europe. In return, Bush offered vague promises on arms control verification (essentially a return to President

Eisenhower's 'open skies' proposal) and possible moves towards obtaining 'most favoured nation' trading status for the USSR. (The latter would involve a temporary Congressional waiver of the Jackson – Vanik amendment.) Conspicuously absent from the Texas speech was any promise of substantial US aid for Soviet restructuring. Speaking in West Germany on the occasion of NATO's fortieth anniversary, on 31 May 1989, Bush made some concessions on European conventional force reductions, and spoke optimistically about the end of divisions in Europe. In July, Bush referred to Gorbachev's talk of a 'common European home'. Such an idea was fine, declared the US President, provided 'you can move from room to room'.[49]

Bush's early defence budgeting, though cautious, was inevitably affected by demands for deficit reduction and by the President's own undertaking that he would not raise taxes. Richard Cheney also ran into demands that the waning of the Cold War should yield a 'peace dividend'. House Armed Services Committee chairman Les Aspin remarked of his colleagues: 'They may like Dick Cheney ... but with Gorbachev and "read my lips" on taxes, defense spending is going to go down.'[50] Bush took every available opportunity to deflate 'peace dividend' expectations. In December 1989, for example, he explained that America's domestic reform agenda would have to be accommodated to the needs of deficit reduction; he condemned 'wild speculation that Congress is going to go in and then take the money in what's called a peace dividend'.[51] (By the same token, Bush also called on Congress to accept that *some* defence reductions were inevitable and could not be entirely painless. In February 1990, he told the Commonwealth Club of San Francisco: 'Longstanding critics of defense spending should not turn around and block the closing of a base in their home districts'.)[52] Bush's initial 1989 proposal was for a real-terms freeze for fiscal year 1990, with 1 per cent real terms growth in the following two years. Following consultation with deficit-cutters in Congress, the White House announced defence cuts of about ten billion dollars, compared with the projected Reagan Administration levels. SDI was to take cuts of seven billion dollars over five years (again compared to the generous Reagan estimates), and the B-2 bomber procurement was to be delayed by one year. On SDI, the Administration appeared to be moving towards the less costly ('Brilliant Pebbles') plan of deploying thousands of small, kinetic weapons in space.[53]

The Bush Administration's slow moves towards a Soviet policy, based on the concepts of 'integration' and 'testing', contrasted sharply with the heady and accelerating collapse of the Soviet empire. On 18 July, Bush sent a secret invitation to Gorbachev to meet 'without thousands of assistants hovering over our shoulders'. By the time they actually met, in Malta in early December, Soviet domination of Eastern Europe was a thing of the past. Moscow had renounced the Brezhnev Doctrine and allowed the people's revolutions to take their course. In late August, Polish Communists, after consulting Moscow, announced that they were forming a coalition with Solidarity oppositionists. On 25 October, Gorbachev told reporters that the USSR had 'no right, moral or political' to interfere in Eastern Europe, adding pointedly: 'We assume others will not interfere either.' Watching the rupturing of the Berlin Wall in early November, Bush remarked to aides: 'If the Soviets are going to let the Communists fall in East Germany, they've got to be really serious – more serious than I realized.'[54] In Czechoslovakia, Alexander Dubcek spoke openly about the evils of Soviet domination: 'Man is the important thing, and there is no socialism without proper living conditions.' As Vaclav Havel (soon to be elected President of Czechoslovakia) contemplated the early December collapse of the interim government in Prague, he announced: 'I think it is time for champagne.'[55]

Washington's voice was muted as the champagne corks popped in Eastern Europe. In this case, the Bush-Baker caution was statesmanlike rather than dilatory. Gorbachev had passed at least one test outlined in the Texas speech in May. For George Bush publicly to dance on the Berlin Wall would have been both unnecessary and potentially damaging to Gorbachev's position within Russia. It would also have provoked criticism of the extent to which the US had abandoned the East European 'captive nations' after World War II. Defending his low-key stance in November 1989, Bush announced: 'I think the lead is being taken by the people in these countries.' It was also important that America's West European allies 'know that I'm not going to go off and prematurely jump out there and try to grandstand by committing them to something. That's not the way you keep an alliance strong … '.[56]

As the Malta summit drew closer, critics like Democratic Senator J. Bennett Johnson of Louisiana continued to charge that 'the president has been a bit too timid in his relations with the Soviets'.[57] The White House did make firm statements in favour of *perestroika* in this period, and managed to stifle Robert Gates's plans to make a series of public anti-Soviet speeches. The Administration busied itself with plans to restructure NATO and to accommodate and integrate a united Germany. Still, however, all the real movement was coming from

Moscow. Interviewed on American television in November 1989, Soviet Foreign Ministry spokesman Gennadi Gerasimov announced that the Malta meeting would see the Cold War 'dumped down to the bottom of the Mediterranean Sea'.[58]

Overshadowing the Malta summit was the question of how to construct a post-Cold War order. Gorbachev advised Bush of his own 'prudent and cautious policy' on German reunification. The Soviet leader was impressed by James Baker's apparent conversion to the idea that US economic aid should be provided to support economic liberalisation in the Soviet Union. According to Gorbachev, the USSR was moving toward the 'Swedish model' of economic management. Bush was informed that Moscow no longer wanted American forces to leave Europe. The US President offered an important, and secret, concession on the Baltic states. In August, the Lithuanian parliament had delcared the 1940 Soviet annexation of Lithuania, Estonia and Latvia to be illegal. Bush now promised that, if Moscow refrained from excessive violence, he would not 'create big problems' for Gorbachev. Some progress was made on strategic nuclear, as well as conventional, force reduction agreements. With the Soviets apparently calling Bush's bluff on 'integration' – and effectively demanding some economic reward for relinquishing control of Eastern Europe – the US delegation undertook to work towards achieving 'most favoured' trading status for Russia, and for Soviet observers to attend meetings of the General Agreement and Tariffs and Trade.[59]

(b) 1990–92

The doctrine of 'status quo plus' – Baker's enthusiasm for *perestroika* had perhaps transformed it into a kind of 'status quo plus plus' by the time of the Malta summit – had just about seen the US through the revolutionary changes of 1989. Yet there was still no START agreement, no real progress on Soviet 'integration', and little clear indication of how potentially damaging superpower differences over the future of Germany could be resolved. Democrats at home looked in vain for the 'peace dividend', while the Administration was forced to accept criticism regarding its niggardly grant of aid to Eastern Europe. (It was noticeable during 1989 that Congress was anxious to increase this aid. Senate Democrats prepared an 840 million dollar Polish and Hungarian aid programme to coincide with the visit to Washington in November, 1989, of Polish Solidarity leader Lech Walesa.)

During 1989, George Bush was able graciously to allow the geopolitical tide to turn in America's favour. Between 1990 and 1992, he seemed more like a post-Cold War King Canute, striving to keep old structures in place and to defend what he called 'our enemy' – 'unpredictability'.[60]

By the early part of 1990, it was clear not only that the Soviet leadership was keen to accept market reforms, but that it would also countenance a multi-party system. Bush's response was to combine a cautious triumphalism with an encouragement to Soviet democracy. He told the World Affairs Council in March 1990: 'Beyond containment lies democracy.' Attempts to 'eliminate the entrepreneurial spirit', argued the President, produce 'neither bread nor freedom'.[61] James Baker announced in Moscow that the enhanced 'power of the Supreme Soviet can be one step forward that advances democracy'.[62] Yet this championing of democracy markedly did not extend to the Baltic states. The official Washington line was that the US would recognise an independent Lithuania only, in the words of State Department spokeswoman Margaret Tutwiler, if the former republic were 'capable of entering into and fulfilling international obligations'.[63] The bargain made at the Malta summit was being maintained, despite intense Congressional criticism. The House of Representatives overwhelmingly passed a non-binding resolution calling for the recognition of Lithuania. Republican Senator Malcolm Wallop condemned the 'Gorbachev-at-any-price policy':

> If maintaining Gorbachev in power takes precedence over all our considerations of principle or prudence, then we have forfeited our freedom to act and given total leverage to the Soviet leader.

Many Congressional liberals, however, were, in effect, prepared to trust Gorbachev not to subject the Baltic states to a brutal crackdown. On the Republican side, Senate Minority Leader Bob Dole was prepared to argue that a crackdown was unlikely; following such action, the Soviets could 'kiss goodbye to the kind of political and economic relations that they so clearly want'.[64] Dole's prophecy proved broadly correct; however, in January 1991, Soviet troops killed fifteen Lithuanian and four Latvian demonstrators. Bush declared in response that 'when we see repression in the Baltics, it is very hard to have business as usual'.[65] Yet recommendations from Congress and from Robert Gates's interagency deputies committee, that sanctions be imposed until Baltic state independence was upheld, were ignored.

This pragmatic bargain extended also to Azerbaijan, whither Soviet troops were dispatched in January 1990 following anti-Armenian riots. Bush privately informed Soviet Ambassador Yuri Dubinin that he would abide by earlier undertakings by James Baker regarding Moscow's response to 'irrational bloodletting and national hatreds'. Bush acknowledged publicly Gorbachev's 'extraordinarily difficult' problems in the republics, which would 'not be made easier by a lot of pontificating from leaders in other countries'.[66]

Early caution about Gorbachev had now given way to a policy, not of Gorbachev-at-any-price, but certainly one of deliberately avoiding any action or statement which might harm the Soviet leader's position. No longer regarded as a 'drugstore cowboy' (in Marlin Fitzwater's memorable phrase of 1989), Gorbachev was held to deserve a degree of Washington's loyalty. During 1990 and 1991, Gorbachev continued to pass important tests, especially regarding support for US action against Iraq in the Gulf region. Moreover, Gorbachev's strategic conservatism – his manifest desire to maintain the territorial integrity of the USSR – suited the Bush Administration's worldview. Neither the apparent setbacks and compromises in his economic reform strategy, nor Shevardnadze's December 1990 resignation (accompanied by warnings of an impending 'dictatorship'), changed Washington's commitment.

Despite this relative closeness in 1990–1, at least three important issues threatened to divide Washington from the increasingly beleaguered leadership in Moscow: the future of Germany, the issue of economic assistance, and arms control. For the first five months of 1990, the Soviets resisted the incorporation of a united Germany into NATO. Shevardnadze told James Baker in March that such incorporation 'would look as if you had won and we had lost'; the 'lessons of history' also suggested, according to the Soviet Foreign Minister, 'that we cannot be relaxed about the Germans'.[67] The US plan for German reunification, originally suggested by Robert Zoellick of the State Department, involved a 'two-plus-four' mechanism. The West and East German leaderships would first determine their internal future; external issues would be resolved by subsequent consultation with the US, France, Britain and the USSR – the victorious Second World War powers. In the event, 'two-plus-four' proved successful in furthering the desire of the US and West German leader Helmut Kohl to see a united Germany in NATO. Grudging Soviet acquiescence was confirmed at the May–June 1990 summit at Washington – Camp David. Gorbachev acknowledged the US argument that NATO membership might actually serve to inhibit German ambitions. In July, Kohl and Gorbachev agreed that a united Germany would belong to NATO, and that the USSR would receive financial help to resettle troops leaving East Germany. The Soviet leader had passed yet another test.

Throughout the whole 'testing' process, it seems to have been presumed in Russia that co-operative behaviour would be rewarded economically. There was even talk of a 'grand bargain', promoted by Soviet economic reformer Grigori Yavlinski and by Graham Allison in the US, whereby American aid would guarantee Soviet political and economic reform. Without a Marshall Plan for the East, argued Yavlinski and Allison, the Soviet economy would collapse. The destruction of the Soviet economy had, of course, precisely been the goal of 'squeeze' strategists in the 1980s. Now, however, the Administration was committed to Gorbachev and worried by Soviet weakness rather than by Soviet strength. However, any progress toward a 'grand bargain', even toward the kind of economic integration foreshadowed in Bush's 1989 Texas A. and M. University speech, was meagre. Various contacts with Soviet supplicants – notably a May 1991 meeting with Yavlinski, Yevgeni Primakov and Vladimir Shcherbakov – convinced Bush both that the Soviets were divided and uncertain about what to do with aid, and that any 'grand bargain' would be prohibitively expensive. The US itself faced 'difficult problems at home in a budgetary sense'.[68] The President had to consider conservative resistance to Soviet aid in Congress. At the July 1991 economic summit in London, Bush insisted that Gorbachev 'didn't come here with a big demand for money' anyway. The slow integration of the USSR into the international financial institutions – the associate status at World Bank and International Monetary Fund meetings – was itself 'very important stuff'. Moreover, once the Soviet people 'see how privatization works, once they see how markets work, once they see how elections work', reforms would 'steamroller' without outside interference.[69] More pointed was James Baker's 1991 comment:

> We believe – we may be wrong – that the Soviets and Gorbachev want to move to a market economy. We think they are convinced it is the only salvation. We are not convinced, however, of two things. One that they know how to do it and, two, that they have the political will to accept the pain that will come from doing it.[70]

A Marshall Plan for the USSR was never given serious consideration within the Bush Administration. Gorbachev's aspirations to join the G-7 club of advanced industrial nations at the July 1991 London summit were politely deflected. Bush confined himself to promoting modest aid programmes, cultural and educational exchanges and a number of bilateral economic initiatives offered at the Moscow summit of July–August 1991. Efforts to lift the Jackson-Vanik restrictions on the granting of Most Favoured Nation status to the USSR were painfully slow. The frenetic pace of change since 1985 had altered expectations so dramatically that a delay of months seemed excessive in the extreme. In December 1990, the Jackson-Vanik restrictions were eventually waived and credit guarantees of one billion dollars in commodity purchases approved. (Only at the 1991 Moscow summit, some three weeks before the coup against Gorbachev, did Bush formally announce the granting of Most Favoured Nation status to the USSR.) Majority Leader Richard Gephardt sounded a by now familiar theme of the Democratic leadership: that the world was being re-created in a way reminiscent of the late 1940s, and that Bush was failing the challenge. 'I can tell you,' declared Gephardt *a propos* the Jackson-Vanik waiver, 'Harry Truman wouldn't have stood around for nine months … . He would have done it.'[71]

Throughout 1989 and 1990, verification and other disputes prevented the signing of a superpower strategic arms (START) treaty. The two sides still could not resolve disagreements on, for example, whether the Soviet Backfire bomber should be regarded as capable of delivering a strategic, long-range weapon. In November 1990, NATO and Warsaw Pact leaders signed a treaty on conventional force levels in Europe. On START, the Bush philosophy seemed to be that delay would favour the US, since Soviet weakness could only increase as the months went by. The START treaty which was signed at the July 1991 Moscow summit seemed to justify Bush's strategy. It reduced nuclear arsenals by 30 per cent (rather than the earlier agreed level of 50 per cent). Most observers saw the treaty as an American victory, especially since it included a Soviet promise to halve the number of warheads carried by their ballistic missiles. Against Gorbachev's wishes, Bush travelled to Ukraine to denounce the ethnic and nationalist fragmentation which was now dismembering Yugoslavia, and which clearly threatened the USSR:

> Americans will not support those who seek independence in order to replace far-off tyranny with a local despotism. They will not aid those who promote a suicidal nationalism based on ethnic hatred … .[72]

Some commentators now see Bush's words as inadvertently encouraging the August coup plotters. Gorbachev had been concerned that Bush's visit to Kiev would be interpreted as support for Ukrainian nationalism. (In March, Bush and Baker had been criticised by Yevgeni Primakov for actually inciting ethnic fragmentation.) Bush's Kiev speech may actually have been viewed by the August plotters as a commitment not to interfere in Soviet internal affairs. The precise impact of American policy on Soviet behaviour and outcomes had always been extremely difficult to assess. Awareness of the complex unpredictability of Soviet power relations lay at the core of Bush's policy of caution. Both Gorbachev and the Americans were aware that too close an identification between US power and the cause of Soviet reform might stimulate a dangerous conservative revanchism in the USSR. Soviet concessions on arms threatened to produce a similar reaction. It is not clear that stronger American support for the cause of reform – possibly involving a 'grand bargain' with Gorbachev, or even unambiguous backing of the ostensibly more radical democratic alternative offered by Boris Yeltsin – would have had the desired effect. Possibly, however, a substantial injection of aid in 1990, coupled with signs that the USSR was being respected as a great power worthy of full participation in international financial fora, would have alleviated Gorbachev's need to compromise with conservative forces in late 1990 and early 1991 – a crucial period, when *perestroika* seemed to be losing its way. In the event, the Bush Administration was open to the charge that it had simply failed to keep pace with the (admittedly almost bewilderingly complex) Soviet changes. The coup, an apparently confused and still obscure attempt to reverse *perestroika*, resulted in the projection of the newly elected Russian President, Boris Yeltsin, into an increasingly unrivalled position of authority. In 1992, Bush recalled the central image of the coup. Saluting Yeltsin as a leader 'committed to democratic reform', Bush declared that the new Soviet leader had 'laid his life on the line on top of a tank to make that message loud and clear'.[73]

The failed coup appeared clearly to have discredited not only reactionaries but also Gorbachev's efforts to save both the Soviet Communist Party and the Soviet Union. At one level, even a Robert Gates could hardly dispute the fact that the Cold War had now ended. Observers spoke of a 'unipolar moment',[74] with the US as Cold War victor and sole remaining superpower. Journalist Patrick Brogan wrote that President Bush 'bestrides the world, a colossus somewhat ill at ease ... not yet sure what to do with the power that has fallen to him'.[75] The coup changed the geopolitical landscape, triggering Soviet collapse and destroying Bush's conservative 'King Canute' strategy. Between August and December 1991, Washington continued to support and deal with Gorbachev, even as the Communist Party and the Union disintegrated. James Baker even toyed with the notion of reviving the 'grand bargain' in order to save Gorbachev. On 29 August, the Soviet Parliament banned the Communist Party. (The sight of an American Republican President joining Gorbachev in mourning the demise of CP-generated stability was something to relish.) US recognition was extended to the Baltic republics. In late September, Bush announced significant unilateral missile reductions; in response, the Soviets began to dismantle tactical nuclear weapons. In early December, Yeltsin informed Bush that a new 'Commonwealth of Independent States' was being formed. On Christmas Day, 1991, Gorbachev accepted his rejection by the Soviet people and a week later the Soviet Union formally ceased to exist.

Yeltsin's triumph excited American fears about post-Soviet fragmentation, especially regarding the loosening of central control over nuclear weapons. Reporters quickly sensed the potential for embarrassing Bush by raising Yeltsin's reputation as 'a loose cannon' and 'a bull in a china shop'.[76] Throughout 1992, Bush defended Yeltsin as a good democrat despite well publicised and long-standing reservations about the new Russian leader.[77] Throughout 1992, Washington tried to develop a policy towards the Soviet successor states. Caution on defence still ruled out any rush into a 'peace dividend'. Still the events of 1991–2 had made their mark. In February 1991, with Gorbachev still in power, Bush proposed a six-year defence plan that would shrink the size of the US military by one quarter. Defence requests for fiscal year 1992 contained the smallest slice of GNP for the Pentagon since the Second World War. Bush's final year defence budgeting combined concessions to the outbreak of peace, with an unwillingness to dismantle the American national security state.[78] Yeltsin confirmed in early 1992 that the US and Russia were 'allies', and that Commonwealth of Independent States ICBMs were no longer targeted at America. At the June 1992 Washington summit, US and Russian leaderships agreed that the Russian Federation should constitute the successor state to the USSR, particularly in the matter of strategic nuclear forces. (In a sense, the 'King Canute' policy was prolonged in the Administration's clear desire to see Russia as the new, post-Soviet guarantor of stability. One of Bush's last acts as President in January 1993 was to issue a communiqué in support of Russian military aid to Armenia in its conflict with

Azerbaijan.) Further strategic arms cuts were agreed, and embodied in the second START treaty (signed in January 1993). START II envisaged joint reduction in strategic arsenals to around 4000 warheads on each side by the end of the century. (START I provided for mutual cuts to a level of 6000 warheads.) The US in the second START treaty achieved the elimination of ex-Soviet SS-18 'heavy' land-based missiles, previously feared as a possible first-strike weapon.[79] Yeltsin continued to press for economic aid and for integration. A measure signed by Bush in December 1991 authorised the President to use Pentagon funds to aid the Soviet successor states (four hundred million dollars for weaponry dismantling and one hundred million for humanitarian assistance). The Freedom Support Act, finalised in October 1992, authorised 410 million dollars to promote democracy in the former Soviet republics. (Russia's share was made contingent upon 'significant progress' being made in removing troops from the Baltic states.) Offering to contribute to a 24 billion dollar multinational aid package, Bush announced that there was not 'enough money in the world instantly to solve the problem of the Russian economy'.[80] By the end of 1992, and despite the progress on START II, Yeltsin appeared to be moving away from strategic partnership with the US, affirming that Russia 'continues to be a great world power' which should not 'shy away from defending our own interests'.[81] Former President Richard Nixon urged Bush to invest more strongly in the cause of Russian democracy in order to deflect the threat of a renewed, populist nationalism. George Bush showed no inclination to revive the idea of a 'grand bargain' for Russia in an election year during which he was being criticised for ignoring America's own domestic difficulties.

THE END OF THE COLD WAR

The termination of the Cold War caused academic and journalistic commentators to re-examine the War's origins, purpose, periodisation – whether there was a 'second' Cold War following detente – and dynamics.[82] 'Reagan victory' interpretations were considered in the previous chapter. As noted there, such interpretations tend seriously to understate the quasi-autonomous features of Soviet decline, as well as to downgrade Gorbachev's role in providing the Cold War with a peaceful denouement. In focusing always on Washington, 'Reagan victory' interpretations tend also to overlook the contribution made by NATO and other allies. Washington never followed a coherent 'squeeze' strategy. If it had, it would presumably have *encouraged* Soviet over-extension in Central America, and discouraged attempts to revive the Soviet economy through market reforms. (The Bush Administration was concerned that *perestroika* might reinvigorate Soviet power, but hardly sought actively to discourage Gorbachev.) Some further interpretations of the Cold War's end may now be considered: notably, theories of the Cold War system; theories of American ideological triumph; and differing accounts of the role played by nuclear weapons.

In an essay published in 1992, Walter LaFeber distinguished four dimensions to the Cold War: firstly, a continuation of 'the ongoing struggle, dating back at least to World War I and the Paris Peace conference, between the United States and the European countries to determine the kind of Europe that should evolve, and to decide how great a role America will have in that determination'; secondly, 'the ongoing struggle between the world's commercial centers and the outlying countries' – the 'periphery' – 'that provide markets and raw materials'; thirdly, a war 'fought within the United States' to turn 'an individualistic, open, commercial and domestic-oriented society into a consensual, secret, militaristic, international force'; and, lastly, 'the long conflict between the United States and the Soviet Union' which, at least in nascent form, predated the Bolshevik Revolution of 1917.[83]

Leaving aside for a moment the 'long conflict' between Russia and the West, we have here the bones of a systemic explanation of the Cold War. It served to contain and discipline allies, as well as to contain communism.[84] Despite the Vietnam War, it kept the developing world in a state of relatively stable subjugation. It served the needs of internal elites (notably the 'military-industrial complex', but also all Americans who stood to benefit from a clear articulation of anti-communist national purpose). LaFeber concentrates on the American side. However, these arguments can be replicated and extended on the Soviet side too. The Cold War arguably fulfilled Soviet elite needs for stability, ally discipline and periphery control. The US and the USSR became partners in a Cold War system, rooted in the militarised economy of massive arms spending. The system may either be seen as essentially a post-1945 invention, fashioned primarily to the nuclear age, or – as with LaFeber – a device designed to serve long-standing needs and impulses. In any case, the system developed its own logic and dynamic.[85] More conservative views of the Cold War system stress, even celebrate, its stability. For John Lewis Gaddis, the Soviet-

American relationship had by its later stages taken on 'a new maturity': 'an increasing commitment on the part of both great nations involved to a "game" played "by the rules"'. The Cold War was actually a 'long peace', comparable to the days of Metternich and Bismarck.[86] Important theories accounting for Cold War stability include the logic of nuclear deterrence; theories of hegemonic stability (where the US, as hegemon, guaranteed the functioning of the international liberal economic order);[87] theories of bipolarity (where the two superpowers practised mutual restraint and imposed order on the anarchic international system);[88] and various theories of regime formation, cooperation and collaboration.[89] In 1990, a widely cited article entitled 'Why We Will Soon Miss the Cold War' argued that the demise of bipolar stability was likely to lead to global fragmentation and insecurity.[90]

Can the end of the Cold War be explained in terms of the disintegration of the 'Cold War system' (rather than in terms of the victory of one side over the other)? To some extent, it can. Theories of Cold War stability usually allowed for the possibility of stability being undermined: for example, in the economic sphere, by a 'benevolent' hegemon becoming transformed into a 'predatory' one. However much the superpowers might learn to respect 'the rules of the game', there was always scope for the kind of mutual misreading of intentions and misperception described by writers like Robert Jervis.[91] To the extent that we accept arguments asserting that American power has declined since about 1970, we can agree that the Cold War system fell through a process of mutual superpower decline. We can agree that this decline was connected to 'imperial overreach' and to the 'revolt of the periphery' (most conspicuous in Vietnam and Afghanistan). More persuasive still, however, is the argument that the Cold War system ended, not through joint US–USSR decline, but primarily through Soviet collapse. To General Colin Powell, chairman of the Joint Chiefs of Staff under Bush, this seemed obvious. He told the Senate Armed Services Committee in September, 1991: 'We have seen our implacable enemy of forty years vaporize before our eyes.'[92] The Cold War's end drew attention to the radical asymmetry which had always characterised the Cold War system. By the 1908s, an earlier more complex asymmetry had given way to a palpable asymmetry in which viable, globalising capitalism – itself beset by internal rivalries and contradictions, though still led by the US – faced a bankrupt state socialism.[93]

If the 'purpose of the Cold War was not victory but the maintenance of a controlled contest',[94] we should expect both sides to make strenuous efforts to keep the system in place. And, indeed, the Bush Administration's conservatism, its 'King Canute' policy, would seem to fit this interpretation. Allen Lynch has argued that the Bush Administration was actually opposed to the collapse of Soviet authority in Eastern Europe.[95] This really confuses strategic conservatism with a conscious intent to conspire in the continued Soviet domination of the 'captive nations'. (One cannot even imagine Ronald Reagan, who lacked Bush's natural caution, doing anything other than rejoicing at the events of 1989.) Lynch's view perpetuates far-off McCarthyite condemnations of Yalta. Nevertheless, the instinctive nervousness of the Bush Administration in seeing the Cold War system erode does add credence to the systemic theories advanced by writers like Mary Kaldor. Perhaps what is more surprising is the relative alacrity with which the Soviets were willing to let the system go. Again, we come back to the fact of Soviet weakness, and the undeniable truth that the globalised, competitive Cold War system – while it strained the US – was actually destroying the USSR.

As noted in the Introduction to this book, the Cold War had geopolitical and ideological dimensions. The contest was, to some degree, a ritualised affair which had certain rules, but it was a contest for all that. The story of the War's ending was most obviously the story of the triumph of one ideology (consumer-oriented, liberal capitalism) over another (bureaucratised state socialism). Fred Halliday writes: 'If communism surrendered, almost without firing a shot, it was because the instrument of international competition in the late twentieth century was as much the T-shirt as the gunboat.'[96] The geopolitical, 'realist' dimension to the great superpower contest was less apparent in the War's dying stages than was liberal capitalism's ideological onrush. Important here was not only the communications revolution but also (to confound 'Reagan victory' analyses) the role of detente, in communicating values and expectations to the Soviet people. To proclaim a victory for liberal capitalist ideology is not the same as pronouncing the death of Marxism, a potentially liberating philosophy to which Stalinist forms were alien. It is not the same as pronouncing the 'end of history' (even in the Hegelian sense intended by former State Department policy planner Francis Fukuyama, in his famous 1989 article celebrating the triumph of liberal capitalism).[97] It is merely to recognise that, in that dimension of the Cold War which was a contest *between* systems, ideology played a key part.[98] One recalls A.J.P. Taylor's comment: 'The greatest crime of the Soviet Union in Western eyes is to have no capitalists and no landlords.'[99] It is to acknowledge that the years after 1985 saw a progressive obliteration of the Stalinist ideology which had guided the USSR since 1945. A version of Stalinism persisted, of course, in China (where, in contrast to the USSR, economic liberalisation preceded political reform). It is even possible that some form of nationalistic Stalinism could recapture some of the Soviet successor states. However, as the statues of Lenin were pulled down in the post-coup USSR, it was evident that – as far as history allows us to make such judgements – the West's ideology had vanquished Moscow's.

Many theorists of Gaddis's 'long peace' assign nuclear deterrence and 'nuclear learning' – increasingly sophisticated superpower skill in crisis avoidance and management – a key role in their explanations. Mearsheimer has even gone so far as to argue that since fear of nuclear war seems to promote stability, nuclear proliferation may produce yet more stability.[100] Theories of 'nuclear peace' as a paradigm for the Cold War have been challenged from several directions. John Mueller has argued, for example, that war actually became unthinkable *before* the advent of nuclear weapons, and that only the aberration of a Hitler could account for the post-1918 use of war as a means to achieve world domination.[101] Less controversially, 'nuclear peace' theories have been attacked as understating the dangers of 'accidental' nuclear war or the temptation that leaders may resort to 'the threat that leaves something to chance'.[102] The superpower tensions of the early 1980s (certainly if we are to believe the testimony of KGB defector Oleg Gordievsky)[103] lend credence to theories of nuclear risk rather than 'nuclear learning'. The ending of the Cold War was not occasioned primarily by nuclear issues, although they did have a role to play. The Soviet perception that a viable Western capitalism would lead to unchallengeable US nuclear superiority probably was an important influence on post-1985 events. The ending of the Cold War also illustrated the extent to which nuclear weapons had become the 'currency' of superpower interchange. The Reagan–Gorbachev 'poker game' at Reykjavik exemplified this. Justified and ever-present fear of nuclear annihilation, however, was not simply a characteristic of the Cold War. It was and is an inescapable part of the post-1945 human condition.

8　Bush: Gulf War and New World Order

The invasion of Panama had shown that George Bush was prepared to go to war. Both in Panama and the Gulf, Bush sought directly to confront the legacy of the Vietnam War. In various remarks made in the closing stages of the Gulf War, Bush announced: 'The specter of Vietnam has been buried in the desert sands of the Arabian peninsula'. And: 'By God, we've kicked the Vietnam syndrome once and for all.'[1] He wished America's options in the post-Soviet New World Order to be those which were appropriate to contemporary US strengths and interests. They should not continue to be affected by memories of defeat, division and humiliation in the early 1970s. Bush achieved much in the Gulf. However, he was as unable to extinguish the legacy of Vietnam as he was to secure his own electoral future.

THE GULF WAR

(a) Desert Shield

On 2 August 1990, Iraqi troops invaded and occupied Kuwait. Iraq's leader, Saddam Hussein, announced that Kuwait, with its vast oil reserves, had assumed its rightful place as a province of Iraq. Bush reacted strongly to this act of brigandage. The UN Security Council, prodded by the US and no longer paralysed by the Soviet veto, imposed the strictest sanctions in its history. A multinational force, from almost thirty nations, was assembled to defend Saudi Arabia. The anti-Saddam coalition included Arab nations, notably Syria and Egypt (who had significant levels of debt to the US cancelled). Two hundred thousand US troops led this defensive operation, titled Desert Shield. Saddam promised the 'mother of all battles' and took Western hostages. By mid-November (following the Congressional elections) the US troop commitment was increased to over half a million – effectively an *offensive* capacity. Talks between James Baker and Iraqi Foreign Minister Tariq Aziz continued almost up until the UN-imposed deadline for Iraqi withdrawal: 15 January 1991. A French mediation effort attempted to link withdrawal from Kuwait with Israeli abandonment of the West Bank and Gaza. In his talks with Aziz, Baker refused to countenance such linkage. On 16 January 1991, a massive allied air bombardment of Iraq and Kuwait signalled that war had begun, and that Desert Shield had transmogrified into Desert Storm.

The brief narrative immediately begs many questions. Why Saddam did invade Kuwait, apparently converting a local conflict into (as Lawrence Freedman and Efraim Karsh put it) 'a feud between Iraq and the entire international community'?[2] Why was the US apparently taken by surprise? Was Saddam, as Bush insisted, the new Hitler? What were Bush's motives? Was the American response appropriate? Should, for example, Bush have put more faith in sanctions, or – as Roger Hilsman has argued[3] – simply have put his diplomatic weight behind a purely Arab military response to the invasion? Was Desert Shield a paradigm for a post-Cold War New World Order?

Several explanations for Saddam's invasion come to mind. The Saudi ambassador to London evoked the Iraqi dictator's personality – burning aggression, persecution mania – and focused on internal Ba'athist and oppositional pressures. At one level, the invasion was an act of pure gangsterism. (Robert Hunter, Middle Eastern specialist on President Carter's NSC staff, commented: 'If you're going to run a protection racket, every once in a while you have to blow up a dry cleaner.')[4] Clearly, however, Saddam felt that the borders of Iraq constituted a Western imperialist legacy, and that Kuwait *was* a part of his country. Fred Halliday wrote that the annexation represented 'the coming together of a long-standing Arab drive for the union of states with the contemporary questioning of state frontiers derived from the end of the cold war'.[5] Saddam also made important miscalculations: about the extent to which the Iran–Iraq war had strengthened ties between the US and the Gulf states;[6] about his own credibility in the Arab world, and the possibility of using the Palestinian cause to promote Arab anti-Americanism; about pressures on Gorbachev to support Iraq;[7] about the feasibility of repairing relations with Iran; about his own military preparedness. He was annoyed by the harm to Iraq consequent upon the apparent desire of the Al Sabahs (Kuwait's ruling family) to drive down oil prices.[8] Saddam was also misled with regard to likely American reactions.

Even prior to the invasion, Congress (for example in the shape of the House Banking Committee chaired by Henry Gonzalez) had begun investigations into the support extended to Baghdad by the Reagan and Bush Administrations. Though historically inclined to look towards Moscow for sponsorship, Baghdad had received significant aid – in the form of credits, military intelligence and assistance – during the 1980s. A pre-inauguration task force had informed George Bush:

> It is up to the new administration to decide whether to treat Iraq as a distasteful dictatorship to be shunned where possible, or to recognize Iraq's present and potential power in the region and accord it relatively high priority. We strongly urge the latter view.[9]

Bruce Jentleson, in the most authoritative study of US–Iraqi relations in this period, argues that Baker and Bush were still concerned to back Baghdad against Tehran.[10] The Ayatollah Khomeini's death sentence on British author Salman Rushdie was seen as a deliberate assault on Western values; Iran was involved in anti-American activities, including the holding of hostages, in Lebanon; and Soviet–Iranian relations were seen (in 1989) to be warming. Secularist Iraq was seen by Washington as at least capable of moving in an acceptable direction. Throughout 1989, Bush deflected calls to impose sanctions following Saddam's chemical weapons assaults on Kurdish oppositionists. In October 1989, Bush signed National Security Directive 26, advocating 'normal relations' with Iraq. While the precise nature of US Ambassador April Glaspie's undertakings to Saddam are disputed, the Iraqi leader was certainly not informed that an invasion of Kuwait would be met with a huge show of American force. By 1 August, both the CIA, and Joint Chiefs of Staff head Colin Powell, were convinced that an invasion was imminent. In the White House, Brent Scowcroft felt that Saddam was blustering. Though the White House later tried to scapegoat Ambassador Glaspie, Bush and his closest advisers – Scowcroft, Cheney and Baker – allowed the view of Iraq implicit in National Security Directive 26 to distort their understanding of Saddam. As S.R. Graubard puts it, they 'deluded themselves about the nature of the world they were seeking to refashion'.[11]

Bush's demonisation of Saddam following the invasion of 2 August was extreme. It disturbed Colin Powell. At one stage, during the November Congressional campaigns, the President even suggested that

Saddam was worse than Hitler. Reporting on Iraq's treatment of the hostages, Bush declared that many 'are reportedly staked out as human shields near possible military targets – something that even Adolf Hitler didn't do'.[12] As C.W. Maynes argued in *Foreign Policy*, the Administration's portrayal of Saddam as the new Hitler was more than a little absurd, despite the unjustified nature of Saddam's actions. Germany under Hitler was the leading industrial state of Europe; land-locked Iraq, with its eighteen million population, was entirely dependent on outside help for its military and scientific development.[13]

The strength of Bush's response was traceable not to the objective evil of Saddam and his regime, but to the poignant intersection of the politics of oil with the perceived demands of the post-Cold War. Administration spokesmen were actually quite frank about the need to protect oil supplies. James Baker warned in October, 1990, that the entire world could 'be thrust into a deep recession by an Iraqi stranglehold on Gulf energy resources'; if this were allowed to happen, 'American industry, farmers and small businesses would be hit especially hard.'[14] Richard Cheney later in the same month dismissed as 'hogwash' the idea that the US was just in the Gulf to protect oil prices. However, there was 'no way the United States ... could allow a man like Saddam Hussein, with his military force and his willingness to use it, to in effect have a chokehold on the lifeline of the world's economy.'[15]

Cheney was correct to insist that Desert Shield was not simply about oil. Coming at a defining moment in the emergence of a post-Cold War order, the invasion was a crucial test of collective security in the new context. The Bush Administration consciously interpreted the crisis in these terms. James Baker told the Los Angeles World Affairs Council that, if Saddam's aggression were not countered, 'the bright promise of the post-Cold War era could be eclipsed by new dangers, new disorders ...'. [16] The need for post-Cold War collective security was a real one. It is difficult to imagine how any effective, precedent-setting collective security could have been achieved without American leadership. (Hilsman's notion of a purely Arab force being able to liberate Kuwait is not convincing.) Yet, almost inevitably, there was an element of hypocrisy in Washington's position. The US President, so it seemed, was to be the sole agency responsible for defining and identifying threats to the New World Order. Saddam's invasion was not the first act of aggression to be condemned by the United Nations, the chosen vehicle of Bush's new diplomacy. Several contributors to the Congressional Gulf War debate of January 1991 pointed to instances where the US had tautly accepted violations of international law: Israeli occupation of the West Bank and Gaza, Moroccan activities in the Sahara, Turkish intervention in Cyprus. Democratic Senator Ernest Hollings of South Carolina contrasted the response to the UN's resolution condemning Saddam with the limited impact effected by anti-*American* resolutions passed by the General Assembly:

> The President likes to ride us all up about the wild man Saddam Hussein, saying that Saddam has attacked two of his neighbors in the last 10 years. But that is exactly what the US had been condemned for in the United Nations in 1983, not by 12 votes as in the case of Resolution 678, but by 109 members of the United Nations condemning the United States for an act of aggression in Grenada, and by 75 votes ... for an act of aggression in Panama.[17]

During the later months of 1990, Congress, despite its generalised support for Desert Shield, reflected public anxieties about the apparent precipitate approach to war. Public backing for Desert Shield declined significantly between August and October. Thereafter it remained fairly steady – around 60 per cent support levels – during the key developments of late 1990: the November troop buildup and UN Security Council vote (setting the deadline and other conditions); the December hostage releases; and the January 1991 war debate in Congress.[18] The legislature was especially exercised about the war powers issue. House and Senate leaders emphasised in October that resolutions in support of Desert Shield did not constitute a 1990s version of the 1964 Gulf of Tonkin resolution. After the November troop escalations, Members became especially concerned that the White House had effectively decided to go to war. A group of Congressional Democrats unsuccessfully filed a lawsuit, citing the War Powers Act, and designed to prevent Bush from pursuing unilaterally the war option.

Despite Bush's promise to go the 'extra mile' for peace, Richard Cheney and Colin Powell appear to have decided in late December that war would come. Such a perception reflected the executive branch's judgment that sanctions alone would not work. As the UN deadline loomed, this judgment became a potent source of controversy. A month before the deadline, former Joint Chiefs chairman William Crowe testified to Senator Sam Nunn's Armed Services Committee that the real issue was 'not whether an embargo will work', but 'whether we have the patience to let it take effect'. Nunn informed Richard Cheney that, if war came, no-one would ever know if sanctions would have worked. The Senator accused Cheney of having been committed, since the post-election buildup, 'to the notion of bringing this thing to a head early on'.[19] Former Defence Secretary Robert McNamara told the Senate Foreign Relations Committee in December that sanctions should be given a chance to work: 'Who can doubt that a year of blockade will be cheaper than a week of war?'[20]

Desert Shield was also afflicted by a malady familiar from the era of Vietnam: 'mission shift'. As early as September 1990, Gulf commander General Schwarzkopf was expressing anxiety at the way operational goals appeared to be shifting beneath his feet. Air Force Chief, General Michael Dugan, was dismissed following a *Washington Post* interview of 16 September 1990 wherein he announced that the Joint Chiefs intended to use 'massive bombing' to defeat Saddam. In public, Bush was careful to stress that objectives were not open-ended. On 18 January 1991 – as the 'massive bombing' described by Dugan was actually taking place – he stated that his goal was, and always had been, precise and limited: 'Iraq's complete and unconditional withdrawal from Kuwait and then full compliance with the Security Council resolutions.'[21] The confusions of the Vietnam era would not be replicated. Yet, since August 1990, goals had shifted in rather random fashion: from defence of Saudi Arabia, to eradication of Saddam's Hitler-like threat to world order, to liberation of Kuwait. Bush's verbal attacks on Saddam clouded the issue without unambiguously marshalling US public opinion behind the war option. The President and his advisers did not see the removal of Saddam as the principal and necessary aim of the operation. However, as America prepared for war, this was not entirely clear. Congress and the public were offered a range of motives and objectives: the need to destroy Saddam's emerging nuclear capability; human rights and New World Order; the need to avoid the mistakes both of 1930s appeasement and of Vietnam; protection of oil supplies and American jobs; elimination of evil.

All these doubts and confusions were aired in the historic Congressional war debate of January 1991. Within the war-making elite, Cheney had long sought to proceed with a minimum of legislative interference, while Powell argued the need to secure Congressional support. In January 1991, as James Baker conducted 'extra mile' talks in Baghdad, Bush requested legislative authority to begin hostilities as soon as the UN Security Council deadline expired. On the anti-Bush side, Hollings asked: 'Are we going to intervene in Lithuania? Not a chance. Oh, Lithuania does not have oil.' Senator Edward Kennedy prophesied heavier casualties than in Vietnam and declared: 'Not a single drop of American blood should be spilled because American automobiles burn too many drops of oil a mile.' Democratic Congressman Esteban Torres of California argued that US soldiers should not 'die in Kuwait and Iraq so that the multinational oil corporations continue to reap huge profits ...'. Senator Biden of Delaware derided Bush's New World Order. It would always be a matter, declared Biden, of the US leading, with Europe and Japan being 'content to hold our coats'. Pro-Bush speakers argued that support for the President would actually promote peace by causing Saddam to undertake a last minute withdrawal. (Many commentators considered this Saddam's best option, and one which would afford him a kind of victory.) Supporters of the Presidential position echoed the White House view on oil and New World Order. Republican Senator Warren Rudman of New Hampshire, identified the 'stakes involved here' as 'nothing less than the creation of a new international security framework'. Several Senators held that Saddam simply could not be allowed to threaten US oil supplies. Republican Senator D'Amato of New York suggested that Iraq was capable of developing 'a crude nuclear device within a few months'.[22] Narrow victories for the Presidential position were achieved in both House and Senate, with Democratic supporters of the resolution providing the margin of success.

(b) Desert Storm

Air bombardment of Kuwait and Iraq began shortly after the expiry of the 15 January deadline, and lasted five weeks.[23] The ground war began on 23 February, and, on 27 February, Bush was able to announce that Kuwait was liberated. Between January and early March, Bush's successes knew no bounds. The anti-Saddam coalition held together. Israel was persuaded not to enter the war, despite Iraqi Scud missile attacks on Israeli targets. In his 1991 State of the Union address, Bush informed Congress that coalition allies had pledged over forty billion dollars for Desert Storm. In February, he assured American taxpayers that, due to further coalition pledges and the relative ease of the ground war victory, Desert Storm would not be charged against them. The Gulf war-managers were able to channel information to the public far more effectively than their Vietnam era counterparts, despite the vast technological changes that had occurred since the earlier war.[24] Oil prices began to fall as soon as the coalition's air attack was launched. Ground war fatalities on the coalition side were far lower than anyone could have anticipated.

As he announced Kuwait's liberation, Bush also made it clear that – aside from a briefly ferocious air assault on Iraqi Republican Guard units – coalition forces would respect the relatively limited objectives outlined in mid-January. The UN had not authorised the US or its allies to occupy Baghdad or to effect Saddam's extinction. The President's understanding of the situation was always imbued with his characteristic strategic conservatism. As Colin Powell later put it, 'our practical intention was to leave Baghdad enough power to survive as a threat to Iran'.[25] Bush contented himself with issuing encouragement to the Iraqi military, and to Kurdish and Shi'ite oppositionists, to depose the dictator. The ensuing rebellions were viciously repressed by the considerable Iraqi military force which survived the war. Somewhat belated and uncertain assistance was extended to Kurdish refugees. Just over a year later, Iraqi aircraft began to bombard Shi'ite rebels in the South of the country. US and European members of the coalition implemented a 'no-fly zone' in the area in August 1992. Saddam's various challenges to the Bush Administration, his 'cheat and retreat' strategy; his circumventions of UN conditions, especially regarding nuclear inspections; his insistence that Iraq had won the war; his very survival as leader: these factors damaged Bush at home, contributing to the extraordinary slide in Presidential popularity between March 1991 (near perfect approval ratings) and the 1992 election defeat. It is, however, impossible to argue with any great conviction that Bush should have ordered allied forces to Baghdad. Not only would there have been no legal basis for such action, any such order would have put the coalition under enormous strain. As it was, it appeared, in Peter Calvocoressi's words, 'that the United States was supremely able to do half a job'.[26]

Bush achieved much in the Gulf. Freedman and Karsh insist that the war 'saw the return of the United States to a self-confident and an effective role at the heart of international affairs'.[27] Unprecedented degrees of international cooperation were achieved (including the recruitment of Gorbachev to bargain, unsuccessfully as it turned out, with Saddam prior to the ground assault). By 1994, American oil companies were again dominating the global oil industry.[28] But memories of Vietnam were not expunged.[29] Bush was continually and wisely concerned that US public support – so uncertain in late 1990 – would not survive a prolonged ground conflict. The survival of Saddam was, in effect, a function of the continuing 'Vietnam syndrome'. It was also far from clear that the war did set the stage for New World Order peacekeeping. Senator Robert Byrd of West Virginia warned Bush against an emerging American role as a permanent 'Middle East riot squad'.[30] Despite important allied financial and military participation, the war was overwhelmingly an American effort. Iraqi military command structures were particularly vulnerable to US air attack.[31] So many special factors – from Saddam's personality to the role of oil and the particular condition of US–Soviet relations – seemed to make the Gulf conflict an exception: perhaps the mother of all exceptions.

NEW WORLD ORDER

As George Bush looked out upon the peace which followed the Cold and Gulf Wars, he did not find himself short of advice as to how he should re-set the compass of American foreign policy. He was told that now was the time to embrace a new agenda: 'the problems of the environment, of drugs, of terrorism, or refugees and immigration, all worldwide problems, requiring world-wide solutions'.[32] Alternatively, he should make the most of the 'unipolar moment' by supporting America's position as the sole remaining superpower (a course of action recommended in the Pentagon's 'No Rivals' plan, leaked in 1992).[33] Others advised him to retrench, even to the point of a new isolationism: essentially to manage America's international decline by adopting a policy of 'selective engagement' (based on clear identification of American national interest) in the world's affairs.[34] American Presidents should not allow the apparent result of the Cold War (the triumph of democracy) to conspire with the putative lesson of the Gulf War (that US-led military action could control post-Cold War disorder) to lead them into a new arrogance of power. Robert Tucker and David Hendrickson thus urged Bush to renounce the 'imperial temptation', with its familiar, Vietnam-era, equation of world order with US security.[35]

Post-Cold War advice proliferated. Voices urged that the US should realise that its destiny lay in the Western hemisphere. New alliance structures needed to be forged. The days of American leadership of NATO were numbered. The idea of 'economic security' should replace that of 'national security'.[36] Robert McNamara urged immediate 50 per cent defence cuts.[37] Now was the time to reinvest in the American social and economic infrastructure and to tackle the reality of decline.[38]

James Chace urged a responsible 'new internationalism' rooted in 'new international economic and financial institutions' designed to safeguard the role of the dollar and the international free trade order.[39] Yet more voices called for American leaders variously to promote international democracy; to maximise world order (with the US military acting as 'globocop' and calling on other nations to fund its peace-keeping activities); to resurrect the 'global community' agenda of the early Carter years; even to defend Western culture and values against new nationalisms and a revived Islam.[40]

Bush Administration officials were aware that they had the opportunity to re-make American foreign policy. In a 1989 interview, Dennis Ross, State Department Policy Planning Director, acknowledged that more was now expected of his staff than at any time since the 1940s. 'The world is changing in very big ways, hour by hour,' declared Ross. 'That keeps you humble when someone says, "Please draw me up three scenarios for the future of Europe."'[41] The Bush Administration's response to the challenges of 1989 and after was the New World Order concept, outlined to Congress during the 1990 Gulf crisis:

> We stand today at a unique and extraordinary moment ... . Out of these troubled times ... a new world order can emerge ... . Today, that new world order is struggling to be born, a world quite different from the one we have known, a world where the rule of law supplants the rule of the jungle, a world in which nations recognize the shared responsibility for freedom and justice, a world where the strong respect the weak.[42]

As the Bush Presidency wore on, its defenders became increasingly reluctant to use the phrase, 'new world order'. Yet the 'new world order' was not just a journalists' creation – certainly less of one than the 'Reagan Doctrine'. Bush frequently used the phrase, as indeed did Gorbachev.[43] The 'new world order' represented the Administration's vision of the future, and of America's role in achieving and sustaining that future. It was a version of 'status quo plus'. The New World Order contained some echoes of Woodrow Wilson, but was certainly not a crusade for global democracy. It represented an adaptation of the *Pax Americana* to a world wherein American power did not hold absolute and undisputed sway. Like its progenitor, the Nixon Doctrine, the New World Order recognised that the US could not do everything. American goals – world order, peaceful adjudication of disputes under international law, the advancement of liberal democracy and market economics, the maintenance of liberal economic regimes – would be achieved through collective action (ideally associated with the United Nations) orchestrated by the United States. (Bush's new vision conveniently ignored continuing US–UN disputes over the scale of dues owed by Washington to the UN.)

To radical critics, all this was simply imperialism in nearly-new clothes. For Noam Chomsky, it was the codification of the rule of the 'rich men of the rich societies ... assisted by the rich men of the hungry nations who do their bidding': a vicious parody of the 1990 call by the South Commission (chaired by Julius Nyerere) for a new, non-exploitative global order.[44] James Petras and Morris Morley described the New World Order as an attempt to recreate 'a world of uncontested U.S. power, in the process subordinating the ambitions of competitor allies to American interest ... '.[45] A cautious reaction to a new era of uncertain opportunities, the New World Order did embody themes from the early days of containment and preponderant power. Bush was concerned, like Harry Truman before him, with isolationist threats. In his farewell foreign policy address in December 1992, Bush argued that 'the alternative to American leadership is not more security for our citizens but less'. The New World Order for democracy and markets should be actively promoted and defended by a United States that was not unmindful of its own security interests: 'Governments responsive to the will of the people are not likely to commit aggression.'[46]

By the time Bush made this valedictory foreign policy address at Texas A. and M., he had been defeated by a Presidential candidate who promised to prioritise the domestic agenda. It now appeared that, as a cautious re-statement of the strategy of preponderant American power, the New World Order was insufficiently attuned both to the economics of global interdependence and to America's domestic needs.

REGIONAL POLICIES FOR A NEW WORLD ORDER

(a) The Middle East

Testifying before the Senate Foreign Relations and House Foreign Affairs Committees in February 1991, Secretary Baker revealed that an important US war aim was the achievement of a new economic and security order in the Middle East. New regional security arrangements would encompass Israeli–Arab reconciliation, 'new and strengthened' regional security ties, together with a role for both post-Saddam Iraq and for Iran.[47] The messy ending to the war frustrated Baker's hopes. However, during the Summer of 1991, Baker achieved an agreement under which the US and Moscow would sponsor an international conference between Syrian, Lebanese, Israeli and joint Jordanian–Palestinian delegations. The conference was scheduled for Madrid on 30 October.

The ending of the Cold War and the liberation of Kuwait had opened a significant window of opportunity for the Middle Eastern peace process. During 1989 and 1990, the Bush Administration had offered little beyond a commitment to incremental bargaining, a suspicion of grand gestures and the assertion that the region's conflicts were not 'ripe' for resolution. Middle Eastern specialist on the NSC staff, Richard Haass, advocated an American policy of 'ripening' the conditions for negotiation: promoting the notion that territory-for-peace was a negotiating paradigm; advocating face-to-face talks; thinking in terms of transitional arrangements rather than comprehensive solutions.[48] During 1989 and much of 1990, Washington followed a policy of working with Israeli leader Yitzhak Shamir, while attempting to prevail upon him to – in Baker's words – 'lay aside, once and for all, the unrealistic vision of a greater Israel'.[49] Bush and Baker in their first year also, in William Quandt's words, 'acted as if the Soviet Union still represented a serious competitor in the Middle East'.[50]

By March 1991, the world had changed. Syria had lost its superpower sponsor, and had cooperated with the US – even in a sense with Israel – against Iraq. Anti-Saddam Arab coalition members were disturbed by the backing given Saddam by the Palestine Liberation Organisation. The US was now clearly the dominant regional power. Though Shamir was frank in his distrust of the Bush Administration, he recognised that there was 'no better candidate' than the US to broker an agreement.[51] Bush and Baker held out the prospect of important loan guarantees to Israel if Shamir moderated his apparent expansive nationalism. The Israeli leader's acceptance of the conditions attached to the Madrid conference seemed to involve acknowledging the principle of land for peace.

Hopes for Madrid, and for the ensuing face-to-face negotiations in Washington and Moscow, were frustrated. The US emphasised that its role was as facilitator rather than as the bringer of substantive proposals. In effect, hopes for any real progress were suspended until after the June 1992 Israeli elections. Bush and Baker were delighted at the victory of Labour leader Yitzhak Rabin, whose undertakings not to establish new settlements were accepted. Important loan guarantees emerged from Congress. However, Bush and Baker were now preoccupied with the *American* elections and were content to abide by the rule that initiatives in the Middle East are best avoided during Presidential campaigns. (In August 1992, Baker handed over the Secretaryship of State to Lawrence Eagleburger in order to devote himself to his boss's re-election.) The Bush Administration expired amid hopes for a settlement, but also amid renewed Israeli–Palestinian violence.

(b) Europe

The conflict in the Gulf rapidly became interpreted in Washington as a test of allied good faith in the New World Order. In Congress, D.E. Bonior (Michigan Democrat) led efforts to tie the US military commitment in the Pacific to Tokyo's funding of the Gulf War.[52] (Japan eventually contributed nearly eleven million dollars.) In Europe, national leaderships took the opportunity to send messages to Washington about how they wished relationships with the US to develop in the post-Cold War era. The British military commitment was the speediest and strongest. Margaret Thatcher, exploiting a public mood in the UK which was actually more hawkish than in the US, saw her role as countering Bush's tendency to 'wobble' in the face of Saddam's aggression.[53] Bush managed to extract a significant French contribution too, despite France's historical ties with Iraq, her traditionally independent role, and the ambivalence of Defence Minister Jean-Pierre Chevenement. Germany witnessed the largest anti-war demonstrations in Europe; eventually, however – following initial reluctance – the German exchequer underwrote about 10 per cent of the war costs.

Observers in Washington were struck by the apparent failure of the European Community to develop a concerted diplomatic response to the Gulf crisis. American adaptation to the uncertain and confusing institutional changes in Europe was to be a major theme of the Bush years. As Michael Smith has put it: 'In both the security and the economic domain, the Bush Administration faced the challenge of a semi-formed "new Europe"' with a 'plethora of institutions ... searching for a new role and meaning.' Against this background, the Administration's position was 'one of engagement, but often without the leverage which could have shaped events into an American model'.[54] Among the new or newly transformed institutions were the reinvented European Community; the government of the reunited Germany; the reactivated Western European Union; the Conference on Security and Cooperation in Europe; plus a host of regional and sub-regional entities. NATO's own force structure, mission, doctrine and organisation were being developed throughout this period. Greater emphasis was now to be placed on crisis management and peacekeeping. A 1991 statement of NATO's strategic concept acknowledged that security risks were now most likely to emerge 'from the adverse consequences of instabilities that may arise from the serious economic, social and political difficulties, including ethnic rivalries and territorial disputes' in central and Eastern Europe.[55] In the same year, the North Atlantic Cooperation Council was created to facilitate civilian-level cooperation between NATO and the Eastern European and Soviet – soon Soviet successor – states. Limited plans for military coordination, stopping short of full NATO membership for the ex-communist states, were bequeathed to the Clinton Administration.

Concerned always to respond to the rise of the single European market as well as to post-Cold War security needs, George Bush continually emphasised the needs for caution and for 'a well-balanced mix of involvement in all dimensions of European affairs'.[56] While there would be no major retreat from NATO, US priorities would inevitably shift from the security to the economic arena. It became conventional wisdom in this period that, in the new context – to quote Robert Hunter – 'foreign policy will be economic policy'.[57] It was also widely assumed that the key relationship would be the bilateral one between the US and Germany. In fact, Washington's early experience with the reunited German leadership under Chancellor Kohl was not especially productive. Apparent understandings that Kohl would cooperate with Washington's case regarding the Uruguay Round of the General Agreement on Tariffs and Trade came to little.[58] Clashes over trade policy appeared to presage a new agenda for transatlantic relations. The decision-making climate in Washington became profoundly affected by the perceived dangers (as well as opportunities) opened by European economic regionalism.[59]

The Bush Administration signalled its views on the 'new Europe' in a number of policy positions: for example, in its evident desire to see the EC take the lead in aiding East European economic reconstruction.[60] At the institutional level, Administration policy centred on

James Baker's 'New Atlantic Architecture' proposals of 1989 and the Transatlantic Declaration of November 1990. Both initiatives involved complex bureaucratic contacts between the US and the new European institutions. Andreas Van Agt (EC Ambassador to the US) dismissed the 1990 Declaration as a 'love letter';[61] it certainly did not give rise to the new, predictable structure of relationships which Baker foresaw in 1989.

The limits both of the 'new Europe' and the new transatlantic relationship were put to the test in the context of the carnage taking place in the former Yugoslavia. Bush's initial conservative reaction to the ethnic warfare in the Balkans was merely to express commitment to the territorial integrity of Yugoslavia. In April 1992, Washington eventually followed the lead of the European Community in recognising that Slovenia, Croatia and Bosnia-Herzegovenia were independent states. The Administration felt that premature EC recognition had led directly to the conflict. US recognition, however, made it difficult for the Administration to ignore the Serbian interventions against the Muslim regime in Bosnia. Bush supported the UN sanctions against the Serbian government in Belgrade, condemned war crimes and 'ethnic cleansing', and expressed support for UN humanitarian and peacekeeping efforts. However, Bush left the world in no doubt that substantial US military intervention was out of the question. There would be, as Democratic Senator Joseph Lieberman of Connecticut put it, no 'Operation Balkan Storm'.[62] Belying his earlier assertion that the 'Vietnam syndrome' had been 'kicked', Bush invoked memories of the earlier conflict: 'I'm old enough to remember Vietnam';[63] 'I am not interested in seeing one single United States soldier pinned down in some kind of guerrilla environment.'[64] While Serbian aggression inescapably violated the New World Order, the US President was adamant that the US would not act as global policeman in every instance – especially where key US interests were uninvolved, and where there was little domestic pressure to intervene. In July 1992, Bush emphasised that the US was 'not in a forward-leaning role in terms of saying our objective is to bring lasting peace to this troubled land' [*sic*]. There was 'no pressure to try to respond fully, from the United States Congress or any citizens here, to say why aren't we putting ... troops into Sarajevo' ... .[65] The US was 'not going to inject itself into every single crisis, no matter how heart-rending, around the world'.[66]

Bush's position on the former Yugoslavia essentially embodied an accurate reading of public and Congressional opinion. In August, candidate Bill Clinton did advocate the use of 'air power against the Serbs to try to restore the basic conditions of humanity'.[67] The Administration in the same month secured Congressional backing for the policy of pressurising Belgrade, by obtaining UN authority for using force for humanitarian ends. In October, Congress voted substantial refugee assistance and – reflecting the view that the universal UN arms embargo was unfair – authorised Bush to provide up to 50 million dollars in military equipment to Bosnia's army. Yet no Administration response ensued. The Balkan situation was perceived to be, in the words of Acting Secretary of State Lawrence Eagleburger, too 'massively mixed up'.[68] At West Point military academy on 5 January 1993, the outgoing President attempted to define conditions for US military interventions to protect the New World Order. Bush consciously attempted to go beyond the familiar post-Vietnam formulation that objectives should be transparent and that the US should possess overwhelming force:

> In the complex world we are entering there can be no single or simple set of fixed rules for using force … . But to warn against a futile quest for a set of hard and fast rules … is not to say there cannot be some principles to inform our decisions … . Using force makes sense as a policy where the stakes warrant, where and when force can be effective, where no other policies are likely to prove effective, where its application can be limited in scope and time, and where the potential benefits justify the potential costs and sacrifice.[69]

Caution, selectivity, multilateralism and interests: these would be the post-Cold War watchwords.

(c) Asia

Policy towards China centred on the need to 'engage' the Communist leadership. Though there were still holdovers from the earlier policy of using the Chinese relationship as a lever against the Soviets, the Bush Administration was primarily concerned to establish ties with a key economic player in the emerging multipolar world. The Administration's operational conservatism invited the charge that human rights concerns were being compromised, and that – if and when the Communist Party gerontocracy fell – the US was yet again failing to keep in step with the world's momentous political changes. The June 1989 massacre of student democracy oppositionists in Tiananmen Square elicited significantly different responses in the White House and on Capitol Hill. Bush suspended arms sales and pro- hibited visits to China by US military personnel. Yet in July he initiated a series of visits (by National Security Adviser Brent Scowcroft, and by James Baker and Lawrence Eagleburger of the State Department) designed to reassure Beijing about American intentions. (At this stage Washington especially welcomed continued Chinese hostility to Soviet influence in Afghanistan. In fiscal year 1991, the US was still providing about a quarter of a million dollars in aid to the Islamic guerrillas in Afghanistan. Washington also sought Beijing's help in resolving the complex situation in Cambodia. Vietnam, under pressure from Moscow, withdrew its troops in 1989. Beijing continued to back Pol Pot's extreme Khmer Rouge movement; while Washington, embar- rassed by its own indulgence towards Pol Pot, sought to encourage 'non-communist' elements. In early 1991, Congress officially con- verted covert aid to non-communist forces to overt aid. In October 1991, the UN agreed to sustain a new coalition regime in Cambodia. Signs of a possible US rapprochement with Vietnam appeared in 1992, when a select Senate Committee concluded that there was no 'com- pelling evidence' that American prisoners were still alive in Southeast Asia.)[70]

Scowcroft's July 1989 visit to China did not become public knowl- edge until December 1989, when it attracted substantial Congressional criticism. Senate Majority Leader George Mitchell declared that the President had 'kowtowed' to Beijing.[71] Congress attempted to strengthen Chinese sanctions and passed a measure (pocket vetoed by Bush) designed to extend sanctuary to Chinese students in the US. Executive–legislative conflicts arose over alleged White House com- plicity in evading the arms sanctions, and over Bush's determination to apply Most Favoured Nation trading status to China. In 1992, Bush twice vetoed bills which sought to limit trade with China because of human rights abuses. The Senate upheld both vetoes, and the White House's preferences in this area prevailed. However, Bush was impelled to make gestures towards Congressional opinion. In April 1991, for example, he became the first US President to receive the exiled Tibetan leader, the Dalai Lama. Signs of emerging Sino–American economic tensions were also evident in the mobilisa- tion of trading sanctions (under the 'Special 301' provisions of the

1988 Omnibus Trade Act) in response to Chinese violations of US computer software copyrights.

By the early 1990s, only Japan and Taiwan had higher American trade surpluses than China. US public opinion was severely exercised by perceptions of America's economic vulnerability and relative decline. A 1990 *New York Times* poll revealed 58 per cent of respondents as seeing Japanese economic competition as more threatening than Soviet military power.[72] By 1990, the US–Japanese trade deficit stood at 38 billion dollars. Attempts to reduce the surplus continued during the Bush years, notably under the rubric of the Structural Impediments Initiative begun in 1989. Anti-Japanese economic nationalism surfaced in Congress (notably over US–Japanese cooperation on developing the FSX fighter support aircraft) and at the level of state governments (some of whom began to consider protectionist, 'buy American' legislation). In March 1990, Bush and Japanese Prime Minister Toshiki Kaifu committed themselves to a 'global partnership' – a phrase which clearly implied greater sharing of the security burden.[73] American perceptions of Japan as a security 'free rider' were strengthened during the Gulf War. Bush's January 1992 mission to Tokyo failed to secure significant trade concessions.

The post-Cold War shakeout promoted an intense debate about the purpose of foreign aid. Bush found it difficult to sell 'security' aid on the Hill. A major overhaul in the Food for Peace programme in 1990 stimulated a Congressional debate on the extent to which Presidents had been allowed extreme leeway.[74] Now at last, argued Members, the process could be subjected to democratic control and the proper role for aid – a mutual enhancement of global development and US interests – identified. Most observers concluded that future aid totals were bound to decline. Congress was also concerned about the need to share more fairly what remained of the security burden – not only in NATO, but also in relation to South Korea. In 1990, the Pentagon announced its intention to move from a leading to a supporting role on the Korean peninsula by the year 2000. Disputes over foreign aid also erupted over the issue of nuclear proliferation (notably in connection with Pakistan's nuclear programme). Finally, in the economic sphere, the Bush Administration lent its support to the Asian Pacific Economic Cooperation process (APEC). The debate over APEC loomed large during the Clinton Administration, and revealed the extent to which, both for President and Congress, issues of economic foreign policy were challenging traditional security concerns.

(d) Africa

George Bush's late 1992 'lame duck' Presidential announcement that a US force was to be sent to Somalia represented the clearest indication that the Administration actually did regard post-Cold War Africa as part of the New World Order. Before November 1991, it seemed that Washington lacked any clear stance on the continent's future. Aid continued to be disbursed to UNITA forces in Angola. A US navy contingent evacuated foreign personnel from Liberia in 1990. The same year saw important debates on Capitol Hill over the human rights records of African aid recipients. In a series of statements issued in November 1991, the Administration signalled that anti-communist dictatorial regimes would no longer be judged as automatically for US aid. Kenya and Zaire were strongly criticised for failure to democratise.[75] Principally, however, the Administration put its faith in the expansion of free enterprise – in an Africa, where, in the words of Assistant Secretary H.J. Cohen, people would be able 'to engage in business activity and investment as free of government interference as possible'.[76] Regarding South Africa, the Bush Administration initially favoured giving the Pretoria government of F.W. de Klerk 'reasonable time to demonstrate' its commitment to reverse apartheid.[77] James Baker warned Pretoria that failure to move on apartheid reform would incite 'pressures ... for more sanctions in the Congress'.[78] Baker and Bush announced their intention to work for a bipartisan policy on South Africa. Nelson Mandela (released from prison in early 1990) and de Klerk both visited the US in 1990. In July 1991, Bush announced that progress in South Africa was 'irreversible' and that sanctions would be lifted. This high-handed overturning of the 1986 sanctions was highly controversial in legal as well as in policy terms. However, Bush's argument was that the conditions set in 1986 had now been met, and a divided Congress failed to mount a challenge to the action.[79]

The Somalian troop commitment was to prove a difficult inheritance for the Clinton Administration. On 4 December 1992, Bush announced that as many as 28 000 US troops would be sent to Somalia to aid food distribution under the auspices of a UN Security Resolution passed the previous day. President-elect Clinton commended Bush 'for taking the lead in this important humanitarian effort'.[80] The civil strife in Somalia – its post-Cold War degeneration into 'warlord' conflicts – was seen as endangering the lives of possibly two million inhabitants. The deployment was supported in Congress. The Somalian situation was seen to be more straightforward than that in Bosnia, and capable of yielding both clear objectives and predictable outcomes. Inevitably, however, the deployment raised questions about the clarity of America's purpose. Was this to be a blueprint for post-Cold War efforts to promote democracy, humanitarianism and regional stability? (In December 1992, Assistant Secretary Cohen revealed that the US was lobbying for unprecedented UN peacekeeping rules of engagement: 'heavily armed' and 'very robust'.)[81] Would America's mission shift to that of Vietnam-era nation-building? Reviewing the Somalia operation (Restore Hope) on 17 December, Representative J.L. Oberstar (Democrat of Minnesota) asked: 'How do we get out?'.[82]

EVALUATING BUSH'S FOREIGN POLICY: PRESIDENT BUSH AND FOREIGN POLICY ACCOUNTABILITY

In many respects, George Bush was far and away the most successful foreign policy President of the post-Vietnam War period. It would be running the risk of damning them with faint praise to observe that the Bush-Baker-Cheney-Scowcroft team worked together more efficiently and harmoniously than their Carter or Reagan era counterparts. Bush's personal diplomacy – admittedly aided by Saddam Hussein's misbehaviour – created and preserved the Gulf War coalition. The Cold War ended in apparent victory for America's liberal capitalist ideology. The Administration's refusal to 'dance on the Berlin Wall' was magnanimous and salutary. Bush's team felt that it had contributed to important breakthroughs in Latin America, the Middle East and South Africa. In Panama, near-humiliation had given way to success. Conceptual foundations had been laid for the New World Order, based on principles of self-determination and multilateral cooperation against aggression. The Administration saw itself also as having made important contributions to a new GATT deal and to a regional free trade order (NAFTA). Yet, as Bush made his West Point speech in January 1993, the debit side to his foreign policy record was clearly evident. Commentators discussed the new world disorder rather than the New World Order. During the 1992 election campaigns, one joke (used most famously in the Democratic primaries by Senator Paul Tsongas) kept recurring: the Cold War is over – Japan won. Saddam was still in power, and the Gulf War's hidden costs (from debt forgiveness to enhanced aid to coalition members) were becoming apparent. Questions were being raised, rather confusingly, both about the wisdom of the Somali intervention and the Bosnian non-intervention.

Bush did not succeed in imbuing the New World Order with purpose and vision. His Administration's cautious conservatism – the familiar refrain that 'our enemy today is uncertainty and instability'[83] – did not serve it too badly. As Kerry Mullins and Aaron Wildavsky wrote in 1992, George Bush knew what he wanted (even if he could not explain what he wanted) – 'to make process of mutual accommodation work at every level, from the family to the family of nations'.[84] Bush's conservatism sought to combine mutual accommodation with support for recognised and apparently predictable central authorities. Such an attitude was not disastrous for American foreign policy, but too often (as in the former USSR and Yugoslavia, even in Iraq) left the Administration lagging behind events. Bush's foreign policy vision was little more than a vague commitment to multilateralism, and a promise that foreign policy would be tied to US interests (themselves grounded vaguely in an asserted coincidence of free markets and liberal democracy). Such a vision could not reverse perceptions of American decline. Perceived (and actual) Presidential neglect of the domestic social and economic fabric lay at the root of Bush's 1992 defeat. Numerous indicators during the Bush years pointed to the continuation of problems with US economic competitiveness. (For example, a 1990 Commerce Department survey of twelve 'cutting-edge' technologies concluded that the US was 'losing badly' to Japan in four areas, 'losing' in six, 'holding' in two, and 'gaining' nowhere. US exports during the Bush years showed little sign of being capable of matching demand for imports.)[85] As the world moved to a Japanese–European–US 'tripolarity' and the US (to quote Michael Bernstein) 'became one member of a new set of major industrial powers', American public opinion became restive and apprehensive.[86] The Bush Presidency was unable to set forth, explain and sell to the US public a vision of America's world role which befitted all the changed international conditions.

Although unquestionably superior to its equivalent in the Reagan years, the Bush foreign policy decision-making process also had its downside. The Bush White House operated with a closely structural National Security Council committee system, designed to optimise interagency coordination and to defer to the President as 'ultimate decider'.[87] Yet many key decisions were made by *ad hoc* groups chaired by Bush. The 1989–90 Panamanian decisions were made entirely outside the NSC system. The 'Gang of Eight' (Bush, Baker,

Cheney, Scowcroft, Robert Gates, White House Chief of Staff John Sununu, Colin Powell and Vice President Dan Quayle) dominated Gulf decisions. The tendency to neglect bureaucratic apparatuses was replicated by Baker at the State Department. Unlike Shultz, Baker was less than keen to draw foreign service officers into important decisions. Raymond Seitz (ironically the first ever career diplomat to serve as US Ambassador to London) declared at his swearing-in that it was a myth that Baker worked through a closed inner circle: 'It's not a circle. It's a trapezoid.' Deputy Secretary Eagleburger and Assistant Secretary for Public Affairs Margaret Tutwiler were particularly influential. Baker's style even evoked comparisons with Henry Kissinger's tenure at Foggy Bottom.[88] (Brent Scowcroft also resembled Kissinger in that he functioned as adviser, manager and foreign policy operator. However, Bush's National Security Assistant tended to deflect any such comparisons by his less visible and more low-key approach.)

Bush and his foreign policy team were frequently intensely secretive, unaccountable and contemptuous of Congress. When Scowcroft visited China in July 1989, not even Presidential Chief of Staff Sununu was informed. We have already noted several examples of Bush's high-handedness and lack of concern for democratic process: for example, in relation to South African sanctions and the post-election Iran-*contra* pardons. Congressional involvement in the Panamanian invasion and the Gulf crisis was kept to a minimum. Both military interventions arguably involved significant transgressions of legislative war powers.[89] Bush denied that he was in any way required to seek Congressional authorisation prior to using forces in the Gulf.[90]

Bush's own position on the Congressional role in foreign policy was expressed in a speech he gave to the conservative lawyers' Federalist Society in 1987:

> Over the last 20 years we have witnessed a departure from the way we have conducted foreign policy for nearly two centuries. Congress has asserted an increasingly influential role in the micromanagement of foreign policy – foreign operations, if you will – and at the same time Congress, through the use of laws ... ushered courts and lawyers into an uncomfortable but very visible role in the development of our foreign policy.[91]

Just as Bush sought to eradicate 'Vietnam syndrome' inhibitions on military intervention, so he consciously attempted as President to reverse the situation he described in 1987. Some of his assaults on Congress were merely partisan, attempting to blame the Democratic controlled legislature for his domestic difficulties. Asked in 1992 why he could not 'bring the same kind of purpose to the domestic scene as you did in Desert Shield and Desert Storm', Bush responded: ' ... the answer is I didn't have to get permission from some old goat in the United States Congress to kick Saddam Hussein out of Kuwait!'[92] However, a series of veto messages and statements from Attorney General Dick Thornburgh's Justice Department encompassed a more measured and concerted drive against Congressional authority in foreign policy. In July 1989, Bush vetoed legislation which sought to regulate the joint US–Japanese production of the FSX jet fighter. He spoke of the need to 'draw the line' between Congress and President and accused the legislature of intruding 'into areas entrusted by the Constitution exclusively to the executive'. In September 1989, the Justice Department informed the Armed Services Committees of Congress that 'the president has exclusive authority to conduct and manage our relations with foreign nations'.[93] Pre-Gulf War policy towards Iraq was promoted through unaccountable National Security Directives, while subsequent Congressional investigations were hampered by deliberate tactics of delay and evasion. Remembering the Nixon experience, the Administration was reluctant to assert an unreviewable 'executive privilege' which enabled it to deny information to Congress. Yet Bush did categorically claim the right to withhold information about covert operations. A 1991 National Security Directive instructed that departmental general counsels should 'review and inventory all requests' from Congress 'to determine which, if any, raise issues of executive privilege (deliberative process, foreign relations, national security, and so on'.)[94] Bush also developed the 'signing statement' – the commentary issued when bills were signed into law – as a significant and unaccountable way of shaping and interpreting the legislative intent. 'Signing statements' appended to foreign aid legislation, for example, made it clear that the Administration would not be bound by restrictions written into the law. Most controversially, these statements negated attempts by Congress in 1989 to cut the implicit link between the giving of aid to Central American allies and their consequent support for the Nicaraguan *contras*. Commenting on an amendment offered by Democratic Representative David Obey, Bush announced: 'I intend to construe this section narrowly.' Implicit linking of aid and policy towards the *contras* would continue. As he stated at

Princeton University in May 1991, George Bush had no hesitation in asserting his own duty to interpret the Constitution and to decide which laws violated the Constitution and thus 'have no binding legal force'.[95]

President Bush's assertion of unaccountable Presidential supremacy in areas of (Presidentially defined) national security recalled the Vietnam years. His underlying assumption – that since the Vietnam War Congress had consistently violated the exclusive grant of power given to the President over foreign policy – was unreliable and misinformed. Cold War foreign policy, with its preoccupation with nuclear crisis and secrecy, always tended to favour the executive branch. Congressional war powers and its funding controls were frequently violated before, during and after the Vietnam War. However, as noted in preceding chapters of this book, the Constitution enjoins President and Congress to share power. It is not a justification for Presidential domination.[96] The struggle continued during the Bush years. From the point of view of democratic foreign policy, it was unfortunate that Congress failed to achieve any authoritative rebuttal of Bush's assertions of Presidential supremacy. However, Congress was far from subservient in this period. In 1992, Bush actually lost 51 per cent of contested national security votes in Congress.[97] The post-Cold War focus on trade and economic issues seemed to favour legislative activism. Bush's assaults involved a constitutionally unacceptable effort to pre-empt a reactivated legislative assertion in this new context.

9 Clinton and Prospects for America's Future: New Priorities for Old?

Describing the debate over post-Cold War priorities in 1992, Norman Ornstein recalled Oscar Wilde's remark that there were two tragedies in human existence: never achieving one's heart's desire – and achieving it. The US had won the Cold War, but the American public was 'bitterly unhappy over the failures of the political and economic processes at home and pessimistic about the future'.[1] The Presidential election did not see a sustained debate over future priorities. Third candidate Ross Perot (who gleaned an extraordinary 19 per cent of votes cast) offered virtually no contribution to the debate over foreign policy priorities. He merely suggested that Germany and Japan might help ease the budget deficit by paying more for their defence. Clinton offered a few specific criticisms of the Bush Administration. It had coddled 'dictators from Baghdad to Beijing' and had missed opportunities accruing from the demise of Soviet communism. Clinton offered also scattered hints that he might embrace some form of modified protectionism (or 'managed trade') and undertook to advance America's economic cause more forcefully than his predecessor.[2]

Rather than offering a positive alternative vision for American foreign relations, Clinton in 1992 presented himself as a candidate concerned pre-eminently with domestic issues. The implication was that he, like the American electorate, was 'homeward bound'. Nevertheless, foreign policy could not be ignored. (That foreign policy mattered was implicit in Clinton's campaign theme: 'Make no mistake, foreign and domestic policy are inseparable.')[3] The choices facing the incoming Administration were well summarised in articles written by British academic Tim Hames. One option was to continue the course set by George Bush: the 'chairman of the board' option, whereby the US would develop an energetic, yet also selective and multilateral, internationalism, rooted in the New World Order. Other options included a

178

'solo superpower' unilateralist, 'globocop' stance, sketched out in the Pentagon's leaked 'No Rivals' plan of 1992; a new isolationism (advanced by 1992 Republican nomination candidate Pat Buchanan); a retrenched internationalism, involving military cutbacks significantly in excess of those envisaged by Bush; a new liberal internationalism (focusing on human rights and environmental issues, essentially a revival of the early Carter agenda); and various strategies based around regional or hemispheric domination.[4] By 1995, ex-Bush NSC staffer Richard Haass was still contending that the US remained suspended between critical choices: between the drive to maximise world order (realism); the view that foreign policy must primarily serve domestic economic ends (economism); concerns for the environment and world poverty (humanitarianism); 'minimalism' – the foreign policy of perceived national decline, amounting to a new isolationist concentration on (left or right wing) domestic agendas; and the export to other countries of US democratic/free market forms (Wilsonianism).[5]

The new Administration's perceptions of American needs and problems inclined it towards some combination of retrenched internationalism, economism and Wilsonianism, with a dash of new, liberal internationalism. The Administration appeared to accept Henry Kissinger's 1993 assertion that 'America now finds herself in a world which she cannot dominate, but from which she also cannot simply withdraw.'[6] Statements made upon the occasion of the naming of Clinton's foreign policy team ran a gamut of various internationalist positions. Warren Christopher, Secretary of State designate, declared that voters had 'embraced Governor Clinton's concept that the strength of the economy is the foundation of our foreign policy'. Yet he seemed also to advocate a reworking of the early Carter human rights agenda (which Christopher had himself, as Cyrus Vance's deputy during the Carter years, formerly promoted): 'We face a world where borders matter less and less, a world that demands we join with other nations to face challenges that range from overpopulation to AIDS to the very destruction of our planet's life support system.' Clinton himself added: 'Mine will be a foreign policy of engagement, one that strengthens democracy, promotes economic reform, opens markets and stands up to aggression and intolerance.'[7]

As the Clinton Administration contemplated these foreign policy options, it was evident that no incoming US Presidency in recent history had enjoyed such freedom of choice. When George Bush took power in 1989, the Cold War was still in process, and the Soviet Union was intact.

However, even Clinton's choices could not be made in a void. The new Administration's policy choices would inevitably be shaped by historical inheritances, received ideas, events, personalities, changing public and Congressional attitudes, mid-term elections and global socio-economic trends (from shifting immigration patterns to the opening of new markets). Just as Clinton was presenting himself in 1992 as a domestic economy-oriented candidate, a reminder of the stubborn power of past international events obtruded. Like a 1990s firebell in the night, Clinton's Vietnam War record became a major campaign theme. Bush charged that Clinton, who had opposed the war while a student at Oxford University, was no better than an unpatriotic draft-dodger. Though Bush's attacks were weakened by the vulnerability of Vice President Quayle on this issue, and by Clinton's choice of Vietnam veteran Al Gore as his 1992 running mate, the 'patriotism' issue revived generational conflicts which now surfaced for the first time at the Presidential level. Gore portrayed Administration searches (with the help of the authorities in London) of Clinton's passport files as the action of a police state. Clinton responded to the attacks in the St Louis Presidential debate:

> When Joe McCarthy went around this country attacking people's patriotism, he was wrong, and a senator from Connecticut stood up to him named Prescott Bush. Your father was right ... . You were wrong to attack my patriotism. I was opposed to the war, but I loved my country.[8]

Clinton's personal Vietnam legacy, together with undertakings to protect the rights of gays in the military, appeared to presage difficulties with America's military establishment. Many commentators interpreted his victory as the coming to power of the anti-Vietnam baby boomers. Journalist Martin Walker wrote that the Friends of Bill – the associates which the new President brought to Washington – represented 'the maturing and ... the vengeance of the anti-Vietnam generation'.[9] Clinton himself forecast that his election would finally heal the wounds: 'If I win, it will finally close the book on Vietnam.'[10]

Due to the incompleteness of perspective, it is impossible here to provide a detailed account or evaluation of US foreign policy during the Clinton Presidency. Instead, it is the intention to sketch out the main themes which emerged in Clinton's first two years, prior to the 1995 Republican takeover on Capitol Hill.

TENDENCIES IN CLINTON'S EARLY FOREIGN POLICY

(a) Economism

President Clinton's most obvious attempt to close the book on Vietnam came in the significant context of promoting the cause of US trade and investment. In July 1993, he announced that, although the 'deep wounds' of Vietnam had 'yet to heal', real progress was being made with a 'full accounting' for those US service personnel who did not return from the war.[11] In February 1994, he announced that America's trade embargo on Vietnam would be lifted and a US liaison office – the first step towards normalisation – established. This announcement, which evoked criticism from the Vietnam Veterans of America organisation, followed a Senate vote to resume trade and pressure from corporations wishing to invest in this sector of the emerging Pacific economy. As Frank Hawke, Citibank representative in Hanoi put it, the Vietnamese were 'emphasising key infrastructure areas such as petrochemicals, … transport and power generation – all areas where US companies excel'.[12]

Strong forces and arguments were pushing the Clinton Administration towards embracing economism as the model for its foreign policy. Following the end of the Cold War, it became conventional wisdom that the American electorate was indeed 'homeward bound', and that the US was in danger of sliding into some form of neo-isolationism, cultural introversion or – as John Gray put it – 'Wilsonianism in one country'.[13] Against this background, economism in foreign policy offered the prospect (providing the approach did not degenerate into protectionist neo-mercantilism) of a sustainable and popular internationalism. Moreover, as C.F. Bergsten pointed out in 1992, exports and imports of goods and services now amounted to almost one quarter of the entire US gross domestic product. Growth in the US economy appeared heavily dependent on exports.[14]

The Administration's concern to place economic interests at the centre of its foreign policy was evident in both its pronouncements and its bureaucratic innovations. Warren Christopher in early 1995 distanced himself from previous Secretaries of State who 'thought of economics as "low policy"', while they dealt with high science like arms control': 'I make no apologies for putting economics at the top of our foreign policy agenda.'[15] Trade Representative Mickey Kantor argued that for too long the US had been too coy about dollar diplomacy: 'For years we have allowed our workers to be hurt and our companies to be left out because we wouldn't pick up the phone.'[16] A new foreign service training curriculum was set in place to emphasise trade promotion. When James Cheek took over as US Ambassador in Buenos Aires in 1993, his first act was to announce that his main job was to lobby for US business in Argentina. Jeffrey Garten, Undersecretary for International Trade at the Commerce Department declared the Administration's intention to 'put other nations on notice that America will no longer make trade concessions in deference to the NATO or US–Japanese security relationship'.[17] Garten was a key player in the ranks of 'economics first' advocates, who also included: Laura D'Andrea Tyson at the Council of Economic Advisers; Commerce Secretary Ron Brown; Labor Secretary Robert Reich; and Theodore Moran of State's Policy Planning Staff. The National Economic Council was set up under Robert E. Rubin (prior to Rubin's move to the Treasury) to factor economic policy considerations into every Presidential decision. Within the Administration, the Commerce Department achieved new prominence. Its main priority – strengthening US involvement in ten 'Big Emerging Markets' (China, including Hong Kong and Taiwan; India; Indonesia; Brazil; Mexico; Turkey; South Korea; South Africa; Poland; and Argentina) – became a key priority for the entire Administration.[18] Zbigniew Brzezinski's policy of fostering 'regional influentials' was being updated to reflect the new economism. Many members of the Clinton economic foreign policy elite were former academics, often associated with 'managed trade', 'market access', 'liberal hawk' or other variants of economic nationalism.[19] Clinton himself asserted that the US was 'like a big corporation competing in the global marketplace'.[20]

Economic nationalism of the kind underscored by Clinton's 'big corporation' remark raises several problems, both conceptual and operational. As Paul Krugman pointed out in an article published in 1994, it is far from self-evident that the US competes with Japan in the same way that Coca-Cola competes with Pepsi. For one thing, Coca-Cola does not sell the majority of its product to its own workers.[21] In practice, the reconciliation of aggressive economic nationalism (involving a concern to achieve exclusive access to markets) with liberal free trade ideals may prove impossible. Moreover, economistic foreign policy may quickly degenerate into an over-rigid quest for quantifiable trade goals. Such degeneration tends to encourage Japan-bashing protectionism and a preoccupation – observed by many during the early Clinton years – with bilateral trade deficits rather than global imbalances. Economism in foreign policy also runs the constant risk of being over-taken by the security agenda (albeit, as in the Gulf, a security agenda with strong economic implications).[22] There is also the obvious problem of economism conflicting with other stated objectives, notably the promotion of democracy and human rights.

Despite all this, the Clinton Administration's advocacy of 'economic security' in foreign policy was clear and unapologetic. In the 1992 election, Clinton criticised Bush's cosiness towards Beijing. In 1993, Clinton announced that China must understand that the new Administration 'has made human rights a cornerstone of our foreign policy'.[23] Yet in the following year, Clinton supported Most Favored Nation trading status for China with little apparent concern for Beijing's human rights record. (Even conservative estimates put the cost to the US of MFN withdrawal at around ten billion dollars.) Subsequent clashes with Beijing revolved around trading practices rather than human rights. The Administration's enthusiasm for Pacific trade – by 1992, 40 per cent of American trade was with Asia – and for regional trade pacts coalesced in its strong endorsement of the Asia Pacific Economic Cooperation. The tension between 'economic security' and human rights was emphasised at APEC's Jakarta summit of November 1994. Students broke into the US Embassy to protest Indonesian violations of human rights in East Timor. Defence Secretary Les Aspin and his successor, William Perry, insisted that post-Cold War arms sales would be geared to human rights considerations. Yet, although the total volume was down, the US share of world arms sales rose from 42 to 70 per cent between 1990 and 1993.[24]

Clinton's major successes with the 1993–4 Congress related to high profile trade issues. (The 103rd Congress actually supported Clinton on 85 per cent of contested national security votes.) In November 1993, Clinton won Congressional endorsement for the North American Free Trade Agreement by a suprisingly wide margin (234–200 in the House; 61–38 in the Senate). NAFTA was conspicuously opposed by Ross Perot, by organised labour – fearful of jobs being exported to Mexico – by some environmental groups, and by many on the conservative right. It opened deep rifts in the Democratic party (still evident in the early 1995 battle over Clinton's rescue plan to save the Mexican peso). However, the 1993 NAFTA vote was a clear Clinton success and a victory for the view that NAFTA could actually create new American jobs. In December 1993, Clinton extended his support to the new

(Uruguay Round) General Agreement on Tariffs and Trade, arguing that it would 'add as much as 100 billion [dollars] to 200 billion per year to our economy'.[25] The ensuing GATT ratification debate involved not only familiar disputes regarding protection *versus* free trade, but also Republican anxiety over US involvement in the World Trade Organization (set up by the GATT to arbitrate international trading disagreements). Some major exporters opposed the agreement's anti-dumping provisions. Again, however, Clinton achieved Congressional approval – in November 1994, following a compromise with Republicans over WTO exit procedures.

(b) Selective Engagement

The Clinton Administration struggled to reconcile its commitment to international leadership with the acceptance of limits imposed by US public opinion, the continuing fear of debilitating entanglement and economic prudence. In its very early statements, the Administration appeared to embrace a kind of 'assertive multilateralism'. When Undersecretary of State Peter Tarnoff sketched out a more restrained form of multilateralism in 1993 – based on 'a case by case decision to limit the amount of American engagement' – he was swiftly admonished by Warren Christopher. According to the Secretary of State: 'our need to lead, our determination to lead, is not constrained by our resources'.[26] Later, reviewing the foreign policy record of 1993–4, Christopher wrote:

> What would the world be like without American leadership just in the last two years? We might have four nuclear states with the breakup of the Soviet Union, instead of one; a North Korea building nuclear bombs; a rising protectionist tide rather than rising trade flows under the Uruguay Round and NAFTA; brutal dictators still terrorizing Haiti and forcing its people to flee; and Iraqi troops very likely back in Kuwait, threatening the world's oil supplies.[27]

Christopher – despite his failure to include in this catalogue a reference to Bosnia, Somalia or Rwanda – was correct to argue that the Administration had not been utterly unable to affect the new world disorder. Yet Clinton's foreign policy elite found it exceedingly difficult to establish criteria to underpin American engagement. Few dissented from the view of Madeleine Albright, US representative to the United Nations that 'the United States is not the world's policeman'.[28] Unfortunately such an assertion merely begs the question: when and how *should* the US intervene? What criteria should determine whether interventions should be diplomatic or military? Were George Bush's West Point principles on military engagement still operative? As the Clinton Presidency wore on, the early assertive multilateralism gave way to a keener recognition of limits. Speaking to the UN in September 1993, Clinton attempted to set criteria for UN interventions (by implication, interventions in which the US would participate). There should be a real threat to international peace, clear objectives, anticipateable costs and an obvious exit-point. As many commentators pointed out, scarcely any military campaign in history has conformed to criteria as restrictive as these. C.W. Maynes wrote in an article published in 1995 that Clinton's criteria (later embodied in Presidential Directive 25) would 'seem to bar the kind of UN force that has successfully monitored the ceasefire on the Golan Heights'.[29] By the middle of the Clinton Presidency a new hierarchy of interests seemed to have emerged to determine the scale and nature of American engagement. There appeared to be a determination to restrict military intervention to but a few areas. In establishing which areas were liable to military attention, the Administration was most likely to prioritise resource access and hemispheric (Monroe Doctrine) concerns. It could not, however, guarantee that arenas of prioritised diplomatic engagement – including alliance obligations – would not, at least in some instances, involve the use of force. Areas of prioritised diplomatic engagement for the Clinton Administration included: regional, hemispheric issues, especially those with a significant domestic overspill involving drugs, immigration or terrorism; particular security concerns, notably nuclear proliferation; the economic foreign policy agenda, including the search for markets and Clinton's vision of the 'new Pacific community'; concern for the future of Russia; and foreign policy issues with strong domestic, usually Democratic party, constituencies attached to them. Piecemeal and uncertain articulation of selective engagement criteria took place against a background of public and elite confusion about America's proper post-Cold War role. (Polls taken in late 1993, for example, tended – in the wake of reversals in Somalia and Haiti – to illustrate extreme public wariness of global involvement. By March 1994, however, an NBC–*Wall Street Journal* poll was showing a majority in favour of sending US ground troops to monitor a Bosnian peace accord. Surveys of opinion-leaders by the *Times–Mirror* Center for the People and the Press showed similar volatility and dissensus.)[30]

There was little evidence in 1993 or 1994 of sustained and widespread public opposition to Clinton's foreign policy leadership. International issues scarcely figured in the 1994 mid-term campaigns. Only in October 1993, after 18 US soldiers were killed in Somalia, did a plurality of poll respondents disapprove of the Presidential foreign policy performance. The inherited involvement in Somalia torpedoed the optimistic assertive multilateralism of Clinton's early period in office. It effectively placed a veto on substantial US intervention following the genocidal slaughter in Rwanda in 1994–5. Somalia typified interventionist uncertainties, where peacekeeping evolves into peace-enforcing, and humanitarian objectives meld into nation-building. (In July 1993, Clinton, presumably in an unconscious echo of the Vietnam era, actually argued that 'we have to have patience in nation-building'.)[31] Somali warlord Mohammad Aidid's forces killed 23 Pakistani 'peace-keepers' in June 1993. (Bush's US-led mission technically ended in May 1993, when it was replaced by a UN operation under Turkish General Cevik Bir. The number of US troops deployed reached its high point of 11 000 – well short of the figure promised by President Bush – in October 1993.) The capture of an injured US helicopter pilot in October 1993 raised the inevitable images of Vietnam. In the face of concerted Congressional opposition to continued deployment, all US troops were withdrawn by April 1994. (Congressional funding cutoffs for US operations in Somalia and Rwanda involved the first such use of its power of the purse since the Vietnam years.)

Regarding the conflict in the former Yugoslavia, the Administration did not deny that US interests were at stake, but recognised that key conditions for US military intervention were lacking. In early 1994, Clinton acknowledged that the US 'has clear interests': 'an interest in helping prevent the spread of a wider war in Europe, an interest in showing NATO remains a credible force for peace, an interest in helping to stem the terrible destabilizing flows of refugees' as well as 'the humanitarian interest we all share'.[32] No powerful domestic lobby favoured intervention, however. If contained to the former Yugoslavian territory, the conflict also raised no immediate problems in relation to US energy access or to nuclear proliferation. The temptation was for the Administration to assert that this was a European problem, which Europeans must themselves resolve. The US would present its good offices and attempt to broker deals between Muslims, Croats and Serbs.

The US was prepared to pressure its European allies, for example against the Vance – Owen peace plan in 1993. In May 1993, the US joined the allies and Russia in a plan to contain the war by creating Muslim enclaves. In February 1994, the US won NATO approval for anti-Serb airstrikes. After failing to secure European agreement to abandon the arms embargo on Bosnian Muslims, Clinton's hand was effectively forced by Congress and, in November 1994, US enforcement of the embargo was terminated. With Senate Republican leader Bob Dole arguing that Serbian intransigence left NATO with no alternative but 'robust bombing', Warren Christopher argued in late 1994 that such a strategy would inevitably lead to ground troops deployments. In December 1994, the Administration announced the possibility of sending troops to help evacuate UN peacekeepers. (US military personnel were already involved in the DENY FLIGHT enforcement of 'no-fly' zones in Bosnia.) In May 1995, NATO airstrikes provoked hostage-taking by the Bosnian Serbs. Clinton raised the possibility of US troop deployment to aid a UN 'reconfiguration'. Generally, US policy on the war between 1993 and early 1995 was less than sure. During the April 1994 siege of Gorazde, for example, the Administration adopted a series of contradictory positions in bewilderingly rapid sequence. Clinton in 1994–5 found himself squeezed between a desire to maintain NATO and UN credibility, and an unwillingness to commit troops. The Republican Congress in early 1995 seemed both committed to the post-Vietnam doctrine of 'overwhelming force', and opposed to involvement with no clear demonstration that US interests were at stake. Between 1993 and mid-1995, Washington essentially endorsed the view that American interests (and the defence of Bosnian sovereignty) warranted neither expanded military involvement, nor even sustained and prioritised diplomatic leadership.[33] This situation changed dramatically with the July–August 1995 Congressional votes to lift the arms embargo on the Bosnian government. Following extended NATO bombing of Bosnian Serb positions, the White House embarked on intense diplomatic activity, coordinated by Assistant Secretary of State Richard Holbrooke. The new policy involved a pragmatic alliance with Croatia, and opened the possibility of a substantial US troop commitment to help guarantee any settlement.

Part of Clinton's selective engagement strategy rested on the idea, enunciated by National Security Adviser Anthony Lake in 1993, of 'backlash states'. According to Lake, the US needed to 'face the reality of recalcitrant and outlaw states' that assault the basic values of the post-Cold War 'family of nations', now committed to the pursuit of democracy and free markets. Lake listed the usual suspects: Iraq, Iran, Cuba, North Korea and Libya.[34] Though offering Saddam a 'new start' with the new Administration, Clinton supported the 13 January 1993 raid (ordered by President Bush on air defence sites in Southern Iraq.) He ordered a cruise missile assault on Baghdad intelligence headquarters to be launched in June 1993 in retaliation for an apparent Iraqi assassination plot against George Bush. The US continued to press for UN inspector access to nuclear sites and for continuation of international sanctions on Iraq, despite evidence that these were inflicting considerable suffering on the population. Swift US response was offered to Iraqi sabre-rattling at the Kuwaiti border in October, 1994. (Due to pre-positioning of heavy equipment, the US Army was able to deploy 4000 soldiers rapidly.) Washington's approach to Iraq and Iran was one of 'dual containment', exploiting geopolitical conditions and alliance structures emanating from the Gulf War. Sanctions were applied in the Spring of 1995 when it appeared that Iran was developing nuclear weapons. Despite the changed relationship with Vietnam, Cuba remained an official pariah during the early Clinton years. An agreement between Washington and Havana on Cuban refugees was reached in September, 1994. However, anti-Castro bureaucratic momentum, the continued vitality of the Monroe Doctrine, and the influence of Cuban exile lobbies in Congress all made the long-overdue normalisation and embargo relaxation difficult to accomplish.[35] If Cuba's 'threat' was mainly symbolic, North Korea certainly did pose a challenge both to nuclear nonproliferation codes and to the security of its Southern neighbour. The Clinton Administration offered a mixture of diplomatic pressure, military threats and bargaining to restrain Pyongyang. A diplomatic initiative headed by ex-President Carter opened the way to a deal in June 1994. Following the death (in July 1994) of North Korean dictator Kim Il Sung, Pyongyang agreed to dismantle its nuclear-weapons-fuel complex in exchange for energy-generating reactors.[36]

Though not enumerated by Anthony Lake as a 'backlash state', Haiti and its problems touched on many of the Administration's key preoccupations: regional security, immigration, drugs, as well as human rights and democracy promotion. Important domestic lobbies were also involved. The Congressional Black Caucus, protesting Clinton's reversal of campaign undertakings to admit Haitian refugees, pushed for active policies to restore Father Aristide. As in North Korea, the Administration tried a variety of means to pressure Haiti's military rulers. The forcible turning back of US and Canadian engineers, on board the USS *Harlan County* in October 1993, was a humiliation for the White House. In April 1994, Randall Robinson, director of TransAfrica, went on hunger strike to protest the Administration's handling of refugees. (The hunger strike was ended a month later, following compromises over the issue.) The US invasion of September 1994, undertaken with the backing of the UN Security Council, occurred against a background of intense Congressional anxiety. Prior mediation by Jimmy Carter and General Colin Powell ensured that the invasion proceeded without severe casualties. By the early part of 1995, the White House was able to claim Aristide's restoration as a success for its version of selective engagement.

(c) 'Enlargement' and Democracy Promotion

Clinton Administration officials repeatedly stressed that economic interests alone could not constitute a successful and popular foreign policy doctrine. Though direct references to the failed Carter Administration were avoided, important cues were picked up from Clinton's Democratic predecessor. US foreign policy needed some moral purpose. President Clinton declared in 1993 that human rights was to be its 'cornerstone'.[37] This search for moral purpose was amplified, and integrated into the Administration's post-Cold War economism, by National Security Adviser Anthony Lake in his 'enlargement' speech of September 1993. The Administration's principal aim was to be 'enlargement of democracy and free markets'.[38] For Clinton: 'The movement toward democracy is the best guarantor of human rights.' Taking up a theme from the Carter years, Clinton argued in 1993 against the view that 'human rights are relative and that they simply mask Western cultural imperialism'.[39] Warren Christopher insisted that democracy promotion was not a 'starry-eyed crusade'.[40] It was, as Deputy Secretary of State Strobe Talbott insisted in a 1994 lecture given at Oxford University, 'in our best interests'.[41]

At times, all this seemed like a reborn Wilsonianism: a restating of old notions about progress, American power, free markets and liberal democracy all advancing together without contradiction. The new Wilsonianism raised familiar doubts, at both the empirical and the theoretical level, about this apparently happy coincidence of democracy, free markets and US influence.[42] (How democratic were the new free market allies in Clinton's 'new Pacific community'?) Messianism, however, was not to be a major Administration characteristic. As we have seen, when democracy promotion conflicted with economic interest, the latter tended to win. Confronting 'backlash states' – the reversal on China policy in 1994 was also linked to the need to contain North Korea; securing markets; recognising post-Cold War limits on US unilateralism: these would have to take their place alongside 'enlargement'. This philosophy of pragmatic accommodation was proudly advertised and defended by Clinton operatives such as Deputy National Security Adviser Samuel R. Berger. None the less, in some parts of the world, the Administration was able to point to diplomatic pressure having headed off military coups, or generally having advanced the cause of democracy. The 1993 recognition of Angola and US policy in Guatemala could be interpreted in this light.[43] Christopher also cited the cases of Mozambique, Malawi and US involvement in the Northern Irish peace process.[44] Clinton was, rather implausibly, able to claim some credit for the agreement (announced in August 1993) between Palestinian leader Yasir Arafat and the Rabin Administration in Israel. Organised around the principle of self-determination for Palestinians in Gaza and the West Bank, the agreement had been brokered by Norway and represented a delayed achievement for Carter's Camp David diplomacy. A further Middle Eastern diplomatic initiative, coordinated by Dennis Ross of the State Department, allowed Clinton to claim more success in September 1995.

Strobe Talbott, architect of the Clinton Administration's policy towards the Soviet successor states, indicated in his 1994 Oxford speech that Russia occupied the centre of the strategy for democracy: 'A military rivalry among the great powers is far more likely to arise should one or more of those powers abandon its commitment to free trade, open markets, and an open society ... .'[45] Integration of Russia and the Soviet successor states into a stable European security system was a key Clinton Administration goal. In July 1993, Clinton declared that 'the crisis in Russia ... overshadowed every other challenge'.[46] Clinton offered a 'strategic alliance' with the cause of Russian reform. To Republicans in Washington this amounted to rather uncritical support for the Russian President – the policy of 'Yeltsin drunk or Yeltsin sober'. Talbott (elevated in January 1994 to second-in-command at State) succeeded in persuading the Administration against the immediate admittance of Poland, the Czech Republic and Hungary into NATO. The 1994 Partnership for Peace proposals were designed to alleviate Russia's anxieties in this area, and to provide a platform for trans-European security integration. The Administration was criticised for its confused response to the rightist gains in the Russian elections of December 1993. The revelations concerning Aldrich Ames and Russian penetration of the CIA also put pressure on Clinton's position. Despite nuclear agreements with Ukraine, Clinton was criticised for neglecting the non-Russian Soviet successors. The American President gained significant grants of aid for Russia. The 2.5 billion dollar package approved by Congress in 1993 for the former Soviet states included over 1.6 billion for Russia (promised by Clinton in his April 1993 Vancouver meeting with Yeltsin). Some of this Russian aid was in the form of low-interest food credits, and some was merely a repackaging of the 1992 Freedom Support Act. Clinton tried with limited success to persuade the G-7 nations to expand their direct aid to Russia. At their Tokyo meeting in 1993, the G-7 pledged over thirty billion dollars in new loans and grants, via the international financial institutions. In 1994, the Administration proposed 900 million dollars in aid to the former Soviet states; Congress appropriated 850 million. In any case, aid could not in any sense 'guarantee' the cause of Russian reform. By the early part of 1995, a host of difficulties – doubts over the viability of Partnership for Peace and even over the START nuclear agreement, the rise of nationalism in Russia, dissension over Moscow's use of force in Chechnya and sale of nuclear materials to Iran, disagreements provoked by the NATO airstrikes on the Bosnian Serbs – cast a deep shadow on the early Clinton vision of 'Russia First'.[47]

(d) Downsizing the Military

Vested interest, international uncertainties and anxieties about the domestic economic effects of cuts all inhibited the Clinton Administration's efforts to achieve a measured reduction in the military budget. For many years, the Pentagon's spending served as the nations's unacknowledged industrial and regional development strategy. Cuts could not be painless. Announcements made in 1993 indicated that, by 1998, Pentagon spending as a percentage of GDP would be less than half what it was in 1970.

The stage for the Clinton defence policy was set by Defence Secretary Les Aspin's 'bottom-up review', issued in September 1993. Aspin's main assumption was that the US needed strength to fight two near-simultaneous 'major regional conflicts'. The review specifically mentioned new aggression by 'a remilitarized Iraq' and by North

Korea.[48] The Administration committed itself to a 1.4 million active-duty military personnel force. Clinton's 263.7 billion defence request for fiscal year 1995 represented the first instalment of a 1.3 trillion five-year defence programme. The projections involved optimistic forecasts regarding Pentagon cost-cutting, inflation and use of the reserves. In 1993, Clinton abandoned SDI in favour of a system of 'theatre' defence, designed to protect American troops abroad. However, the defence requests involved the termination of only a few important programmes. In September 1994, the President sided with the military to oppose nuclear cutbacks to a 'core strategic force' of 500 each for Russia and the US. However, in early 1995, it was calculated that the Pentagon's real purchasing power had dropped by nearly one-third since fiscal year 1985.[49]

The debate over Clinton's defence strategy centred around the question of how spending levels related to commitments (including the commitment to keep 100 000 troops in Europe). Both Aspin and his successor, William Perry, acknowledged that there was a significant shortfall. In 1994, Perry promised that, beginning in fiscal year 1997, there would have to be a sharp increase in Pentagon procurement. The Republican victories in the 1994 mid-term elections opened up bitter battles over defence spending levels and anti-missile programmes. (The foreign and defence flank in the Republican 'Contract with America', promoted by House Speaker Newt Gingrich, passed the House, 241–181, on 17 February 1995 as the National Security Revitalization Act. The measure included generalised attempts to reverse defence cuts; to promote anti-missile programmes; to prevent US troops serving under UN command; and to aid the admission of Poland, Hungary, Slovakia and the Czech Republic to NATO. The Senate version, Senator Bob Dole's 1995 Peace Powers Act, was less sweeping, but also involved an assault on US participation in UN peacekeeping.)

FOUR THEMES AND THE NEW CONTEXT FOR US FOREIGN POLICY

We now return, in this book's final pages, to our four unifying themes: the legacy of the Vietnam War; the Cold War and its aftermath; democratic foreign policy; and arguments concerning American decline. The first two themes have been emphasised throughout this book, and may be disposed of briefly. The Vietnam War left a legacy of doubt (only temporarily deflected by Reagan) about America's international purpose; of inhibitions on the use of military power; and of the kind of generational conflict which surfaced in the 1992 Presidential election. The 'Vietnam syndrome' was no more extinguished by the Gulf War than by Reagan's military buildup in the early 1980s. During the Clinton years, crises in Somalia, Haiti and Bosnia all evoked Vietnam-related memories which still inhabited the national consciousness. Regarding our second theme, it is manifest that containment and the Cold War (despite Carter's attempt to break away) dominated US foreign policy until the later Bush years. The ending of the Cold War, despite the ensuing problems of disorder and fragmentation, created new opportunities for US foreign policy. From 1991 onwards, US foreign policy leaders began searching for a new paradigm to replace anti-communist containment: a new formula for reconciling ideals and interest, and for maintaining consensus at home and between allies. Bush's New World Order and Clinton's combination of economism and 'enlargement' were attempts to achieve this.

The search for a post-Cold War foreign policy has, and will continue to be, deeply affected by our two remaining themes: the claims and constraints of democratic foreign policy, and of American decline. It has been a major thesis of this book that recent Presidents – Reagan and Bush, certainly, and even Carter after 1978 – have failed to respect the claims of democratic and accountable foreign policy. Defined in terms of respecting the law, sharing power and information with Congress, avoiding excessive power concentration in the White House and controlling the intelligence agencies, democratic foreign policy is not – as is commonly supposed – the enemy of efficiency. It is salutary for foreign policy leaders to be forced seriously to consider policy alternatives. Persistence in error is a feature of over-centralised, secretive decision-making.[50] Contempt for the law and for Congress leads to the dislocations experienced in the later Reagan years. It has become a commonplace observation in literature on the CIA that legislative oversight can actually increase intelligence effectiveness, by building a supportive constituency for responsible Agency behaviour.[51] Similar effects may be felt in other areas. Only through stimulating trans-bureaucratic, inter-branch and public debate, can Presidents secure the kind of consensus needed to sustain effective policy. Moreover, the entire cast of post-Cold War foreign policy-making militates against tight executive direction. It is often argued that the international system itself tends to encourage Presidential domination.[52] However, the growth of international interdependence has provoked a disaggregation of the policy process. Trade deficits and increased trade dependency, energy dependency, increasing levels of foreign direct investment and the rise of economic opponents have all affected the process as well as the substance of US foreign policy. Productive, financial and informational 'global webs'[53] have little consonance with national boundaries. In areas stretching from economic competitiveness to immigration, domestic and foreign agendas interwine. Global news-reporting, pioneered by Cable News Network, can focus public and Congressional attention on international issues in an unpredictable way. Alongside globalisation, there has developed a localisation of the process, with sub-national actors (including the state governments) taking an increasingly important role.[54]

The Clinton Administration has been ambivalent about this new context. On the one hand, actions against Iraq and Haiti were taken with scant concern for Congressional war powers. Identical measures passed in House and Senate in September, 1994, criticised Clinton for failing to seek legislative authorisation before sending troops to Haiti. (The continued relevance of the 1973–4 war powers legislation was considered by three Senate committees in 1993. Republican Senator Dole's 1995 Peace Powers Act included a provision to repeal the legislation.) Clinton's inclinations certainly were not to invite Congress into a foreign policy-making partnership. On the other hand, the more that the White House promotes 'economic security' above traditional 'national security', the more it trumpets the interpermeability of domestic and foreign policy, the more must the executive be prepared to live with legislative activism and a disaggregated process. The ending of the Cold War prompted calls (notably from Senator Moynihan of New York) for the abolition of the traditional secret arm of Presidentially determined national security, the CIA. The whole debate about post-Cold War democratic foreign policy, of course, was re-cast by the Republican victories in 1994. The Republican majority's challenge to US participation in United Nations peacekeeping represented a major challenge to Clinton's authority. The challenge appeared to reflect a narrow and illiberal nationalism. Attacks on the 1995 foreign aid budget – only Israeli, Egyptian and Irish aid seemed relatively safe – evidenced a new unilateralism, if not yet a full-blown isolationism. What must be emphasised, however, is that Congress has every right to challenge the President. Supporters of democratic foreign policy must recognise that neither branch – neither President nor Congress – is always 'right' nor always 'wrong'. The commitment to democracy and to legal propriety must override substantive policy preference.

Lastly, we consider the most problematic of this book's four themes: American decline. The catalogue of American woes is familiar. Since the Reagan era, the country has borne massive budget deficits. There are problems of international competitiveness, low savings and investment, and trade deficits. (As well as with Japan, the US has high deficits with China, South Korea, Taiwan, Germany and Italy.) Manufacturing and farm employment have been in decline, though output has increased over the last ten years. The US has a rampant and expensive legal system, as well as a ramshackle and burdensome health care provision. There are problems deriving from the historical over-concentration on defence. As Bush found in Los Angeles in 1992, urban tensions will not disappear. The US also has a political process which is far from well suited to the addressing of long-term structural, and infrastructual, weaknesses.[55] Much of the declinist literature has, however, exaggerated the scale of America's economic (less so its social) difficulties. Traditional measures of economic strength are not always appropriate in an age of economic globalisation. One-sixth of all US trade is made up by transfers between branches of multinational corporations. US-based multinationals are generally more profitable than foreign-owned firms operating in the United States. The American worker is highly productive, particularly in the finance, insurance and real estate sector. Between 1980 and 1993, the growth in America's industrial production was greater than that in any of the G-7 countries apart from Japan. In key sectors, the US economy is innovative and dynamic. Important re-investment has occurred in many regions and industries. The US economy is complex and diverse: high-tech and low-tech, high and low wage. As in the past, immigration remains a potent source of cheap and productive labour. Defence conversion is a major problem, and the political system does make it difficult to achieve ordered restructuring. It does not make it impossible.[56]

The social dislocations which are consequent upon untrammelled capitalism point to the need for governmental action at home, as well as raising the prospect that any post-Cold War free market consensus (whether in Russia or elsewhere) will be unstable and temporary. However, the Cold War certainly did end in an immediate victory for orthodox American free market ideology. The immediate post-Cold War world, however, was also a world of fragmentation, hypernationalism and (especially in Asia) clear evidence that liberal economics do not invariably go alongside liberal democratic political forms. Fragmentation in the new world order was balanced by interdependence, 'global webs' and rapid communications. Apparent 'American decline' in the 1990s may be explained in terms of the need to adjust to these various developments. Though shaken to the roots by the Vietnam War, America's sense of universalism and national mission was sustained during the Cold War. However, the demise of Soviet communism did not automatically reveal American political liberalism as the model for the world. Nationalist and religious fundamentalism, as well as autocratic capitalism, were apparently equally beguiling options. *Pari passu*, global interdependence also called American exceptionalism into question. Perhaps the US was an 'ordinary country' after all? Christopher Thorne declared in 1991 that 'the growing menace of vast environmental hazards' might 'foster a greater sense that Americans are in the same boat as the rest of humankind rather than being the owner-passengers on a separate and uniquely privileged ship of state'.[57] The US cannot now (if it ever could) bend the world to its will. We live, as President Carter recognised in the 1970s, in an age of limits. A more hemispherically oriented, Pacificised, economistic American foreign policy is probably inevitable in contemporary conditions, and is indeed desirable. What is undesirable is a movement towards narrow nationalism and cultural introversion. The task of US foreign policy leaders – in both the White House and Congress – is to rescue America's democratic mission, to amputate from it the accretions of imperialism, thus fitting it to the new requirements of leadership.

Bibliographical Note

Much of the important secondary literature on recent US foreign policy may be found in specialist journals, notably *Foreign Affairs, Foreign Policy, International Security* and *International Affairs*. Memoirs also constitute a vital source for the writer of contemporary history. George Shultz's *Turmoil and Triumph* (New York: Scribner's Sons, 1993) is indispensable. The following memoirs also proved of value in writing this book: Zbigniew Brzezinski, *Power and Principle* (London: Weidenfeld and Nicolson, 1983); Cyrus Vance, *Hard Choices* (New York: Simon and Schuster, 1983); Alexander Haig, *Caveat* (New York: Macmillan, 1984); and Colin Powell, *A Soldier's Way* (London: Hutchinson, 1995). Anatoly Dobrynin's *In Confidence* (New York: Random House, 1995) also contains much that is revealing of changing Soviet perceptions of American policy. Detailed suggestions for further reading are given in the footnotes to my main text. However, special mention may be made of important works relating to this book's four main themes. On the lasting impact of the Vietnam War, see Richard Melanson, *Reconstructing Consensus* (New York: St Martin's, 1991). The best single volume history of the Cold War is Richard Crockatt's *The Fifty Years War* (London: Routledge, 1995). The literature on the ending of the Cold War is already vast, but important aspects of it are well represented in the following: Raymond Garthoff, *The Great Transition* (Washington DC: Brookings, 1994); J.L. Gaddis, *The United States and the End of the Cold War* (New York: Oxford University Press, 1992); R.N. Lebow and T. Risse-Knappen, eds, *International Relations Theory and the End of the Cold War* (New York: Columbia University Press, 1995); and R. Summy and M.E. Salla, eds, *Why The Cold War Ended* (Westport, Connecticut: Greenwood Press, 1995). On subsequent developments, see Michael Cox, *US Foreign Policy After the Cold War* (London: Pinter/Royal Institute of International Affairs, 1995). The decline debate may be followed in: Paul Kennedy, *The Rise and Fall of the Great Powers* (London: Unwin Hyman, 1988); H.R. Nau, *The Myth of American Decline* (Oxford: Oxford University Press, 1990); J.S. Nye, *Bound to Lead* (New York: Basic Books, 1991); and E.N. Luttwack, *The Endangered American Dream* (New York: Simon and Schuster, 1993). On the possibilities for democratic foreign policy, see: Harold H. Koh, *The National Security Constitution* (New Haven: Yale University Press, 1990); Miroslav Nincic, *Democracy and Foreign Policy* (New York: Columbia University Press, 1992); and Louis Fisher, *Presidential War Power* (Lawrence: University Press of Kansas, 1995). Lastly, a particular recommendation for Gaddis Smith, *Morality, Reason and*

Power (New York: Hill and Wang, 1986), still the best single book on Jimmy Carter's foreign policy, and for Thomas J. McCormick, *America's Half-Century* (Baltimore: Johns Hopkins University Press, 1989).

Notes

Chapter 1

1. *American Foreign Policy Current Documents 1987* (Washington DC: Department of State, 1988) p. 29.
2. R. Reagan, *An American Life* (New York: Simon and Schuster, 1990) p. 715.
3. Cited in C.W. Kegley and E.R. Wittkopf, *American Foreign Policy: Pattern and Process* (London: Macmillan, 1987) p. 75.
4. Reprinted in G.F. Kennan, *American Diplomacy 1900–1950* (New York: Mentor, 1951) pp. 99, 105.
5. L.H. Gelb, 'What Exactly is Kissinger's Legacy?', *New York Times Magazine* (31 October 1976).
6. In 1982 constant dollars (see M.M. Ball, *National Security Planning: Roosevelt Through Reagan* (Lexington: University Press of Kentucky, 1988) p. 192.
7. See generally F. Halliday, *The Making of the Second Cold War* (London: Verso, 1983) chapter 2; F. Halliday, 'The Cold War as Inter-systemic Conflict', in M. Bowker and R. Brown (eds), *From Cold War to Collapse* (Cambridge: Cambridge University Press, 1993); M. Cox, 'The Cold War as a System', *Critique*, 17 (1986) 17–82; J. Dumbrell, *The Making of US Foreign Policy* (Manchester: Manchester University Press, 1990) chapters 1 and 2; R. Crockatt, *The United States and the Cold War 1941–53* (British Association for American Studies pamphlet, 1989).
8. See *National Journal* (19 January 1980) (Harris polling); R.A. Melanson, *Reconstructing Consensus: American Foreign Policy Since the Vietnam War* (New York: St Martins, 1991) p. 15.
9. See J. Dumbrell, *Vietnam: American Involvement at Home and Abroad* (British Association for American Studies pamphlet, 1992); O.R. Holsti and J.N. Rosenau, *American Leadership in World Affairs: Vietnam and the Breakdown of Consensus* (Boston: Allen and Unwin, 1984).
10. Reagan, *An American Life*, p. 451.
11. See, for example, H. Cardoso and E. Falletto, *Dependency and Underdevelopment in Latin America* (Berkeley: University of California Press, 1971).
12. *Congressional Quarterly (CQ) Almanac 1971*, p. 770.
13. G. Vidal, *Armageddon? Essays 1983–1987* (London: Grafton, 1989) pp. 115–25.

14. See P. Kennedy, *The Rise and Fall of the Great Powers* (London: Unwin Hyman, 1988); D. Calleo, *The Imperious Economy* (Cambridge, Mass: Harvard University Press, 1982); D. Calleo, *Beyond American Hegemony: The Future of the Western Alliance* (New York: Basic Books, 1987); P.G. Cerny, 'Political Entropy and American Decline', *Millenium*, 18 (1989) 47–63; E.N. Luttwack, *The Endangered American Dream* (New York: Simon and Schuster, 1993).
15. See G. Smith, 'A Future for the Nation-State?', in L. Tivey (ed.), *The Nation-State* (Oxford: Robertson, 1981).
16. S. Gill, 'The Rise and Decline of the Great Powers: The American Case', *Politics*, 8 (1988) 3–9, 5.
17. S. Strange, 'The Future of the American Empire', *Journal of International Affairs*, 42 (1988) 1–17, 5.
18. J.S. Nye, *Bound to Lead: The Changing Nature of American Power* (New York: Basic Books, 1991) pp. 259–60. See also H.R. Nau, *The Myth of American Decline* (Oxford: Oxford University Press, 1990).
19. H.H. Koh, *The National Security Constitution* (New Haven: Yale University Press, 1990) p. 211.
20. *US v. Curtiss-Wright Export Corp.*, 299 US 304 (1936).
21. Final Report of the Senate Select Committee to Study Governmental Operations with Respect to Intelligence Activities (Church Committee Report), 1976, Book 1 ('Foreign and Military Intelligence') p. 9.
22. Cited in N.A. Graebner, *America as a World Power* (Wilmington: Scholarly Resources, 1984) p. 259.
23. G.W. Ball, *Diplomacy for a Crowded World* (Boston: Little, Brown, 1976) p. 14.

Chapter 2

1. See M. MacPherson, *Long Time Passing: Vietnam and the Haunted Generation* (Garden City, NY: Doubleday, 1984) p. 350.
2. *Public Papers of the Presidents of the United States: Jimmy Carter, 1977*, vol. 2 (Washington DC: US Government Printing Office, 1978) p. 956.
3. Cited in J. Carter, *Keeping Faith: Memoirs of a President* (London: Collins, 1982) p. 120.
4. *Public Papers ... 1977*, vol. 2, p. 956.
5. *The Presidential Campaign 1976*, vol. 1, part 2 (Washington DC: US Government Printing Office, 1978) p. 994. The phrase, 'wheeler-healer' was coined by Eric Sevareid (see M. Janeway, 'Campaigning', *Atlantic Monthly* (October 1976) 6–14).
6. *Congressional Quarterly Weekly Report*, 15 January 1977, p. 79.
7. *Ibid.*, p. 77.
8. Cited in J.M. Burns, *The Power to Lead* (New York: Simon and Schuster, 1986) pp. 23–4.
9. J. Carter, Miller Center (University of Virginia) interview transcript, p. 69 (available at Carter Presidential Library, Atlanta, Georgia).

10. *The Presidential Campaign 1976*, vol. 1, part 2, p. 735 (September 1976 interview).
11. *Congressional Quarterly Weekly Report*, 15 January 1977, p. 79.
12. See, for example, T.E. Mann and N.J. Ornstein, eds, *The New Congress* (Washington DC: American Enterprise Institute, 1981).
13. *Congressional Quarterly Weekly Report*, 21 Febuary 1977, p. 361.
14. Memo to the President from Jordan, June 1977, box 34, Jordan (Carter Library).
15. *Ibid.*.
16. See P. Warnke, 'Apes on a Treadmill', *Foreign Policy*, 18 (1975) 12–29.
17. See C.O. Jones, *The Trusteeship Presidency: Jimmy Carter and the United States Congress* (Baton Rouge: Louisiana State University Press, 1988).
18. Memo cited at note 14.
19. K.W. Thompson (ed.), *The Carter Presidency* (Lanham: University Press of America, 1990) p. 142.
20. Jordan interview, *Playboy* (November, 1976).
21. See R.A. Melanson, *Writing History and Making Policy* (Lanham: University Press of America, 1983) p. 248.
22. 'Sailing Without an Anchor', BBC (Radio 3) broadcast, 14 March 1990; see also G.A. Andrianopoulos, *Kissinger and Brzezinski: The NSC and the Struggle for Control of US National Security Policy* (London: Macmillan, 1991).
23. Cited in F.J. Smist, *Congress Oversees the Intelligence Community* (Knoxville: University of Tennessee Press, 1990) p. 110.
24. Z. Brzezinski, *Power and Principle* (London: Weidenfeld and Nicolson, 1983) p. 3, 52–4.
25. See especially R.O. Keohane and J.S. Nye, *Power and Interdependence* (Boston: Little, Brown, 1977); S. Hoffman, *Primacy or World Order* (New York: McGraw-Hill, 1978); Z. Brzezinski, *Between Two Ages: America's Role in the Technetronic Era* (New York: Viking, 1970).
26. See Z. Brzezinski, 'The Deceptive Structure of Peace', *Foreign Policy*, 14 (1974) 73–85. On the Trilateral Commission, see S. Gill, *American Hegemony and the Trilateral Commission* (Cambridge: Cambridge University Press, 1990).
27. Z. Brzezinski *et al.*, Miller Center interview transcript, p. 52.
28. *Congressional Quarterly Weekly Report*, 22 January 1977, p. 106.
29. Z. Brzezinski *et al.*, Miller Center interview transcript, p. 49.
30. *Ibid.*
31. D.P. Moynihan, 'The Politics of Human Rights', *Commentary* (August 1977) 22.
32. Memo to the President from Jordan, 3 December 1977, box 34, Jordan.
33. *American Foreign Policy: Basic Documents, 1977–1980* (Washington DC: US Government Printing Office, 1983) p. 433.
34. Memo to S. Elizenstat from Daft, 22 November 1977, box 208, Elizenstat.
35. See generally J. Muravchik, *The Uncertain Crusade* (Lanham: Hamilton Press, 1986); A.G. Mower, *Human Rights and American Foreign Policy:*

202   *Notes*

The Carter and Reagan Experiences (Westport: Greenwood, 1987); E.S. Maynard, 'The Bureaucracy and Implementation of US Human Rights Policy', *Human Rights Quarterly*, 11 (1989) 175–248.

36. *American Foreign Policy: Basic Documents*, p. 415.
37. Memo to Z. Brzezinski from Matthews, 7 July 1978, box HU-2, White House Central File: Human Rights.
38. *Department of State Bulletin*, September 1979, p. 46.
39. Memo to the President from Powell, 21 Febuary 1977, box 46, Lipshutz.
40. Memo to Z. Brzezinski from Pastor, 4 May 1979, box CO-9, White House Central File: Countries.
41. Cited in J. Pearce, *Under The Eagle* (London: Latin American Bureau, 1982) p. 119.
42. *American Foreign Policy: Basic Documents*, p. 293.
43. Cited in J. Rosati, 'Jimmy Carter, a Man Before his Time?', *Presidential Studies Quarterly*, 23 (1993) 459–76.
44. *Department of State Bulletin*, 24 October 1977, p. 552.
45. This view was also expressed by 'neo-realist' writers like R.E. Feinberg, (*The Intemperate Zone: The Third World Challenge to US Foreign Policy* (New York: Norton, 1983)).
46. *American Foreign Policy: Basic Documents*, p. 1131.
47. *Ibid.*, pp. 292–3.
48. See R.A. Pastor, *Whirlpool* (Princeton: Princeton University Press, 1992) pp. 60–4.
49. *American Foreign Policy: Basic Documents*, p. 14; also, Pastor, *Whirlpool*, p. 3.
50. Cited in J.D. Cockcroft, *Neighbors in Turmoil* (New York: Harper and Row, 1989) p. 214.
51. Z. Brzezinski *et al.*, Miller Center interview transcript, p. 89.
52. D. Skidmore, 'Foreign Policy Interest Groups and Presidential Power', *Presidential Studies Quarterly*, 23 (1993) 477–97.
53. *American Foreign Policy: Basic Documents*, p. 1131.
54. Special briefing at Department of State, 15 August 1979, box 79, Powell.
55. Hearings before the Subcommittee on Africa of the House Committee on Foreign Affairs, 'US Interests in Africa', October–November 1979, p. 3.
56. Brzezinski, *Power and Principle*, p. 139.
57. Hearings, 'US Interests in Africa', p. 48.
58. Hearings before the Subcommittees on Africa, Internationl Economic Policy and International Organisations of the House Committee on Foreign Affairs, 'US Policy toward South Africa', April–June 1980, p. 7.
59. See R.J. Barnet, *The Alliance: America, Europe, Japan* (New York: Simon and Schuster, 1983) p. 388.
60. D. Owen, *Time to Declare* (London: Penguin, 1992) p. 320.
61. See M.F. Goldman, 'President Carter, Western Europe, and Afghanistan in 1980', in H.D. Rosenbaum and A. Ugrinsky (eds), *Jimmy Carter: Foreign Policy and Post-Presidential Years* (Westport: Greenwood, 1994). On Northern Irish issues, see J. Dumbrell, *The Carter Presidency: A Re-evaluation* (Manchester: Manchester University Press, 1993) pp. 130–41.

62. Owen, *Time to Declare*, p. 320.
63. Carter, *Keeping Faith* p. 235.
64. Department of State Bulletin, Febuary 1978, p. 34 (R.N. Cooper).
65. *Ibid.*, October 1980, p. 53 (H. Kopp).
66. R.C. Thornton, *The Carter Years: Toward a New Global Order* (New York: Paragon House, 1991) p. 86.
67. R. Drifte, *Japan's Foreign Policy* (London: Routledge, 1990) p. 29.
68. Report of a Study Group, *Toward Peace in the Middle East* (Washington DC: Brookings, 1975).
69. W.B. Quandt, *Peace Process* (Washington DC: Brookings, 1993) p. 257.
70. C. Vance, *Hard Choices: Critical Years in America's Foreign Policy* (New York: Simon and Schuster, 1983) p. 165.
71. Quandt, *Peace Process*, p. 267.
72. *American Foreign Policy: Basic Documents*, p. 650.
73. Thornton, *The Carter Years*, p. 288. See also T.G. Fraser, *The USA and the Middle East since World War 2* (London: Macmillan, 1989) pp. 141–58.
74. See, for example, W.B. Quandt, *Camp David: Peacemaking and Politics* (Washington DC: Brookings, 1986); M. Dayan, *Breakthrough: A Personal Account of the Egypt–Israel Peace Negotiations* (New York: Knopf, 1981); E. Weizman, *The Battle for Peace* (New York: Bantam, 1981); Carter, *Keeping Faith*, pp. 269–430. See also S. Segev, 'Did President Carter Miss an Opportunity for Peace?', in Rosenbaum and Ugrinsky (eds), *Jimmy Carter*.
75. Quandt, *Peace Process*, p. 308.
76. J. Carter, *The Blood of Abraham* (Boston: Houghton Mifflin, 1985) p. 45.
77. Memo to the President from Donovan, 7 Febuary 1980, box 2, Donovan.
78. Quandt, *Peace Process*, p. 315.

Chapter 3

1. Z. Brzezinski *et al.*, Miller Center (University of Virginia) interview transcript, p. 52 (available at Carter Presidential Library, Atlanta, Georgia).
2. See R.C. Thornton, *The Carter Years: Toward a New Global Order* (New York: Paragon House, 1991) p. 8.
3. See T.J. McCormick, *America's Half Century* (Baltimore: Johns Hopkins University Press, 1989) p. 206.
4. Cited in J. Ranelagh, *The Agency: The Rise and Decline of the CIA* (London: Weidenfeld and Nicolson, 1986) p. 653.
5. K. Thompson (ed.), *The Carter Presidency* (Lanham: University Press of America, 1990) p. 125.
6. Cited in H. Jordan, *Crisis: The Last Year of the Carter Presidency* (New York: Putnam's Sons, 1982) p. 60.
7. Memo to Z. Brzezinski from Tarnoff, 23 September 1977, box CO-31, White House Central Files: Countries.

8. G. Sick, *All Fall Down: America's Tragic Encounter with Iran* (New York: Random House, 1985) p. 25.

9. Cited in G. Smith, *Morality, Reason and Power: American Diplomacy in the Carter Years* (New York: Hill and Wang, 1986) p. 186.

10. See A. Taheri, *The Spirit of Allah: Khomeini and the Islamic Revolution* (London: Hutchinson, 1985) pp. 211–14.

11. Z. Brzezinski *et al.*, Miller Center interview transcript, p. 69.

12. G.W. Ball, *The Past Has Another Pattern* (New York: Norton, 1982), p. 460.

13. J. Carter, Miller Center interview transcript, p. 37.

14. Z. Brzezinski, Miller Center interview transcript, p. 90.

15. W. Christopher *et al.*, *American Hostages in Iran: Conduct of a Crisis* (New Haven: Yale University Press, 1985) p. 7.

16. See G. Sick, *October Surprise* (London: I.B. Tauris, 1991); R. Parry, *Trick or Treason* (New York: Sheridan Square Press, 1993).

17. C. Vance, *Hard Choices: Critical Years in America's Foreign Policy* (New York: Simon and Schuster, 1983) p. 347.

18. *Ibid.*

19. Ball, *The Past Has Another Pattern*, p. 456. See also J.A. Bill, *The Eagle and the Lion: The Tragedy of American–Iranian Relations* (New Haven: Yale University Press, 1988); W.H. Sullivan, *Mission to Iran* (New York: Norton, 1981).

20. See R.A. Pastor, *Condemned to Repetition: The United States and Nicaragua* (Princeton: Princeton University Press, 1988); J. Theberge, 'The Collapse of the Somoza Regime', in D. Pipes and A. Garfinkle (eds), *Friendly Tyrants: An American Dilemma* (London: Macmillan, 1991).

21. Pastor, *Condemned to Repetition*, p. 79.

22. Letter to L. Hamilton from Bennet, 24 Oct. 1978, box CO-46, White House Central Files: Countries.

23. A. Lake, *Somoza Falling* (Boston: Houghton Mifflin, 1989) p. 263.

24. *Ibid.*, p. 261.

25. Memo to Z. Brzezinski and D. Aaron from Pastor, 20 September 1979, box CO-47, White House Central File: Countries.

26. Cited in W. LaFeber, *Inevitable Revolutions: The United States in Central America* (New York: Norton, 1983) p. 239. See also L. and R. Pezzullo, *At the Fall of Somoza* (Pittsburgh: University of Pittsburgh Press, 1994).

27. Memo to Z. Brzezinski and D. Aaron from Pastor, 15 August 1980, box CO-47, White House Central File: Countries.

28. See M.L. Cottam, 'The Carter Administration's Policy toward Nicaragua: Images, Goals and Tactics', *Political Science Quarterly*, 107 (1992) 123–46.

29. Cited in A.R. Hybel, *How Leaders Reason: US Intervention in the Caribbean Basin and Latin America* (Oxford: Blackwell, 1990) p. 239.

30. Z. Brzezinski, 'From Cold War to Cold Peace', in G.B. Urban (ed.), *Detente* (London: Temple Smith, 1976) p. 265.

31. Cited in B.I. Kaufman, *The Presidency of James Earl Carter, Jr.* (Lawrence: University Press of Kansas, 1993) p. 39.

32. See S. Gill, *American Hegemony and the Trilateral Commission* (Cambridge: Cambridge University Press, 1990) p. 233; also B. Buzan, *People, States and Fear* (London: Harvester Wheatsheaf, 1991) p. 302.
33. Brzezinski, 'From Cold War to Cold Peace', p. 268.
34. Z. Brzezinski *et al.*, Miller Center interview transcript, p. 56.
35. Presidential Review Memorandum 10: see B. Garrett, 'China Policy and the Constraints of Triangular Logic', in K.A. Oye *et al.* (eds), *Eagle Defiant: United States Foreign Policy in the 1980s* (Boston: Little, Brown, 1983) p. 246.
36. Z. Brzezinski, *Power and Principle* (London: Weidenfeld and Nicolson, 1983) p. 148.
37. S. Talbott, *Endgame: The Inside Story of SALT II* (London: Harper and Row, 1979) pp. 49, 76.
38. Brzezinski, *Power and Principle*, p. 148.
39. *Ibid.*
40. Memo to Z. Brzezinski from Brown, 8 March 1978, box 77, Presidential Handwriting File.
41. R.C. Thornton, *The Carter Years: Toward A New Global Order* (New York: Paragon House, 1991). See also R.L. Garthoff's review, *American Historical Review*, 98 (1993) 979.
42. Brzezinski, *Power and Principle*, p. 147.
43. Talbott, *Endgame*, p. 78.
44. A. Moens, *Foreign Policy under Carter: Testing Multiple Advocacy Decision-Making* (Boulder: Westview, 1990) p. 171.
45. Cited in R.D. Schulzinger, *American Diplomacy in the Twentieth Century* (New York: Oxford University Press, 1990) p. 328.
46. Talbott, *Endgame*, p. 136. See also E.L. Rowny, *It Takes One To Tango* (Washington DC: Brassey's, 1992).
47. J. Carter, *Keeping Faith: Memoirs of a President* (London: Collins, 1982) p. 241.
48. Vance, *Hard Choices*, p. 349.
49. D. Caldwell, *The Dynamics of Domestic Politics and Arms Control: The SALT II Treaty Ratification Debate* (Columbia: University of South Carolina Press, 1991) pp. 47, 184.
50. Report of the Senate Foreign Relations Committee, 'The SALT II Treaty', November 1979, p. 282.
51. Cited in Smith, *Morality, Reason and Power*, p. 93.
52. Brzezinski, *Power and Principle*, p. 515.
53. *Ibid.*, p. 40.
54. Moens, *Foreign Policy under Carter*, p. 173.
55. Goldwater *et al.* v. Carter *et al.*, 444 US 996 (1979) (The Supreme Court dismissed the case.)
56. See M. Oksenberg, 'A Decade of Sino-American Relations', *Foreign Affairs*, 61 (1982) 175–95.
57. *Morality, Reason and Power*, p. 97.
58. Ibid.
59. R.L. Garthoff, *Detente and Confrontation: American–Soviet Relations from Nixon to Reagan* (Washington DC: Brookings, 1985) p. 742.

60. C. Gershman, 'The Rise and Fall of the New Foreign-Policy Establishment', *Commentary*, (July, 1980) p. 22.
61. D. Yankelovich and L. Kaagan, 'Assertive America', *Foreign Affairs*, 60 (1981) 696–713, 696.
62. See D.D. Newsom, *The Soviet Brigade in Cuba* (Bloomington: Indiana University Press, 1987).
63. Interview with G.F. Kennan, *US News and World Report*, 10 March 1980, p. 33.
64. Memo to T. Sand from Jody Powell, undated, box 79, Powell (on key issues for Administration speakers).
65. Memo to the President from A. McDonald, 8 January 1980, box 78, Powell ('Possible briefing ideas').
66. Briefing in Cabinet room, 15 January 1980, box 79, Powell.
67. *Department of State Bulletin*, January 1980 (Carter Address, 4 January 1980).
68. *Congressional Quarterly Weekly Report*, 26 January 1980, p. 201.
69. Cited in C.V. Crabb, *The Doctrines of American Foreign Policy* (Baton Rouge: Louisiana State University Press, 1982) p. 332.
70. *Department of State Bulletin*, August [*sic*] 1980, p. 62.
71. Memo to the President from Donovan, 2 January 1980, box 2, Donovan.
72. *Department of State Bulletin*, May 1980, p. 27.
73. Kennedy, speech at Georgetown University, 28 January 1980 (box 13, Speechwriters: Special File).
74. Jordan, *Crisis*, p. 47.
75. See S. Turner, *Secrecy and Democracy* (Boston: Houghton Mifflin, 1985).
76. H.H. Koh, *The National Security Constitution* (New Haven: Yale University Press, 1990) p. 122.
77. See J. Dumbrell, *The Carter Presidency: A Re-evaluation* (Manchester: Manchester University Press, 1993); J. Rosati, 'Jimmy Carter, a Man Before his Time?', *Presidential Studies Quarterly*, 23 (1993) 459–76.
78. In 1982 constant dollars (see M.M. Boll, *National Security Planning: Roosevelt Through Reagan* (Lexington: University Press of Kentucky, 1988) p. 192).

Chapter 4

1. See W. Schneider, 'The November 4 Vote for President', in A. Ranney ed., *The American Elections of 1980* (Washington DC: American Enterprise Institute, 1981); R.D. Schulzinger, *American Diplomacy in the Twentieth Century* (New York: Oxford University Press, 1984) p. 339.
2. Cited in R. Dugger, *On Reagan: The Man and His Presidency* (New York: McGraw-Hill, 1983) p. 344.
3. Cited in R. Dallek, *Ronald Reagan: The Politics of Symbolism* (Cambridge, Massachusetts: Harvard University Press, 1984) p. 49.
4. L.J. Barrett, *Gambling With History: Ronald Reagan in the White House* (Garden City: Doubleday, 1983) p. 207.

5. Dallek, *Ronald Reagan*, p. 58.
6. *Congressional Quarterly Weekly Report*, 24 January 1981, p. 188.
7. See C. Bell, *The Reagan Paradox: American Foreign Policy in the 1980s* (Aldershot: Elgar, 1989); M. Smith, 'The Reagan Presidency and Foreign Policy', in J. Hogan ed., *The Reagan Years: The Record in Presidential Leadership* (Manchester: Manchester University Press, 1990).
8. See, for example, M. Poster ed. and trans., *Jean Baudrillard: Selected Writings* (London: Blackwell, 1990).
9. M. Schaller, *Reckoning With Reagan: America and its President in the 1980s* (New York: Oxford University Press, 1992), p. 122.
10. G. Wills, *Reagan's America: Innocents at Home* (London: Heinemann, 1988) p. 4.
11. W. Schneider, 'Rambo and Reality: Having it Both Ways', in K.A. Oye, R.J. Lieber and D. Rothchild, eds, *Eagle Resurgent? The Reagan Era in American Foreign Policy* (Boston: Little, Brown, 1987) p. 70.
12. *American Foreign Policy Current Documents 1984* (Washington DC: Department of State, 1986) p. 61 (April 1984 speech at Georgetown University).
13. Cited in M. Turner, 'Foreign Policy and the Reagan Administration', in J.D. Lees and M. Turner, eds, *Reagan's First Four Years: A New Beginning?* (Manchester: Manchester University Press, 1988) p. 127.
14. See W.K. Muir, 'Ronald Reagan: The Primacy of Rhetoric', in F.I. Greenstein, ed., *Leadership in the Modern Presidency* (Cambridge, Massachusetts: Harvard University Press, 1988).
15. *Department of State Bulletin*, June 1981, p. 33.
16. Cited in R. Melanson, *Reconstructing Consensus: American Foreign Policy Since the Vietnam War* (New York: St Martins, 1991) p. 149 (Haig, 1982).
17. Cited in J.W. Sanders, *Peddlers of Crisis* (London: Pluto Press, 1983) p. 277. See also H.C. Tyroler, ed., *Alerting America* (Washington DC: Pergamon-Brassey's, 1984) and S. Dalby, *Creating the Second Cold War: The Discourse of Politics* (London: Pinter, 1990).
18. Cited in Sanders, *Peddlers of Crisis*, p. 279.
19. *National Journal*, 25 April 1981, p. 729.
20. Sanders, *Peddlers of Crisis*, pp. 16, 20.
21. *Ibid.*, p. 10.
22. *Ibid.*, p. 330.
23. *National Journal*, 29 May 1982, p. 960.
24. See, for example, D. Bandow *et al.*, *US Aid to the Developing World: A Free Market Agenda* (Washington DC: Heritage, 1985).
25. *National Journal*, 15 May 1982, p. 763.
26. *National Journal*, 12 September 1981, p. 1631.
27. *Ibid.*
28. *National Journal*, 15 May 1982, p. 763.
29. See J.J. Kirkpatrick, 'Dictatorship and Double Standards', in H.J. Wiarda, ed., *Human Rights and U.S. Human Rights Policy* (Washington DC: American Enterprise Institute, 1981).

30. Cited in C.W. Kegley and E.R. Wittkopf, *American Foreign Policy: Pattern and Process* (London: Macmillan, 1987) p. 186.
31. See A. Tonelson, 'Nitze's World', *Foreign Policy*, 35 (1979) 74–90; R. Kolkowicz, 'The Strange Career of the Defense Intellectuals', *Orbis*, 31 (1987) 179–92.
32. Cited in L. Cannon, *President Reagan: The Role of a Lifetime* (New York: Simon and Schuster, 1991) p. 134.
33. D.T. Regan, *For the Record* (London: Arrow, 1988).
34. Cannon, *President Reagan*, pp. 137–8.
35. Regan, *For The Record*, p. 294.
36. Cannon, *President Reagan*, p. 132.
37. *National Journal*, 28 November 1981, p. 2114.
38. L. Speakes, *Speaking Out* (New York: Scribner's Sons, 1984) p. 265.
39. Cannon, *President Reagan*, p. 189.
40. A.M. Haig, *Caveat: Realism, Reagan and Foreign Policy* (New York: Macmillan, 1984) p. 73.
41. M.K. Deaver, *Behind The Scenes* (New York: Morrow, 1987) p. 43.
42. R. Reagan, *An American Life* (New York: Simon and Schuster, 1990) p. 284.
43. J. Spanier and E.M. Uslaner, *American Foreign Policy and the Democratic Dilemmas* (Pacific Grove: Brooks Cole, 1989) pp. 55–6.
44. G.P. Shultz, *Turmoil and Triumph: My Years as Secretary of State* (New York: Scribner's Sons, 1993) pp. 275, 1133.
45. See I.M. Destler, 'The Evolution of Reagan's Foreign Policy', in F.I. Greenstein ed., *The Reagan Presidency: An Early Assessment* (Baltimore: Johns Hopkins University Press 1983) p. 118.
46. See C.H. Percy, 'The Partisan Gap', *Foreign Policy*, 45 (1981–2) 82–103.
47. See D.C. Waller, *Congress and the Nuclear Freeze* (Amherst: University of Massachusetts Press, 1987).
48. B.D. Berkowitz and A.E. Goodman, *Strategic Intelligence for American National Security* (Princeton: Princeton University Press, 1989) p. 46.
49. *Congressional Quarterly Weekly Report*, 14 April 1984, p. 823; B. Woodward, *Veil: The Secret Wars of the CIA 1981–1987* (New York: Simon and Schuster, 1987) p. 200; L.K. Johnson, 'Legislative Reform of Intelligence Policy', *Polity*, 17 (1985) 549–73, p. 566.
50. See W.W. Kaufmann, 'A Defense Agenda for Fiscal Years 1990–1994' in J.D. Steinbruner ed., *Restructuring American Foreign Policy* (Washington DC: Brookings, 1989) p. 57.
51. Haig, *Caveat*, p. 29; *American Foreign Policy Current Documents 1984*, p. 181 (Reagan April 1984 speech at Georgetown University).
52. *Department of State Bulletin*, December 1982, p. 33.
53. *Department of State Bulletin*, April 1981, p. 16.
54. Cited in R.A. Stubbing, *The Defense Game* (New York: Harper and Row, 1986) p. 376. See also D. Wirls, *Buildup: The Politics of Defense in the Reagan Era* (Ithaca: Cornell University Press, 1992).
55. Stubbing, *The Defense Game*, p. 391.

56. P.M. Smith, *Assignment: Pentagon* (Washington DC: Pergamon-Brassey's, 1989) p. 169.
57. Cited in F. Halliday, *The Making of the Second Cold War* (London: Verso, 1983) p. 124.
58. P. Williams, 'The Reagan Administration and Defence Policy' in D.M. Hill, R.A. Moore and P. Williams, eds, *The Reagan Presidency: An Incomplete Revolution?* (London: Macmillan, 1990) p. 205.
59. C.W. Weinberger, 'U.S. Defense Strategy', *Foreign Affairs*, 64 (1986) 675–97; M.M. Ball, *National Security Planning: Roosevelt Through Reagan* (Lexington: University Press of Kentucky, 1988) p. 218.
60. *National Journal*, 7 November 1981, p. 1995. See also P.G. Boyle, *American–Soviet Relations: From the Russian Revolution to the Fall of Communism* (London: Routledge, 1993) p. 203.
61. Reagan, *An American Life*, p. 547. See also D.R. Baucom, *The Origins of SDI, 1944–1983* (Lawrence: University of Kansas Press, 1992).
62. *Ibid.*, p. 548.
63. *American Foreign Policy and the Democratic Dilemmas*, p. 318.
64. *American Foreign Policy Current Documents 1982* (Washington DC: Department of State, 1986) p. 47.
65. Cited in M. Walker, *The Cold War and the Making of the Modern World* (London: Fourth Estate, 1993) p. 275.
66. Cited in Turner, 'Foreign Policy and the Reagan Administration', p. 189; Bell, *The Reagan Paradox*, p. 52. (The 'dominoes' remark came from the 1980 election campaign; the 'right ... to lie' quotation from Reagan's first Presidential press conference).
67. Walker, *The Cold War*, p. 267.
68. Cited in Boyle, *American–Soviet Relations*, p. 200.
69. *Department of State Bulletin*, August 1981, p. 23.
70. *American Foreign Policy Current Documents 1982*, p. 16.
71. S. Bialer and J. Afferica, 'Reagan and Russia', *Foreign Affairs*, 61 (1982–3) 249–71, 271; S. Bialer and J. Afferica, 'Gorbachev's World', *Foreign Affairs*, 64 (*America and the World*, 1985) 605–44. See also M. Cox, 'The Collapse of Soviet Studies', in P. Dunleavy and J. Stanyer eds, *Contemporary Political Studies 1994*, Vol. 1 (Belfast: Political Studies Association, 1994) p. 39.
72. See R.W. Tucker, *The Purposes of American Power; An Essay on National Security* (New York: Praeger, 1981).
73. Department of State Bulletin, September 1982, p. 30. See also R. Leugold, 'Containment without Confrontation', *Foreign Policy*, 40 (1980) 74–98.
74. Haig, *Caveat*, p. 220.
75. *National Journal*, 28 November 1981, p. 2128.
76. *American Foreign Policy Current Documents 1985* (Washington DC: Department of State, 1986) p. 47.
77. *American Foreign Policy Current Documents 1983* (Washington DC: Department of State, 1985) p. 98.
78. *National Journal*, 28 November 1981, p. 2128.

79. Reagan, *An American Life*, p. 296.
80. Shultz, *Turmoil and Triumph*, p. 123.
81. *National Journal*, 2 January 1982, p. 10.
82. Cannon, *President Reagan*, p. 305.
83. *National Journal*, 9 May 1981, p. 842.
84. *The Reagan Paradox*, p. 46. But see also C. Andrew and O. Gordievsky, *KGB: The Inside Story* (New York: Harper Collins, 1990) p. 150 (on Soviet fears of a US nuclear attack in the early 1980s).
85. *American Foreign Policy Current Documents 1985*, p. 47 (McFarlane speech to Overseas Writers Association, 7 March 1985).
86. R. Perle, 'The Continuing Threat', in G.F. Treverton ed., *Europe and America Beyond 2000* (New York: Council on Foreign Relations, 1990) p. 133.
87. See J. Peterson, *Europe and America in the 1990s: The Prospects for Partnership* (Aldershot: Elgar, 1993) pp. 88–9; L. Tyson, 'Making Policy for Competitiveness in a Changing World', in A. Furino ed., *Cooperation and Competition in the Global Economy* (Cambridge, Massachusetts: Ballinger, 1988).
88. Shultz, *Turmoil and Triumph*, pp. 135–45.
89. See W.C. Cromwell, *The United States and the European Pillar* (London: Macmillan, 1992) p. 120; A.W. DePorte, 'France's New Realism', *Foreign Affairs*, 63 (1984) 258–73; W. Goldstein, ed., *Reagan's Leadership and the Atlantic Alliance* (Washington DC: Pergamon-Brassey's, 1986).
90. S. Kober, 'Can NATO Survive?', *International Affairs*, 59 (1983) 339–49, 345.
91. M. Thatcher, *The Downing Street Years* (London: Harper Collins, 1993) p. 472.
92. *Ibid.* See also I.H. Daalder, *The Nature and Practice of Flexible Response* (New York: Columbia University Press, 1991); F. Costigliola, *France and the United States: The Cold Alliance since World War II* (New York: Twayne, 1992) p. 215.
93. Shultz, *Turmoil and Triumph*, p. 190.

Chapter 5

1. G.P. Shultz, *Turmoil and Triumph* (New York: Scribner's Sons, 1993) pp. 552–3; *Public Papers of the Presidents of the United States, 1985*, vol. 1 (Washington DC: US Government Printing Office, 1986) p. 454. See also G.C. Herring, 'The "Vietnam Syndrome" and American Foreign Policy', *Virginia Quarterly Review*, 57 (1981) 587–601.
2. C. Weinberger, *Fighting For Peace: Seven Critical Years at the Pentagon* (London: Michael Joseph, 1990) pp. 22, 253–4.
3. R.A. Melanson, *Reconstructing Consensus* (New York: St Martin's, 1991) p. 145. See also *Time*, 1 April 1985 (C. Krauthammer); B.W. Jentleson, 'The Reagan Administration and Coercive Diplomacy', *Political Science Quarterly*, 106 (1991) 57–82.

4. *Congressional Quarterly Almanac 1985*, p. 8D.
5. Cited in *American Foreign Policy Current Documents 1983* (Washington DC: Department of State, 1985) p. 28.
6. Cited in M. Turner, 'Foreign Policy and the Reagan Administration', in J.D. Lees and M. Turner, eds, *Reagan's First Four Years* (Manchester: Manchester University Press, 1988) p. 141.
7. Weinberger, *Fighting For Peace*, p. 98.
8. Shultz, *Turmoil and Triumph*, pp. 106–7. See also G.W. Ball, *Error and Betrayal in Lebanon* (Washington DC: Foundation for Middle East Peace, 1984).
9. *Congressional Quarterly Almanac 1983*, p. 114.
10. *Ibid.*, p. 115.
11. See T.G. Fraser, *The USA and the Middle East Since World War 2* (London: Macmillan, 1989) p. 183.
12. See W.B. Quandt, *Peace Process* (Washington DC: Brookings, 1993) p. 365.
13. Shultz, *Turmoil and Triumph*, pp. 650–1.
14. See D.C. Martin and J. Walcott, *Best Laid Plans: The Inside Story of America's War against Terrorism* (New York: Harper and Row, 1988) p. 192.
15. *Department of State Bulletin*, June 1986, p. 5.
16. *Congressional Quarterly Weekly Report*, 19 April 1986, p. 839. See also H.H. Koh, *The National Security Constitution: Sharing Power after the Iran-Contra Affair* (New Haven: Yale University Press, 1990) p. 126.
17. M. Thatcher, *The Downing Street Years* (London: Harper Collins, 1993) pp. 444, 449.
18. Cited in T.L. Deibel, 'Why Reagan is Strong', *Foreign Policy*, 62 (1986) 108–25, at p. 116.
19. See T. Jacoby, 'Reagan's Turnaround on Human Rights', *Foreign Affairs*, 64 (1986) 1066–84. On comparisons between the Carter and Reagan foreign aid record, see M. Stohl and D. Carleton, 'The Foreign Policy of Human Rights: Rhetoric and Reality from Jimmy Carter to Ronald Reagan', *Human Rights Quarterly*, 7 (1985) 205–29; S.C. Poe, 'Human Rights and Economic Aid Allocation under Ronald Reagan and Jimmy Carter', *American Journal of Political Science*, 36 (1992) 147–67; J.M. Lindsay, 'Congress, Foreign Policy and the New Institutionalism', *International Studies Quarterly*, 38 (1994) 281–304, at p. 292.
20. See K.W. Thompson, ed., *Foreign Policy in the Reagan Presidency* (Lanham: University Press of America, 1993) pp. 107–8 (E. Abrams); M. Falcoff, 'Uncomfortable Allies: US Relations with Pinochet's Chile, in D. Pipes and A. Garfinkle, eds, *Friendly Tyrants: An American Dilemma* (London: Macmillan, 1991) p. 277; Americas Watch, *Failure: the Reagan Administration's Human Rights Policy in 1984* (New York: Helsinski Watch Lawyers' Committee, 1984).
21. See D. Cingranelli, *Ethics, American Foreign Policy and the Third World* (New York: St Martin's, 1993) p. 199; also, R.H. Johnson, 'Misguided Morality: Ethics and the Reagan Doctrine', *Political Science Quarterly*, 103 (1988) 509–29.

22. See P.S. Khoury, 'The Reagan Administration and the Middle East', in D.E. Kyvig, ed., *Reagan and the World* (New York: Praeger, 1990) p. 75.
23. *Congressional Quarterly Weekly Report*, 12 March 1982, p. 563.
24. See A. Acharya, *US Military Strategy in the Gulf* (London: Routledge, 1989) p. 133.
25. E. Hooglund, 'Reagan's Iran: Factions Behind US Policy in the Gulf', *Middle East Report*, April 1988, p. 29. See also M. Viorst, 'Iraq at War', *Foreign Affairs*, 65 (1986–7) 349–65.
26. The Committee of Santa Fe, *A New Inter-American Policy for the Eighties* (Washington DC: Council for Inter-American Security) p. 2.
27. Cited in R.A. Pastor, *Whirlpool: US Foreign Policy toward Latin America and the Caribbean* (Princeton: Princeton University Press, 1992) p. 67. See also R. Gutman, *Banana Diplomacy: The Making of American Policy in Nicaragua 1981–1987* (New York: Simon and Schuster) p. 19.
28. Pastor, *Whirlpool*, p. 68.
29. Ibid.
30. Cited in R. Dallek, *Ronald Reagan: The Politics of Symbolism* (Cambridge, Massachusetts: Harvard University Press, 1984) p. 177.
31. *New York Times*, 6 March 1986 (B. Weinraub).
32. *Department of State Bulletin*, March 1982, p. 61.
33. *Ibid.*, September 1982, p. 28.
34. *New York Times*, 17 March 1986.
35. *Department of State Bulletin*, June 1984, p. 25; Pastor, *Whirlpool*, p. 66.
36. *Ibid.*, April 1986, p. 32. See also E. Kenworthy, 'Where Pennsylvania Avenue meets Madison Avenue', *World Policy Journal* 5 (1987–8) 107–27.
37. *Ibid.*, March 1987, p. 16.
38. Cited in R.D. Schulzinger, *American Diplomacy in the Twentieth Century* (New York: Oxford University Press, 1994) p. 338.
39. Cited in T.G. Paterson, 'Historical Memory and Illusive Victories: Vietnam and Central America', *Diplomatic History* 12 (1988) 1–18, p. 14.
40. *Ibid.*, p. 3 (1983).
41. *Ibid.*, p. 18 (1986).
42. V.P. Vaky, 'Positive Containment in Nicaragua', *Foreign Policy* 68 (1987) 42–58, at p. 50. See also L. Schoultz, *National Security and United States Policy towards Latin America* (Princeton: Princeton University Press, 1987) p. 143. See also T. Carothers, *In The Name of Democracy: US Policy toward Latin America in the Reagan Years* (Berkeley: University of California Press, 1991).
43. See S. Welch, 'American Public Opinion: Consensus, Cleavage and Constraint', in D.P. Forsythe, ed., *American Foreign Policy in an Uncertain World* (Lincoln: University of Nebraska Press, 1984) p. 22; R. Sobel, 'Public Opinion about United States intervention in El Salvador and Nicaragua', *Public Opinion Quarterly* 53 (1989) 114–28; E.C. Ladd, 'Where the Public stands on Nicaragua', *Public Opinion* 9 (1987) 2–4, 59–60; E.R. Wittkopf, *Faces of Internationalism: Public*

Opinion and American Foreign Policy (Durham: Duke University Press, 1990); B.W. Jentleson, 'The Pretty Prudent Public', *International Studies Quarterly*, 36 (1992) 49–74, at p. 56.

44. See V. Gosse, '"The North American Front"': Central American Solidarity in the Reagan Era', in M. Davis and M. Sprinkler, eds, *Reshaping the US Left: Popular Struggles in the 1980s* (London: Verso, 1988).

45. H. Sklar, *Washington's War on Nicaragua* (Boston: South End Press, 1988) p. 68; J. Kwitny, *Endless Enemies: The Making of an Unfriendly World* (New York: Penguin, 1984) p. 369.

46. Vaky, 'Positive Containment', p. 43.

47. P. Gleijeses, 'Resisting Romanticism', *Foreign Policy* 54 (1984) 122–38, at p. 133.

48. C.H. Fairbanks, 'Gorbachev's Global Doughnut', in F.J. Fleron, E.P. Hoffman and R.F. Laird, eds, *Contemporary Issues in Soviet Foreign Policy: From Brezhnev to Gorbachev* (New York: De Gruyter, 1991) p. 603; Editors of *Congressional Quarterly, US Foreign Policy: The Reagan Impact* (Washington DC: Congressional Quarterly, 1988) p. 73 (Wright). See also W. LaFeber, *Inevitable Revolutions: The United States in Central America* (New York: Norton, 1993) pp. 292–95; W. Luers, 'The Soviets and Latin America', in R.F. Laird and E.P. Hoffman, eds, *Soviet Foreign Policy in a Changing World* (New York: Aldine, 1986) at p. 839; W.R. Duncan, 'Soviet Interests in Latin America', *Journal of Inter-American Studies and World Affairs*, 26 (1984) 163–98, at p. 186; J.S. Adams, *A Foreign Policy in Transition: Moscow's Retreat from Central America and the Caribbean* (Durham: Duke University Press, 1992) at p. 24.

49. See J.A. Nathan and J.K. Oliver, *Foreign Policy Making and the American System* (Boston: Little, Brown, 1987) p. 185; B. Woodward, *Veil: The Secret Wars of the CIA 1981–1987* (New York: Simon and Schuster, 1986) at p. 49.

50. See M. Damer, *The Massacre at El Mozote* (New York: Vintage, 1992); J. Didion, 'Something Horrible Happened in El Salvador', *New York Review of Books*, 14 July 1994, pp. 8–13.

51. Cited in J.D. Cockcroft, *Neighbors in Turmoil* (New York: Harper and Row, 1989) p. 148. See also R. Bonner, *Weakness and Deceit: US Policy and El Salvador* (New York: Times Books, 1984); M. McClintock, *The American Connection: State Terror and Popular Resistance in Guatemala* (London: Zed Books, 1986).

52. S. Jones, 'Reagan Administration Policy in Central America', in Kyvig, ed., *Reagan and the World*.

53. Pastor, *Whirlpool*, pp. 79–80.

54. Cockcroft, *Neighbors in Turmoil*, p. 598.

55. C.C. Menges, *Inside the National Security Council* (New York: Simon and Schuster, 1988) p. 104.

56. K. Roberts, 'Bullying and Bargaining: The United States, Nicaragua, and Conflict Resolution in Central America', *International Security* 15 (1990) 67–93, p. 71. See also W.M. LeoGrande, 'Rollback or Contain-

ment? The United States, Nicaragua and the Search for Peace in Central America', *International Security* 11 (1986) 77–99.

57. N. Reagan, *My Turn: The Memoirs of Nancy Reagan* (London: Weidenfeld and Nicolson, 1989) p. 242. See also A.M. Haig, *Caveat* (New York: Macmillan, 1984) p. 129.

58. See R. Gutman, 'America's Diplomatic Charade', *Foreign Policy* 56 (1984) 3–23; W. Goodfellow and J. Morrell, 'From Contadora to Esquipulas to Sapoa and Beyond', in T.W. Walker, ed., *Revolution and Counterrevolution in Nicaragua* (Boulder: Westview, 1991).

59. Pastor, *Whirlpool*, p. 76. See also T.M. Leonard, 'The United States, Costa Rica and Nicaragua, 1980–1984', in H. Jones, ed., *The Foreign and Domestic Dimensions of Modern Warfare* (Tuscaloosa: University of Alabama Press, 1988).

60. Cited in J. Muravchik, 'The Nicaragua Debate', *Foreign Affairs* 65 (1986–7) 366–82, p. 372.

61. *Congressional Quarterly Weekly Report*, 14 April 1984, p. 833; Shultz, *Turmoil and Triumph*, p. 406.

62. P. Rodino, 'International Law', *Christian Science Monitor*, 27 February 1985. See also D.P. Forsythe, *The Politics of International Law* (Boulder: Lynne Rienner, 1990) ch. 3.

63. Hearing before the Senate Committee on Foreign Relations, *US Policy toward Nicaragua*, August 1986, p. 5.

64. *New York Times*, 24 May 1985. See also C.J. Arnson, *Crossroads: Congress, the Reagan Administration, and Central America* (New York: Pantheon, 1989).

65. Shultz, *Turmoil and Triumph*, p. 953.

66. Ibid., pp. 950–69.

67. See T.W. Walker, 'Introduction', in Walker, ed., *Revolution and Counterrevolution in Nicaragua*, p. 3.

68. Cited in Sklar, *Washington's War on Nicaragua*, p. 217 (March, 1986).

69. *Ibid.*, p. 177 (April, 1985).

70. Cited in M. Vanderlaan, 'The Dual Strategy Myth in Central American Policy', *Journal of Inter-American Studies and World Affairs*, 26 (1984) 199–222, at p. 201.

71. Cited in Didion, 'Something Horrible Happened in El Salvador', p. 9.

72. Vanderlaan, 'The Dual Strategy Myth', p. 202.

73. See *Department of State Bulletin*, September 1982, p. 28; see also J. Cohen and J. Rogers, *Inequity and Intervention: The Federal Budget and Central America* (Boston: South End Press, 1986) p. 22.

74. *The Report of the President's National Bipartisan Commission on Central America* (New York: Macmillan, 1984) (extracts printed in Cockcroft, *Neighbors in Turmoil*, pp. 584–93).

75. See J.S. Fitch, 'The Decline of US Military Influence in Latin America', *Journal of Inter-American Studies and World Affairs*, 35 (1993) 1–51; W. Little, 'International Conflict in Latin America', *International Affairs*, 63 (1986–7) 589–602, at p. 596; L.D. Langley, *America and the Americas: The United States in the Western Hemisphere* (Athens: University of Georgia Press, 1989) p. 248.

76. R.J. Beck, *The Grenada Invasion: Politics, Law and Foreign Policy Decisionmaking* (Boulder: Westview, 1993) p. 227.
77. See M.H. Morley, *Imperial State and Revolution: The United States and Cuba 1952–1986* (Cambridge: Cambridge University Press, 1987) pp. 317–66; P. Shearman, 'The Soviet Union and Grenada under the New Jewel Movement', *International Affairs*, 61 (1984–5) 661–73.
78. See R.W. Burrowes, *Revolution and Rescue in Grenada* (New York: Westport, 1988) p. 115; S. Davidson, *Grenada: A Study in Politics and the Limits of International Law* (Aldershot: Avebury, 1987). C.L. Powell, *A Soldier's Way*, (London: Hutchinson, 1995) p. 292.
79. Shultz, *Turmoil and Triumph*, p. 1052.
80. See M.E. Scranton, *The Noriega Years: US–Panamanian Relations, 1981–1990* (London: Lynne Rienner, 1991) pp. 105–7. See also R. Millett, 'Looking Beyond Noriega', *Foreign Policy*, 71 (1988) 46–64.
81. Shultz, *Turmoil and Triumph*, p. 1086.
82. Cited in R. Crockatt, *The Fifty Years War: The United States and the Soviet Union in World Politics, 1941–1991* (London: Routledge, 1995) p. 362.
83. Shultz, *Turmoil and Triumph*, p. 692.
84. See ibid.. Also, T.G. Paterson, 'Oversight or Afterview? Congress, the CIA, and Covert Operations since 1947', in M. Barnhart, ed., *Congress and United States Foreign Policy* (Albany: State University of New York Press, 1987); T. Draper, *A Very Thin Line: The Iran-Contra Affairs* (New York: Hill and Wang, 1991) p. 596; L.K. Johnson, *Americas Secret Power: The CIA in a Democratic Society* (New York: Oxford University Press, 1989) p. 247; D. Oberdorfer, *The Turn: How the Cold War Came to an End* (London: Cape, 1992) pp. 274–82.
85. C. Baxter, 'The United States and Pakistan: The Zia Era and the Afghan Connection', in Pipes and Garfinkle, eds, *Friendly Tyrants*.
86. Cited in R.J. Kessler, 'Marcos and the Americans', *Foreign Policy*, 63 (1986) 40–57, at p. 57.
87. Cited in R.J. Kessler, *Rebellion and Repression in the Philippines* (New Haven: Yale University Press, 1989) p. 100.
88. D.B. Schirmer and S.R. Shalom, eds, *The Philippine Reader* (Boston: South End Press, 1987) pp. 322–3.
89. See S. Karnow, *In Our Image: America's Empire in the Philippines* (New York: Random House, 1989) ch. 15.
90. R.A. Manning, 'China: Reagan's Chance Hit', *Foreign Policy*, 54 (1984) 83–101, p. 84.
91. See D. Shambaugh, 'Patterns of Interaction in Sino-American Relations' and T.W. Robinson, 'Chinese Foreign Policy 1940s–1990s', in T.W. Robinson and D. Shambaugh, eds., *Chinese Foreign Policy: Theory and Practice* (Oxford: Clarendon Press, 1994); D. Shambaugh, *Beautiful Imperialist: China Perceives America, 1972–1990* (Princeton: Princeton University Press, 1991) ch. 6.
92. Shultz, *Turmoil and Triumph*, p. 1132.
93. See A. Iriye, 'US–Asian Relations in the 1980s', in Kyvig, ed., *Reagan and the World*; S.B. Linder, *The Pacific Century* (Stanford: Stanford University Press, 1986).

94. See R.E. Bissell, *South Africa and the United States: The Erosion of an Influence Relationship* (New York: Praeger, 1982) p. 42.
95. Cited in P.J. Schraeder, *United States Foreign Policy toward Africa: Incrementalism, Crisis and Change* (Cambridge: Cambridge University Press, 1994) p. 220.
96. Cited in Shultz, *Turmoil and Triumph*, p. 1122.
97. C.A. Crocker, *High Noon in Southern Africa: Making Peace in a Rough Neighborhood* (New York: Norton, 1992) p. 319.
98. See J. Davidow, 'Zimbabwe is a Success', *Foreign Policy*, 49 (1982/3) 93–106.
99. *A US Policy toward South Africa: The Report of the Secretary of State's Advisory Committee* (Washington DC: Department of State, 1987) pp. 3–4.
100. *Department of State Bulletin*, January 1984, p. 43.
101. Crocker, *High Noon*, p. 76. See also C.A. Crocker, 'Southern Africa: Eight Years Later', *Foreign Affairs*, 68 (1989) 144–64.
102. *Department of State Bulletin*, June 1982, pp. 46–7.
103. Remark cited in Schraeder, *United States Foreign Policy toward Africa*, p. 221.
104. Crocker, *High Noon*, p. 170.
105. Crocker, 'Southern Africa: Eight Years Later', p. 160.
106. Crocker, *High Noon*, p. 314; K. Somerville, 'Darkness at Noon in Africa?', *The World Today*, June 1993, p. 115.
107. R.G. Lugar, *Letters to the Next President* (New York: Simon and Schuster, 1988) p. 238.
108. See A. Lake, 'Do the Doable', *Foreign Policy*, 54 (1984) 102–1; P.H. Baker, 'Facing up to Apartheid', *Foreign Policy*, 64 (1986) 37–62.
109. Crocker, *High Noon*, p. 261.
110. See *ibid.*, p. 462 for Crocker's defence. Also, C.A. Crocker, 'Peacemaking in Southern Africa: the Namibia–Angola Accord of 1988', in D.D. Newsom, ed., *The Diplomatic Record, 1989–1990* (Boulder: Westview, 1991); M.G. Schatzberg, 'Zaire under Mobutu', in Piper and Garfinkle, eds., *Friendly Tyrants*.
111. See J.A. Lefebvre, *Arms For the Horn: US Security Policy in Ethiopia and Somalia, 1953–91* (Pittsburgh: University of Pittsburgh Press, 1991) p. 222.
112. Schraeder, *United States Policy toward Africa*, p. 157; see also D. Laitin, 'Security, Ideology and Development on Africa's Horn', in R.I. Rotberg, ed., *Africa in the 1990s and Beyond: US Policy Opportunities and Changes* (Algonac, Mich: Reference Publications, 1988).

Chapter 6

1. R.L. Garthoff, *The Great Transition: American–Soviet Relations and the End of the Cold War* (Washington DC: Brookings, 1994) pp. 204–5.
2. M. Gorbachev, *Perestroika: New Thinking for Our Country and the World* (New York: Harper and Row, 1987) p. 51.

3. G.P. Shultz, *Turmoil and Triumph* (New York: Scribner's Sons, 1993) p. 864.
4. Garthoff, *The Great Transition*, p. 355.
5. Shultz, *Turmoil and Triumph*, p. 703.
6. *Ibid.*, p. 571.
7. D.T. Regan, *For The Record* (London: Arrow, 1988) p. 298.
8. D. Oberdorfer, *The Turn: How The Cold War Came to an End* (London: Cape, 1992) p. 111; Shultz, *Turmoil and Triumph*, p. 6.
9. K.W. Thompson, ed., *Foreign Policy in the Reagan Presidency* (Lanham: University Press of America, 1993) p. 165.
10. Oberdorfer, *The Turn*, p. 144.
11. Garthoff, *The Great Transition*, pp. 332–3.
12. Oberdorfer, *The Turn*, p. 203.
13. See Regan, *For The Record*, p. 344.
14. J. Mayer and D. McManus, *Landslide: The Unmaking of the President, 1984–1988* (Boston: Houghton Mifflin, 1988) p. 357.
15. Cited in Oberdorfer, *The Turn*, p. 183.
16. Gorbachev, *Perestroika*, p. 240; R. Reagan, *An American Life* (New York: Simon and Schuster, 1990) p. 683; Shultz, *Turmoil and Triumph*, p. 776.
17. J. Schlesinger, 'Reykjavik and Revelations', in W.G. Hyland, ed., *America and the World, 1986* (New York: Council on Foreign Relations, 1987) p. 434.
18. M. Mandelbaum and S. Talbott, *Reagan and Gorbachev* (New York: Vintage, 1987) p. 175.
19. Thompson, ed., *Foreign Policy in the Reagan Presidency*, pp. 54–5.
20. See J.L. Gaddis, *The United States and the End of the Cold War* (New York: Oxford University Press, 1992) p. 128; S. Talbott, *The Master of the Game: Paul Nitze and the Nuclear Peace* (New York: Knopf, 1988) pp. 315–25.
21. Garthoff, *The Great Transition*, p. 530.
22. See B. Russett, 'Doves, Hawks and US Public Opinion', *Political Science Quarterly*, 105 (1990–91) 515–38, p. 536.
23. Regan, *For The Record*, p. 303.
24. *Annual Report to the Congress, Fiscal Year 1987, Caspar W. Weinberger, Secretary of Defense*, 5 February 1986, pp. 3, 38.
25. See Garthoff, *The Great Transition*, p. 532.
26. Oberdorfer, *The Turn*, p. 213.
27. Cited in Garthoff, *The Great Transition*, p. 352.
28. *Ibid.*, p. 357.
29. *Ibid.*, p. 358.
30. *Ibid.*, p. 365.
31. *Ibid.*, p. 367.
32. *Ibid.*, p. 371.
33. See Oberdorfer, *The Turn*, p. 438.
34. D. Deudney and G.J. Ikenberry, 'Who Won the Cold War?', *Foreign Policy*, 87 (1992) 123–38, p. 127.
35. For an exception, see M. Cox, 'Radical Theory and the New Cold War', in M. Bowker and R. Brown, eds, *From Cold War to Collapse: Theory*

and World Politics in the 1980s (Cambridge: Cambridge University Press, 1993), at p. 48.

36. Thompson, ed., *Foreign Policy in the Reagan Presidency*, p. 170. See also G. Lapidus and A. Dallin, 'The Pacification of Ronald Reagan', in P. Boyer, ed., *Reagan as President* (Chicago: I.R. Dee, 1990).

37. 'Who Won the Cold War?', p. 127.

38. Cited in S. Blumenthal, *Pledging Allegiance: The Last Campaign of the Cold War* (New York: Harper Collins, 1990) p. 86.

39. *Daily Telegraph*, 11 August 1988.

40. (New York: Atlantic Monthly Press, 1993). See also A.R. Dolan, *Undoing the Evil Empire: How Reagan Won the Cold War* (Washington DC: Washington Institute Press, 1990); and Patrick Glynn, *Closing Pandora's Box: Arms Races, Arms Control and the History of the Cold War* (New York: Atlantic Monthly Press, 1992).

41. P. Nitze, 'Security and Arms Control': A Number of Good Beginnings', *NATO Review*, 36 (1988) 1–6, p. 4.

42. Cited in Blumenthal, *Pledging Allegiance*, p. 249.

43. S.E. Ambrose, 'The Presidency and Foreign Policy', *Foreign Affairs*, 70 (1992) 118–37, p. 135.

44. See Garthoff, *The Great Transition*, p. 40.

45. See M. Cox, 'Whatever Happened to the Second Cold War? Soviet-American Relations: 1980–1988', *Review of International Studies*, 16 (1990) 155–72, p. 164.

46. See O. Roy, 'The Lessons of the Soviet–Afghan War', *Adelphi Papers*, 259 (1991).

47. See J. Checkel, 'Ideas, Institutions, and the Gorbachev Foreign Policy Revolution', *World Politics*, 45 (1993) 271–300. On the roots of the 'new thinking', see also A. Lynch, *Gorbachev's International Outlook: Intellectual Origins and Political Consequences* (New York: Institute for East–West Security Studies Occasional Paper, 1989); J. Snyder, 'The Gorbachev Revolution: A Waning of Soviet Expansionism', *International Security*, 12 (1987–8) 93–131.

48. 'East–West Relations and Eastern Europe', *Problems of Communism*, 27 (1988) 55–68, p. 66.

49. Ascherson review of T. Garton Ash, *In Europe's Name: Germany and the Divided Continent* (London: Cape, 1993), *The Independent on Sunday*, 5 December 1993. See also M. McGwire, *Perestroika and Soviet National Security Policy* (Washington DC: Brookings, 1991); R. Lebow and J. Stein, *We All Lost the Cold War* (Princeton: Princeton University Press, 1993); G. Segal, 'Ending the Cold War', *Diplomacy and Statecraft*, 1 (1990) 35–57.

50. T. Risse-Knappen, 'Did "Peace Through Strength" End the Cold War: Lessons from INF', *International Security*, 16 (1991) 162–88, p. 185. But see also J.L. Gaddis, 'Hanging Tough Paid Off', *Bulletin of the Atomic Scientists*, 45 (1989) 11–14.

51. F. Fukuyama, *The End of History and the Last Man* (London: Hamish Hamilton, 1992) p. 75. See also J. Voas, 'Soviet Attitudes towards Ballistic Missile Defence and the ABM Treaty', *Adelphi Papers*, 255 (1990).

52. S. Talbott, ed., *Krushchev Remembers: The Last Testament* (Boston: Little, Brown, 1974) p. 532.
53. A.K.I. Shevchenko, *Breaking with Moscow* (New York: A. Knopf, 1985) p. 278.
54. M. Bowker, 'Soviet Foreign Policy in the 1980s', in Bowker and Brown, eds, *From Cold War to Collapse*, p. 102.
55. This point is made forcefully in Lebow and Stein, *We All Lost the Cold War*. See also, Garthoff, *The Great Transition*, pp. 758, 764.
56. Bowker, 'Soviet Foreign Policy', p. 103. A good critique of 'Reagan victory' interpretations is contained in F. Chernoff, 'Ending the Cold War', *International Affairs*, 67 (1991) 111–26.
57. Garthoff, *The Great Transition*, p. 765.
58. See M. Cox, 'The Rise and Fall of the "Soviet Threat"', *Political Studies*, 33 (1985) 484–98.
59. A. Wroe, *Lives, Lies and the Iran-Contra Affair* (London: I.B. Tauris, 1991) p. 194.
60. Ibid.
61. T. Draper, *A Very Thin Line: The Iran-Contra Affair* (New York: Hill and Wang, 1991) p. 589.
62. Ibid., p. 596.
63. Ibid., p. 76.
64. Wroe, *Lives, Lies and the Iran-Contra Affair*, p. 195.
65. P. deLeon, *Thinking About Political Corruption* (London: M.E. Sharpe, 1993) p. 166.
66. L. Cannon, *President Reagan: A Role of a Lifetime* (New York: Simon and Schuster, 1991) p. 666.
67. Ibid., p. 703; Draper, *A Very Thin Line*, p. 549.
68. *Under Fire: An American Story* (New York: Harper Collins, 1991).
69. L. Fisher, 'The Foundations of Scandal', *Corruption and Reform*, 3 (1988–9) 154–71, p. 168; see also L. Fisher, 'Foreign Policy Powers of the President and Congress', *Annals of the American Academy*, 500 (1988) 148–62.
70. Draper, *A Very Thin Line*, p. 340.
71. T. Draper, 'Iran-Contra: The Mystery Solved', *New York Review of Books*, 10 June 1993, p. 53. See also C. Weinberger, *Fighting For Peace* (London: Michael Joseph, 1990) pp. 383–4.
72. From Fourth Interim Report to Congress by L.E. Walsh, Independent Counsel for Iran-Contra Matters, 8 February 1993, cited in Draper, 'Iran-Contra', p. 53.
73. Shultz, *Turmoil and Triumph*, pp. 816–18.
74. E. Meese, *With Reagan: The Inside Story* (New York: Regnery Gateway, 1993) p. 260. See also E. Abrams, *Undue Process: A Story of How Political Differences are Turned into Crimes* (New York: Free Press, 1994).
75. Cited in Draper, 'Iran-Contra', p. 57.
76. See deLeon, *Thinking About Political Corruption*, p. 179.
77. Draper, 'Iran-Contra', p. 59.
78. See H.H. Koh, *The National Security Constitution: Sharing Power after the Iran-Contra Affair* (New Haven: Yale University Press, 1990).

79. *The Tower Commission Report* (New York: Bantam Books edition, 1987) pp. 78–9.
80. *Final Report of the Independent Counsel for Iran-Contra Matters by Lawrence E. Walsh* (Washington DC: US Government Printing Office, 1993) vol. 1, p. 562.
81. S. Dash, 'Saturday Night Massacre II', *Foreign Policy*, 96 (1994) 173–86, p. 186. See also T. Draper, 'Walsh's Last Stand', *New York Review of Books*, 3 March 1994.
82. L. Speakes, *Speaking Out: The Reagan Presidency from Inside the White House* (New York: Scribner's Sons, 1988) p. 307.
83. C.L. Powell, *A Soldier's Way* (London: Hutchinson, 1995) p. 292.
84. *Washington Post*, 18 January 1993. See also I.M. Destler, 'Reagan and the World: An "Awesome Stubbornness"', in C.O. Jones, ed., *The Reagan Legacy* (Chatham: Chatham House, 1988).
85. R.W. Tucker, 'Reagan's Foreign Policy', *Foreign Affairs*, 68 (1988–89) 1–27, p. 27. See also H. Johnson, *Sleepwalking Through History: America in the Reagan Years* (New York: Norton, 1992).
86. See G.T. Hammond, 'US International Economic Policy: Past Neglect and Uncertain Future', in J.E. Winkates *et al.*, eds, *US Foreign Policy in Transition* (Chicago: Nelson-Hall, 1994).
87. D.P. Calleo, 'America's Federal Nation State', *Political Studies*, 42 (1994 Special Issue, ed., J. Dunn), 16–34, p. 24.
88. Cited in M. Walker, *The Cold War* (London: Fourth Estate, 1993) p. 330. See also S. Burman, *America in the Modern World: The Transcendence of United States Hegemony* (London: Harvester Wheatsheaf, 1991) ch. 8.
89. See D.P. Calleo, *The Bankrupting of America: How the Federal Budget is Impoverishing the Nation* (New York: Morrow, 1992). See also D. Stockman, *The Triumph of Politics* (London: Bodley Head, 1986).
90. S. Huntington, 'The US – Decline or Renewal?', *Foreign Affairs*, 67 (1988–9) 76–96.
91. *Sleepwalking Through History*, p. 177.
92. I.W. Morgan, *Beyond The Liberal Consensus* (London: Hurst, 1994) p. 205. See also R. Lekachman, *Visions and Nightmares: America after Reagan* (New York: Macmillan, 1987).

Chapter 7

1. Cited in R. Rose, *The Postmodern President: George Bush Meets the World* (Chatham: Chatham House, 1991) p. 334.
2. M. Mandelbaum, 'The Bush Foreign Policy', *Foreign Affairs*, 70 (1990–1) 5–22, p. 5.
3. See S. Blumenthal, *Pledging Allegiance: The Last Campaign of the Cold War* (New York: Harper and Collins, 1990).
4. *Public Papers of the Presidents of the United States: George Bush: 1989:* Book I (Washington DC: US Government Printing Office, 1990) p. 2.

5. *American Foreign Policy Current Documents: 1989* (Washington DC: Department of State, 1990) p. 3.
6. See, for example, P.C. Light, *Vice-Presidential Power* (Baltimore: Johns Hopkins University Press, 1984) pp. 265–70.
7. Cited in R.L. Garthoff, *The Great Transition: American–Soviet Relations and the End of the Cold War* (Washington DC: Brookings, 1994) p. 128.
8. B.A. Rockman, 'The Leadership Style of George Bush', in C. Campbell and B.A. Rockman, eds, *The Bush Presidency: First Appraisals* (Chatham: Chatham House, 1991) p. 17.
9. 'The Fabulous Bush and Baker Boys', *New York Times Magazine*, 6 May 1990.
10. M. Thatcher, *The Downing Street Years* (London: Harper Collins, 1993) p. 783.
11. N. Polsby in 'IGS Panel Assesses Bush Administration', *Public Affairs Report*, September 1990.
12. W.D. Burnham, 'The Legacy of George Bush: Travails of an Understudy', in G.M. Pomper *et al., The Election of 1992* (Chatham: Chatham House, 1993), p. 32.
13. See J.M. Scolnick, 'The Bush Approach to American Foreign Policy', in J.E. Winkates *et al.*, eds, *US Foreign Policy in Transition* (Chicago: Nelson-Hall, 1994); C.W. Kegley, 'The Bush Administration and the Future of Foreign Policy: Pragmatism or Procrastination?', *Presidential Studies Quarterly*, 19 (1989) 710–22.
14. M. Duffy and D. Goodgame, *Marching in Place: The Status Quo Presidency of George Bush* (New York: Simon and Schuster, 1992) p. 40.
15. *Public Papers of the Presidents ... 1989:* Book I, pp. 3–4.
16. *Public Papers of the Presidents of the United States: George Bush: 1989:* Book I (Washington DC: US Government Printing Office, 1990) p. 3.
17. M. Duffy and D. Goodgame, *Marching in Place* (New York: Simon and Schuster, 1992) p. 139.
18. P. Calvert, *The International Politics of Latin America* (Manchester: Manchester University Press, 1994) p. 176.
19. *Congressional Quarterly Weekly Report (CQWR)*, 23 December 1989, p. 3534.
20. C. Maechling, 'Washington's Illegal Invasion', *Foreign Policy*, 79 (1990) 113–31, p. 123.
21. Ibid., p. 124. See also J. Dinges, *Our Man in Panama: The Shrewd Rise and Brutal Fall of Manuel Noriega* (New York: Random House, 1991).
22. *CQWR*, 23 Dec. 1989, pp. 3532–5. See also L. Fisher, 'Congressional Checks on Military Initiatives', *Political Science Quarterly*, 109 (1994–5) 739–62.
23. R.A. Pastor, *Whirlpool*, (Princeton: Princeton University Press, 1992) p. 94.
24. See R.L. Millett, 'The Aftermath of Intervention: Panama 1990', *Journal of InterAmerican Studies and World Affairs*, 32 (1990) 1–15.

25. Cited in Pastor, *Whirlpool*, p. 91.
26. *Ibid.*, p. 94.
27. *CQWR*, 23 December 1989, p. 3535.
28. Cited in Pastor, *Whirlpool*, p. 98.
29. See L. Diamond, 'Promoting Democracy', *Foreign Policy*, 87 (1992) 25–40.
30. *Public Papers of the Presidents of the United States: George Bush: 1991: Book II* (Washington DC: US Government Printing Office, 1992) p. 1658.
31. *CQWR*, 10 February 1990, p. 401.
32. See Pastor, *Whirlpool*, p. 87. Also, D. Ryan, *US–Sandinista Diplomatic Relations: Voice of Intolerance* (London: Macmillan, 1995) chs 7–8.
33. *Public Papers of the Presidents of the United States: George Bush: 1990: Book I* (Washington DC: US Government Printing Office, 1991) p. 501.
34. See D.N. Farnsworth, 'The United States Again Confronts the Americas', in J.E. Winkates *et al.*, *US Foreign Policy in Transition* (Chicago: Nelson-Hall, 1994).
35. P. Hollingworth, 'Colombia: Modernity and the Drugs', *The World Today*, 47 (1991) 90–2, p. 92.
36. See W.A. Nitze, 'Swords into Ploughshares: Agendas for Change in the Developing World', *International Affairs*, 69 (1993) 39–53.
37. M. Naim, 'Latin America: Post-Adjustment Blues', *Foreign Policy*, 92 (1993) 133–50, p. 134. See also A. Hurrell, 'Latin America in the New World Order', *International Affairs*, 68 (1992) 121–39.
38. A.L. Horelick, 'US–Soviet Relations: Threshold of a New Era', *Foreign Affairs*, 69 (1989–90) 51–69, p. 56.
39. See M.R. Beschloss and S. Talbott, *At the Highest Levels: The Inside Story of the End of the Cold War* (Boston: Little, Brown, 1993) p. 47.
40. Horelick, 'US–Soviet Relations', p. 55.
41. Cited in M. Cox, 'From Superpower Detente to Entente Cordiale? Soviet–US Relations, 1989–90', in B. George, ed., *Jane's NATO Handbook* (Surrey: Jane's Information Group, 1990) p. 279.
42. Beschloss and Talbott, *At the Highest Levels*, p. 48.
43. *Ibid.*, p. 54.
44. 'Preface' to *Soviet Military Power: 1990* (Washington DC: Department of Defense, Sept. 1990).
45. *Public Papers ... 1989: Book II*, p. 1219 (18 September 1989); Beschloss and Talbott, *At the Highest Levels*, p. 55.
46. *Public Papers ... 1989: Book I*, p. 23 (27 January 1989).
47. Thatcher, *The Downing Street Years*, p. 786.
48. Beschloss and Talbott, *At the Highest Levels*, pp. 50–6; P. Williams and C. Miller, 'The Bush Administration's Foreign Policy Review', in M. Pugh and P. Williams, eds, *Superpower Politics: Change in the United States and the Soviet Union* (Manchester: Manchester University Press, 1990); G.T. Allison, 'Testing Gorbachev', *Foreign Affairs*, 67 (1988) 18–32.

49. See *Public Papers ... 1989:* Book I, pp. 540–3; Williams and Miller, 'The Bush Administration's Foreign Policy Review', pp. 93–6; *Public Papers ... 1989:* Book II, p. 973.

50. *Congressional Quarterly Weekly Report (CQWR)*, 4 November 1989, p. 2964.

51. *Public Papers ... 1989:* Book II, p. 1673 (8 December 1989).

52. *American Foreign Policy Current Documents: 1990* (Washington DC: Department of State, 1991) p. 34.

53. See S. Smith 'US Defence: The Reagan Legacy and the Bush Predicament', in Pugh and Williams, eds, *Superpower Politics*; G. Adams and S.A. Cain, 'Defense Dilemmas in the 1990s', *International Security*, 13 (1989) 5–15.

54. Beschloss and Talbott, *At the Highest Levels*, p. 132.

55. N. Hawkes, ed., *Tearing down the Curtain* (London: Hodder and Stoughton, 1990) pp. 119–20. See also G. Stokes, *The Walls Came Tumbling Down: The Collapse of Communism in Eastern Europe* (New York: Oxford University Press, 1993).

56. *Public Papers ... 1989:* Book II, p. 1593 (28 November 1989).

57. *CQWR*, 4 November 1989, p. 2967.

58. *Ibid.*

59. Beschloss and Talbott, *At the Highest Levels*, ch. 7.

60. Cited in M. Singer and A. Wildavsky, *The Real World Order* (Chatham: Chatham House, 1993) p. 139.

61. *American Foreign Policy Current Documents: 1990*, pp. 12–13 (30 March 1990).

62. *Ibid.*, p. 372 (10 February 1990).

63. *Ibid.*, p. 376 (12 March 1990).

64. *CQWR*, 7 April 1990, pp. 1084–5.

65. Garthoff, *The Great Transition*, p. 447.

66. Beschloss and Talbott, *At the Highest Levels*, p. 176.

67. *Ibid.*, p. 198. See also R.D. Asmus, 'A United Germany', *Foreign Affairs*, 69 (1990–1) 63–76.

68. *Public Papers of the Presidents of the United States: George Bush: 1991:* Book II (Washington DC: US Government Printing Office, 1992) p. 907 (17 July press conference with Gorbachev).

69. *Ibid.*, pp. 908, 912, 914 (17 July London press conference).

70. Cited in M. Cox, 'East–West Relations in a Year of Uncertainty', in B. George, ed., *Jane's NATO Handbook* (Surrey: Jane's Information Group, 1991) p. 332. See also G. Allison and R. Blackwill, 'America's Stake in the Soviet Future', *Foreign Affairs*, 70 (1991) 81–98.

71. *CQWR*, 8 December 1990, p. 4087. See also M. Brement, 'Reaching Out to Moscow', *Foreign Policy*, 80 (1990) 56–76.

72. See Beschloss and Talbott, *At the Highest Levels*, p. 418. Also, M. Almond, *Europe's Backyard War: The War in the Balkans* (London: Mandarin, 1994) p. 36.

73. *Public Papers of the Presidents of the United States: George Bush: 1992:* Book I (Washington DC: US Government Printing Office, 1993) p. 180 (1 February 1992).

74. C. Krauthammer, 'The Unipolar Moment', *Foreign Affairs*, 70 (1990–1) 5–33. See also C. Layne, 'The Unipolar Illusion', in S.M. Lynn-Jones and S.E. Miller, eds, *The Cold War and After: Prospects for Peace* (London: MIT Press, 1993).

75. *The Observer*, 25 August 1991.

76. *Public Papers ... 1992:* Book I, p. 1100 (reporter questions, 8 July 1992).

77. See Beschloss and Talbott, *At the Highest Levels*, p. 471: 'If Gorbachev was the mask of Russia and Yeltsin its real face, Bush preferred the mask'.

78. Pentagon planning now centred on the 'base force' concept. See J.E. Winkates, 'US Defense Policy in the 1990s', in Winkates *et al.*, eds, *US Foreign Policy in Transition*.

79. See C. Bluh, 'American–Russian Strategic Relations: From Confrontation to Cooperation?', *The World Today*, March 1993, 47–51.

80. *Public Papers ... 1992:* Book I, p. 1102 (8 July 1992).

81. See H. Adomeit, 'Russia as a "Great Power" in World Affairs: Images and Reality', *International Affairs*, 71 (1995) 35–68, p. 45.

82. See, for example, M.J. Hogan, ed., *The End of the Cold War: Its Meaning and Implications* (Cambridge: Cambridge University Press, 1992); A. Lynch, *The Cold War is Over – Again* (Boulder: Westview Press, 1992); J.L. Gaddis, *The United States and the End of the Cold War* (New York: Oxford University Press, 1992; M.P. Leffler and D.S. Painter, eds, *Origins of the Cold War: An International History* (London: Routledge, 1994).

83. W. LaFeber, 'An End to *Which* Cold War', in Hogan, ed., *The End of the Cold War*, pp. 14–17.

84. On 'double containment', see C. Layne and B. Schwarz, 'American Hegemony – Without an Enemy', *Foreign Policy*, 92 (1993) 5–21; M.P. Leffler, *A Preponderance of Power* (Stanford: Stanford University Press, 1992); M.P. Leffler and D.S. Painter, eds, *Origins of The Cold War* (London: Routledge, 1994).

85. See M. Kaldor, *The Imaginary War: Was There an East–West Conflict* (Oxford: Blackwell, 1990); T.J. McCormick, *America's Half-Century: United States Foreign Policy in the Cold War* (Baltimore: Johns Hopkins University Press, 1989); N. Chomsky, *Towards a New Cold War* (New York: Pantheon Books, 1982); M. Kaldor, 'After the Cold War', *New Left Review*, 180 (1990) 25–40; M. Cox, 'Radical Theory and the New Cold War', in M. Bowker and R. Brown, eds, *From Cold War to Collapse: Theory and World Politics in the 1980s* (Cambridge: Cambridge University Press, 1993).

86. J.L. Gaddis, 'The Long Peace', in Lynn-Jones and Miller, eds, *The Cold War and After* pp. 42, 44; J.L. Gaddis, *The Long Peace: Inquiries into the History of the Cold War* (New York: Oxford University Press, 1982).

87. See J. Dumbrell, *The Making of US Foreign Policy* (Manchester: Manchester University Press, 1990) pp. 19–21.

88. See K.N. Waltz, *Theory of International Politics* (New York: Random House, 1979) (for example, p. 173).

89. See S.D. Krasner, *Defending the National Interest* (Princeton: Princeton University Press, 1978); A.L. George, P.J. Farley and A. Dallin, eds,

US–Soviet Security Cooperation: Achievements, Failures, Lessons (New York: Oxford University Press, 1988).

90. J.J. Meirsheimer, *The Atlantic*, August 1990.

91. See R. Jervis, *Perception and Misperception in International Politics* (Princeton: Princeton University Press, 1976).

92. *Washington Post*, 28 September 1991. On 'imperial overreach', see P. Kennedy, *The Rise and Fall of the Great Powers* (London: Unwin Hyman, 1988).

93. On complex asymmetry, see R. Crockatt, 'Theories of Stability and the End of the Cold War', in Bowker and Brown, eds, *From Cold War to Collapse*.

94. M. Cox, 'From the Truman Doctrine to the Second Superpower Detente: The Rise and Fall of the Cold War', *Journal of Peace Research*, 27 (1990) 25–41, p. 30.

95. Lynch, *The Cold War is Over – Again*, p. 56. See also M. Cox, 'Rethinking the End of the Cold War', *Review of International Studies*, 20 (1994) 187–200.

96. F. Halliday, *Rethinking International Relations* (London: Macmillan, 1994) p. 215.

97. F. Fukuyama, 'The End of History', *The National Interest*, 16 (1989) 3–18.

98. For alternative views, see A. Filitov, 'Victory in the Postwar Era: Despite the Cold War or Because of it?', in Hogan, ed., *The End of the Cold War;* R. Crockatt, *The Fifty Years War* (London: Routledge, 1995) pp. 356–66.

99. A.J.P. Taylor, *The Russian War* (eds, D. Mrazkova and V. Remes) (London: Cape, 1978) p. 11.

100. See J.J. Mearsheimer, 'Back to the Future', *International Security*, 15 (1990) 48–61. On 'nuclear learning', see J.S. Nye, 'Nuclear Learning and US–Soviet Security Regimes', *International Organization*, 41 (1987) 371–402; M. Bundy, *Danger and Survival* (New York: Random House, 1988); M. Trachtenberg, 'The Past and Future of Arms Control', *Daedelus*, 120 (1991) 203–16.

101. J. Mueller, *Retreat From Doomsday: The Obsolescence of Major War* (New York: Basic Books, 1989). See also Gaddis, *The United States and the End of the Cold War*, pp. 105–18.

102. T. Schelling, *The Strategy of Conflict* (Cambridge, Massachusetts: Harvard University Press, 1960) p. 187. See also S.D. Sagan, *The Limits of Safety: Organizations, Accidents and Nuclear Weapons* (Princeton: Princeton University Press, 1993).

103. See C. Andrew and O. Gordievsky, *KGB: The Inside Story* (New York: Harper Collins, 1990) p. 150.

Chapter 8

1. Cited in R.W. Tucker and D.C. Hendrickson, *The Imperial Temptation* (New York: Council on Foreign Relations, 1992) p. 152.

2. L. Freedman and E. Karsh, *The Gulf Conflict, 1990–1991: Diplomacy and War in the New World Order* (London: Faber and Faber, 1994) p. 69.

3. See R. Hilsman, *George Bush vs. Saddam Hussein: Military Success! Political Failure?* (Novato: Lyford Books, 1992).

4. See G.A. Algosaibi, *The Gulf Crisis: An Attempt to Understand* (London: Kegan Paul, 1993). Also, *Time*, 13 August 1990, p. 12.

5. F. Halliday, 'The Crisis of the Arab World', *New Left Review*, 184 (1990) 69–75, p. 71.

6. See S.A. Yetiv, 'The Outcomes of Desert Shield and Desert Storm: Some Antecedent Causes', *Political Science Quarterly*, 107 (1992) 195–212.

7. See G. Golan, 'Gorbachev's Difficult Time in the Gulf', *Political Science Quarterly*, 107 (1992) 213–22.

8. D. Hiro, *Desert Shield to Desert Storm: The Second Gulf War* (London: Paladin, 1992) ch. 2.

9. B.W. Jentleson, *With Friends Like These: Reagan, Bush and Saddam: 1982–1990* (New York: Norton, 1994) pp. 95–6.

10. See ibid., p. 97; also, K. Timmerman, *The Death Lobby: How the West Armed Iraq* (London: Fourth Estate, 1992); A. Friedman, *The Spider's Web: The Secret History of How the White House Illegally Armed Iraq* (New York: Bantam Books, 1993).

11. S.R. Graubard, *Mr. Bush's War: Adventures in the Politics of Illusion* (London: I.B. Tauris, 1992) p. 108; B. Woodward, *The Commanders* (New York: Simon and Schuster, 1991) pp. 219–21.

12. Cited in Freedman and Karsh, *The Gulf Conflict*, p. 462. See also C.L. Powell, *A Soldier's Way* (London: Hutchinson, 1995) p. 491.

13. C.W. Maynes, 'Dateline Washington: A Necessary War?', *Foreign Policy*, 82 (1991) 159–77, p. 166.

14. *American Foreign Policy Current Documents*: 1990 (Washington DC: Department of State, 1991), p. 526.

15. *Ibid.*, pp. 528–9.

16. *Ibid.*, p. 525 (29 October 1990).

17. *Congressional Record* (1991), S332.

18. J. Mueller, *Policy and Opinion in the Gulf War* (Chicago: University of Chicago Press, 1994) pp. 23–4.

19. *Congressional Record* (1991), S340 (extract from Nunn hearings); hearings transcript (14 December 1990) p. 2. For Powell's view, see *A Soldier's Way*, p. 491.

20. D. Shapley, *Promise and Power: The Life and Times of Robert McNamara* (Boston: Little, Brown, 1993) p. 611. The case for persisting with sanctions is presented in K.L. Vaux, *Ethics and the Gulf War: Religion, Rhetoric and Righteousness* (Boulder: Westview, 1992).

21. *Public Papers of the Presidents of the United States: George Bush*: 1991: Book I (Washington DC: US Government Printing Office, 1992) p. 48. See also B.L. Nacos, 'Presidential Leadership During the Persian Gulf Conflict', *Presidential Studies Quarterly*, 24 (1994) 543–60; Woodward, *The Commanders*, p. 298 (Schwarzkopf).

22. *Congressional Record* (1991) S232; S272; S332–6; S365–75; H406. See also citations in J. Dumbrell, 'The US Congress and the Gulf War', in J. Walsh, ed., *The Gulf War Did Not Happen* (Aldershot: Arena, 1995);

F. Halliday, 'If Saddam Pulls Out', *New Statesman and Society*, 2 November 1990.

23. For differing interpretations of the air campaign, see R.P. Hallion, *Storm Over Iraq: Air Power and the Gulf War* (Washington DC: Smithsonian Institution Press, 1992) and J. Record, *Hollow Victory: A Contrary View of the Gulf War* (New York: Brassey's, 1993).

24. See W.L. Bennett and D.L. Paletz, eds, *Taken by Storm: The Media, Public Opinion and US Foreign Policy in the Gulf War* (Chicago: University of Chicago Press, 1994).

25. Powell, *A Soldier's Way*, p. 531.

26. P. Calvocoressi, 'After Kuwait', *International Relations*, 10 (1991) 287–300, p. 295. See also R.A. Divine, 'Historians and the Gulf War', *Diplomatic History*, 19 (1995) 117–34.

27. *The Gulf Conflict*, p. 441.

28. See P.R. Odell, 'International Oil: A Return to American Hegemony', *The World Today*, November 1994, pp. 208–10.

29. See J. Roper, 'Overcoming the Vietnam Syndrome: The Gulf War and Revisionism', in J. Walsh, ed., *The Gulf War Did Not Happen*.

30. *Congressional Quarterly Almanac*: 1991, p. 450.

31. See Record, *Hollow Victory*, pp. 134–5; M.T. Clark, 'The Trouble with Collective Security', *Orbis*, 39 (1995) 237–58.

32. J.C. Whitehead, 'The Place of the United States in the World Today', *Presidential Studies Quarterly*, 19 (1989) 703–4, p. 704.

33. See note 54. Also, S.P. Huntington, 'Why International Primacy Matters', *International Security*, 17 (1993) 68–83.

34. See A.C. Goldberg, 'Selective Engagement: US National Security Policy in the 1990s', *The Washington Quarterly*, Summer 1992.

35. Tucker and Hendrickson, *The Imperial Temptation*, pp. 11, 55. See also R. Steel, *Temptations of a Superpower* (Cambridge, Massachusetts: Harvard University Press, 1995).

36. See B. Kemp, 'The Regionalisation of Conflict', in B. Roberts, *US Security in an Uncertain Era* (Cambridge, Massachusetts: MIT Press, 1993); C. Fred Bergsten, 'The Primacy of Economics', *Foreign Policy*, 87 (1992) 3–24; C. Layne and B. Schwarz, 'American Hegemony without an Enemy', *Foreign Policy*, 92 (1993) 5–23.

37. R. McNamara, *Out of the Cold* (New York: Pantheon, 1989).

38. See P. Kennedy, 'Fin-de-Siecle America', *New York Review of Books*, 28 June 1990.

39. J. Chace, *The Consequences of the Peace: The New Internationalism and American Foreign Policy* (New York: Oxford University Press, 1992) p. 16.

40. Various options emerge from: Krauthammer, 'The Unipolar Moment'; W.G. Hyland, 'America's New Course', *Foreign Affairs*, 69 (1990) 1–12; J.L. Gaddis, 'Toward the Post-Cold War World', *Foreign Affairs*, 70 (1991) 102–22; T.G. Carpenter, 'The New World Disorder', *Foreign Policy*, 84 (1991) 24–39; W.S. Lind, 'Defending Western Culture', *Foreign Policy*, 84 (1991) 40–50; L. Diamond, 'Promoting Democracy', *Foreign Policy*, 87 (1992) 25–40; S.P. Huntington, 'The Clash of Civilizations',

Foreign Affairs, 72 (1993) 22–49; T. Hames, 'Foreign Policy and the Election of 1992', *International Relations*, 11 (1993) 315–30.

41. *New York Times*, 17 November 1989.

42. *Public Papers of the Presidents of the United States: George Bush: 1990*: Book II, (Washington DC: US Government Printing Office, 1991) p. 1219.

43. See Garthoff, *The Great Transition*, p. 435.

44. N. Chomsky, *World Orders, Old and New* (London: Pluto Press, 1994) p. 5.

45. J. Petras and M. Morley, *Empire or Republic? American Global Power and Domestic Decay* (New York: Routledge, 1995) p. 21.

46. *Public Papers of the Presidents of the United States: George Bush: 1992–3*, Book II (Washington DC: US Government Printing Office, 1993) pp. 2191–2.

47. *COWR*, 9 February 1991, pp. 381–2. See also A. Bennett and J. Lepgold, 'Reinventing Collective Security after the Cold War and Gulf Conflict', *Political Science Quarterly*, 108 (1993) 213–37.

48. R.N. Haass, *Conflicts Unending: The United States and Regional Conflicts* (New Haven: Yale University Press, 1990) pp. 51–2.

49. Cited in W.B. Quandt, *Peace Process* (Washington DC: Brookings, 1993) p. 389.

50. *Ibid.*, p. 411.

51. Cited in M. Indyk, 'Watershed in the Middle East', *Foreign Affairs*, 71 (1991–2) 70–93, p. 89.

52. See B. Stokes, 'How Tokyo's Being Tested in the Gulf', *National Journal*, 13 October 1990.

53. M. Thatcher, *The Downing Street Years* (London: Harper Collins, 1993) ch. 27.

54. M. Smith, 'The United States and Western Europe: Empire, Alliance and Interdependence', in A. McGrew, ed., *Empire* (London: Hodder and Stoughton, 1994) p. 127. See also P. Williams, P. Hammond and M. Brenner, 'Atlantic Lost, Paradise Regained?', *International Affairs*, 69 (1993) 1–17; P. Duignan and L.H. Gann, *The United States and the New Europe: 1945–1993* (Oxford: Blackwell, 1994) ch. 7; M. Smith, '"The Devil You Know": The United States and a Changing European Community', *International Affairs*, 68 (1992) 103–20.

55. *The Transformation of an Alliance: The Decisions of NATO's Heads of State and Government* (Brussels: NATO, 1992) p. 34.

56. *Public Papers ... 1990*: Book I, p. 626 (4 May 1990).

57. Cited in B. Stokes, 'Continental Shift', *National Journal*, 18 August 1990, p. 1998. See also M. Smith and S. Woolcock, *The United States and the European Community in a Transformed World* (London: Pinter, 1993); C.F. Bergsten, 'The Primacy of Economics', *Foreign Policy*, 87 (1992) 3–24.

58. See W.R. Smyser, *Germany and America: New Identities, Fateful Rift?* (Boulder: Westview, 1993) p. 80.

59. See, for example, M. Silva and B. Sjogren, *Europe 1992 and the New World Power Game* (New York: Wiley, 1990); J. Bergner, *The New*

Superpowers: Germany, Japan, the US and the New World Order (New York: St Martin's, 1991).

60. See R.O. Keohane, 'The Diplomacy of Structural Change', in H. Haftendorn and C. Tuschhoff, eds, *America and Europe in an Era of Change* (Boulder: Westview, 1993).
61. Cited in *National Journal*, 21 March 1992, p. 725.
62. *Congressional Quarterly Almanac*: 1992, p. 534.
63. M. Almond, *Europe's Backyard War: The War in the Balkans* (London: Mandarin, 1994) p. 255.
64. *Public Papers of the Presidents of the United States: George Bush*: 1992: Book I (Washington DC: US Government Printing Office, 1993) p. 1069.
65. *Ibid.*, pp. 1066, 1068.
66. *Congressional Quarterly Almanac*: 1992, p. 533.
67. *Ibid.*, p. 534.
68. Cited in S. Brown, *The Faces of Power: United States Foreign Policy from Truman to Clinton* (New York: Columbia University Press, 1994) p. 569.
69. *Public Papers of the Presidents of the United States: George Bush*: 1992–3: Book II (Washington DC: US Government Printing Office, 1993) p. 2228–9.
70. *CQ Almanac* 1992, p. 560.
71. *CQWR*, 16 December 1989, p. 3434.
72. *New York Times*, 10 July 1990.
73. Cited in J.R. Walsh, 'From Patron to Partner: US Policy in East Asia', in Winkates *et al.*, *US Foreign Policy in Transition*, p. 119. See also I.M. Destler, 'A Government Divided: The Security Complex and the Economic Complex', in D.A. Deese, ed., *The New Politics of American Foreign Policy* (New York: St Martin's, 1994) p. 133.
74. *CQ Almanac* 1990, p. 803.
75. *Ibid.*, p. 790; M. Chege, 'Remembering Africa', *Foreign Affairs*, 71 (1991–2) 146–63.
76. Cited in K.P. Magyar, 'Sub-Saharan Africa: Political Marginalization and Strategic Realignment', in Winkates *et al.*, eds, *US Foreign Policy in Transition* p. 247.
77. *CQ Almanac* 1989, p. 625 (Cohen). See also P.J. Schraeder, *United States Foreign Policy toward Africa* (Cambridge: Cambridge University Press, 1994) p. 237.
78. *CQ Almanac* 1989, p. 625.
79. *CQ Almanac* 1991, pp. 478–80.
80. *CQ Almanac* 1992, p. 536.
81. *Ibid.*, p. 537.
82. *Ibid.*
83. *Public Papers ... 1990*: Book I, p. 627 (4 May 1990).
84. K. Mullins and A. Wildavsky, 'The Procedural Presidency of George Bush', *Political Science Quarterly*, 107 (1992) 31–50, p. 36.
85. See J. Petras and M. Morley, *Empire or Republic? American Global Power and Domestic Decay* (New York: Routledge, 1995) pp. 36, 39. (See pp. 25–62 for statistics on declining US competitiveness). See also

J.G. Ruggie, 'Third Try at World Order? America and Multilateralism after the Cold War', *Political Science Quarterly*, 109 (1994) 553–70.

86. M.A. Bernstein, 'Understanding American Economic Decline', in M.A. Bernstein and D.E. Adler, eds, *Understanding American Economic Decline* (Cambridge: Cambridge University Press, 1994) p. 28. See also C.F. Bergsten, 'Japan and the United States in the New World Economy', in T. Rueter, ed., *The United States in the World Political Economy* (New York: McGraw-Hill, 1994) p. 174.

87. F.H. Hartmann and R.L. Wendzel, *America's Foreign Policy in a Changing World* (New York: Harper Collins, 1994) p. 166.

88. See C. Madison, 'Baker's Inner Circle', *National Journal*, 13 August 1991; J.P. Burke, *The Institutional Presidency* (Baltimore: Johns Hopkins University Press, 1992) pp. 168–71.

89. See L. Fisher, 'Congressional Checks on Military Initiatives', *Political Science Quarterly*, 109 (1994–5) 739–62. See generally L. Fisher, *Presidential War Power* (Lawrence: University of Kansas Press, 1995).

90. See *Congressional Quarterly Almanac*: 1992, p. 533.

91. *CQWR*, 3 February 1990, p. 293. See also L.G. Crovitz and J.A. Rabkin, eds, *The Fettered Presidency* (Washington DC: American Enterprise Institute, 1989); R. Cheney, 'Congressional Overreaching in Foreign Policy', in R.A. Goldwin and R.A. Licht, eds, *Foreign Policy and the Constitution* (Washington DC: American Enterprise Institute, 1991).

92. *Congressional Quarterly Almanac*: 1992, p. 533.

93. *CQWR*, 3 February 1990, pp. 293–4.

94. Cited in C. Tiefer, *The Semi-Sovereign Presidency: The Bush Administration's Strategy for Governing without Congress* (Boulder: Westview, 1994) p. 108.

95. *Ibid.*, p. 38.

96. See J. Dumbrell, *The Making of US Foreign Policy* (Manchester: Manchester University Press, 1990) ch. 5. Also, B. Hinckley, *Less Than Meets the Eye: Foreign Policy-making and the Myth of the Assertive Congress* (Chicago: University of Chicago Press, 1994).

97. See J.D. Rosner, *The New Tug-of-War* (Washington DC: Carnegie Endowment, 1995) p. 17. Also R.B. Ripley and J.M. Lindsay, eds, *Congress Resurgent: Foreign and Defense Policies on Capitol Hill* (Ann Arbor: University of Michigan Press, 1993); J.M. Lindsay, *Congress and the Politics of US Foreign Policy* (Baltimore: Johns Hopkins University Press, 1994); J.T. Tierney, 'Congressional Activism in Foreign Policy', in D.A. Deese, ed., *The New Politics of American Foreign Policy* (New York: St Martin's, 1994); S.R. Weissman, *A Culture of Deference: Congress's Failure of Leadership in Foreign Policy* (New York: Basic Books, 1995).

Chapter 9

1. N.J. Ornstein, 'Foreign Policy and the 1992 Election', *Foreign Affairs*, 71 (1992) 1–16, p. 2.

2. See T. Hames, 'Foreign Policy and the American Elections of 1992', *International Relations*, 11 (1993) 315–30.
3. O. Robison, 'The Presidential Election and American Foreign Policy', *The World Today*, July 1992, p. 121.
4. T. Hames, 'Foreign Policy and the American Elections of 1992'.
5. R.N. Haass, 'Paradigm Lost', *Foreign Affairs*, 74 (1995) 43–58.
6. *Newsweek*, 1 February 1993, p. 12.
7. Quotations from C. Madison, 'Juggling Act', *National Journal*, 9 January 1993, p. 63–4.
8. J. Germond and J. Witcover, *Mad as Hell: Revolt at the Ballot Box* (New York: Warner, 1993) p. 475.
9. *The Guardian*, 5 November 1992. See also J. Kitfield, 'Closing the Gap', *National Journal*, 18 June 1994, pp. 1401–3.
10. *Time*, 16 November 1992, p. 50. See also K.A. Frankovic, 'Public Opinion in the 1992 Presidential Campaign', in G.M. Pomper *et al.*, *The Election of 1992* (Chatham: Chatham House, 1993) p. 123.
11. *Public Papers of the Presidents of the United States: Bill Clinton*: 1993: Book I (Washington DC: US Government Printing Office, 1994) pp. 990–1.
12. *The Guardian*, 4 February 1994.
13. *Ibid.*, 9 November 1993.
14. C.F. Bergsten, 'The Primacy of Economics', *Foreign Policy*, 87 (1992) 3–24.
15. *Newsweek*, 6 March 1995, p. 10. See also I.M. Destler, 'Foreign Policy-Making with the Economy at Centre Stage', in D. Yankelovich and I.M. Destler, eds, *Beyond the Beltway* (New York: Norton, 1994).
16. *Newsweek*, 6 March 1995, p. 14.
17. J. Garten, 'Clinton's Emerging Trade Policy', *Foreign Affairs*, 72 (1993) 181–9, p. 183.
18. See J. Stremlau, 'Clinton's Dollar Diplomacy', *Foreign Policy*, 97 (1994–5) 18–35.
19. See L. D'Andrea Tyson, *Who's Bashing Whom: Trade Conflict in High-Technology Industries* (Washington DC: Institute for International Economics, 1992); I.C. Magaziner and R.B. Reich, *Minding America's Business: The Decline and Rise of the American Economy* (New York: Vintage Books, 1983); J.E. Garten, *A Cold Peace: America, Japan, Germany, and the Struggle for Supremacy* (New York: Times Books, 1992); T. Moran, 'International Economics and National Security', *Foreign Affairs*, 69 (1990–1) 74–90. Also, P.F. Cowley and J.D. Aronson, *Managing the World Economy: The Consequences of Corporate Alliances* (New York: Council on Foreign Relations, 1993); B. Crawford, 'The New Security Dilemma under International Economic Interdependence', *Millenium*, 23 (1994) 25–55; P.S. Nivola, *Regulating Unfair Trade* (Washington DC: Brookings, 1994).
20. P. Krugman, 'Competitiveness: A Dangerous Obsession', *Foreign Affairs*, 73 (1994) 28–44, p. 29.
21. *Ibid.*, p. 34.

22. See Haass, 'Paradigm Lost', p. 47; H. Harding, 'Asia Policy to the Brink', *Foreign Policy*, 96 (1994) 57–74.
23. *Public Papers ... 1993*: Book I, p. 773 (28 May 1993).
24. See B. Morris, 'Clinton Cramped on Foreign Trade', and 'Ideals Give Way to Jobs', *Independent on Sunday*, 13 and 20 November 1994.
25. *Congressional Quarterly* (CQ) *Almanac:* 1993, p. 182.
26. S. Brown, *The Faces of Power* (New York: Columbia University Press, 1994) p. 609.
27. W. Christopher, 'America's Leadership, America's Opportunity', *Foreign Policy*, 98 (1995) 6–28, p. 8.
28. *National Journal*, 28 January 1995, p. 231.
29. C.W. Maynes, 'Relearning Intervention', *Foreign Policy*, 98 (1995) 96–115, p. 109.
30. See *CQ Weekly Report*, 26 March 1994, p. 752; also, *National Journal*, 8 April 1995, p. 889.
31. *Public Papers ... 1993*, p. 987 (2 July 1993); see also L. Miller, 'The Clinton Years: Reinventing US Foreign Policy?', *International Affairs*, 70 (1994) 621–34. For a positive verdict on the Somalia intervention, see C.A. Crocker, 'The Lessons of Somalia', *Foreign Affairs*, 74 (1995) 2–8.
32. *CQ Weekly Report*, 26 March 1994, p. 752.
33. See M. Mandelbaum, 'The Reluctance to Intervene', *Foreign Policy*, 95 (1994) 3–18. Also, R. Steel, *Temptations of a Superpower* (Cambridge: Harvard University Press, 1995).
34. A. Lake, 'Confronting Backlash States', *Foreign Affairs*, 73 (1994) 45–55.
35. See D. Bernell, 'The Curious Case of Cuba in American Foreign Policy', *Journal of InterAmerican Studies and World Affairs*, 36 (1994) 65–103.
36. On the background and context to the North Korean diplomacy, see H. Harding, 'Asia Policy to the Brink'.
37. *Public Papers ... 1993*: Book I, p. 773 (28 May 1993).
38. Miller, 'The Clinton Years', p. 626.
39. *Public Papers ... 1993*: Book I, p. 1024 (7 July 1993).
40. Christopher, 'America's Leadership, America's Opportunity', p. 15.
41. S. Talbott, 'The New Geopolitics: Defending Democracy in the Post-Cold War Era', *The World Today*, January 1995, pp. 7–10.
42. See J. Dumbrell, *The Making of US Foreign Policy* (Manchester: Manchester University Press, 1990) ch. 1; A. Tonelson, 'Jettison the Policy', *Foreign Policy*, 97 (1994–5) 121–32; M. Posner, 'Rally Round Human Rights', *Foreign Policy*, 97 (1994–5) 133–9.
43. See R.J. Barnet, 'Promoting Democratic Stability', in R. Caplan and J. Feffer, eds, *State of the Union 1994: The Clinton Administration and the Nation in Profile* (Boulder: Westview, 1994).
44. Christopher, 'America's Leadership, America's Opportunity', p. 15.
45. Talbott, 'The New Geopolitics', p. 9.
46. *Public Papers ... 1993*: Book I, p. 987 (2 July 1993).
47. See M. Cox, 'The Necessary Partnership? The Clinton Presidency and Post-Soviet Russia', *International Affairs*, 70 (1994) 635–58.

48. *CQ Weekly Report*, 23 July 1994, p. 1993. For a review of post-Cold War defence conversion issues, see A. Markusen and J. Yudken, *Dismantling the Cold War Economy* (New York: Basic Books, 1992).
49. See *CQ Weekly Report*, 14 January 1995, p. 167; A. Tonelson, 'Superpower without a Sword', *Foreign Affairs*, 72 (1993) 166–80.
50. See Dumbrell, *The Making of US Foreign Policy*, chs. 2, 5, 9; R. Jervis, *Perception and Misperception in International Politics* (Princeton: Princeton University Press, 1976).
51. See F.J. Smist, *Congress Oversees the Intelligence Community: 1947–1989* (Knoxville: University of Tennessee Press, 1990).
52. See P.E. Peterson, 'The International System and Foreign Policy', in Peterson, ed., *The President, the Congress and the Making of Foreign Policy* (Norman, Oklahoma: University of Oklahoma Press, 1994).
53. R.B. Reich, *The Work of Nations* (New York: Knopf, 1991) ch. 10.
54. See B. Hocking, 'Globalization and the Foreign–Domestic Policy Nexus', in A. McGrew, ed., *Empire* (London: Hodder and Stoughton, 1994). Also, S.A. Shull, ed., *The Two Presidencies: A Quarter Century Assessment* (Chicago: Nelson-Hall, 1991); B. Hocking, *Localizing Foreign Policy: Non-Central Governments and Multilayered Diplomacy* (London: Macmillan, 1993); D.A. Deese, ed., *The New Politics of American Foreign Policy* (New York: St Martin's, 1994).
55. See E.N. Luttwak, *The Endangered American Dream* (New York: Simon and Schuster, 1993).
56. See S. Burman, 'America in Transition: Domestic Weakness and International Competitiveness', in G. Thompson, ed., *Markets* (London: Hodder and Stoughton, 1994); K. Ohmae, 'The Rise of the Region State', *Foreign Affairs*, 72 (1993) 78–87; P. Duignan and L.H. Gann, *The United States and the New Europe: 1945–1993* (Oxford: Blackwell, 1994) ch. 8.
57. C. Thorne, 'American Political Culture and the End of the Cold War', *Journal of American Studies*, 26 (1992) 303–30, p. 327 (1991 Albert Shaw Lecture). See also R. Rosencrantz, ed., *America as an Ordinary Power* (Ithaca: Cornell University Press, 1976); J. Citrin, E.B. Haass, C. Muste and B. Reingold, 'Is American Nationalism Changing?', *International Studies Quarterly*, 38 (1994) 1–31.

Index